DEVELOPING MENTAL TOUGHNESS
IN YOUNG PEOPLE

DEVELOPING MENTAL TOUGHNESS IN YOUNG PEOPLE

Approaches to Achievement, Well-being, Employability, and Positive Behaviour

Edited by

Doug Strycharczyk and Peter Clough

KARNAC

First published in 2014 by
Karnac Books Ltd
118 Finchley Road
London NW3 5HT

British Library Cataloguing in Publication Data

A C.I.P. for this book is available from the British Library

ISBN-13: 978-1-78220-005-5

Typeset by V Publishing Solutions Pvt Ltd., Chennai, India

www.karnacbooks.com

CONTENTS

PART IV: DEVELOPING MENTAL TOUGHNESS

ACKNOWLEDGEMENTS

It's almost twenty years since Peter and I started a journey to develop a model of mental toughness that is universally applicable. That journey has taken us to one of the model's most important applications—the development of young people—which is the theme of this book. For both of us this is perhaps the most satisfying application.

What is especially gratifying is that this application now receives acknowledgment all over the globe. It resonates with a good deal of current thinking. Dweck (2012), Seligman and Csikszentmihalyi (2000) and others all write about the same themes—although they give them different names—grit, character, resilience and mindset, these are all essentially the same as mental toughness.

We couldn't have made our contribution without the support and encouragement of many who have shown us aspects of the world of developing young people about which we had little knowledge. Pleasingly, most have agreed to contribute as authors in this book.

One contributor deserves a special mention. Kieran Gordon, CEO for Greater Manchester Connexions Partnership (GMCP), who in 2007, was the first to identify the potential for the model and the measure, MTQ48, in the development of young people. He organised the first trial. It worked and the rest, as they say, is history.

Anyone who has written or authored a book knows that this is a challenging task requiring copious amounts of mental toughness. All authors need collaborators. We are very grateful to Monika Czwerenko who has diligently coordinated the assembly of this work, liaising with all the featured authors to deliver on time! And once again we thank Helen Murray for her work in proofreading the compilation and tidying up our mistakes and grammatical errors.

Above all I dedicate this book to my grandchildren Jay, Charlie, Bella, and Axel who are exactly the young people for whom this book is written.

Peter Clough
Doug Strycharczyk

ABOUT THE EDITORS AND CONTRIBUTORS

Editors

Professor Peter Clough holds the Chair in Applied Psychology at Manchester Metropolitan University. Before taking this position Peter was Reader and Head of Department at the University of Hull. He is a chartered sport and exercise psychologist and a chartered occupational psychologist. His main research interests are in performance in high-pressure environments. He is co-developer, with Keith Earle, of the mental toughness model and of the MTQ48 the mental toughness questionnaire.

Again, working with AQR, Peter is supervising the ongoing development of the world's first integrated psychometric measure for leadership style and behaviour. The ILM72 maps to all major leadership models. Supported by the Institute of Leadership and Management, it was published in January 2008.

Peter's consultancy experience in the world of work embraces a wide variety of projects with major organisations in the UK and elsewhere including the design and implementation of assessment and development centres, workplace counselling, employee and culture surveys, leadership development and psychometric testing and training.

Peter's first degree is in psychology and his masters degree (awarded by Sheffield University) is in occupational psychology. Peter earned his PhD at Aberdeen University.

Doug Strycharczyk is CEO for AQR international, now recognised as one of the most innovative test publishers in the world. Doug has a background in organisational development and people development with global blue chip organisations. AQR publishes very accessible, reliable, and valid measures and development programmes for mental toughness, leadership, personality, and team working.

The focus of AQR's and Doug's activity is on improving performance, wellbeing and positive behaviours.

Working with Dr Peter Clough, Doug has been instrumental in taking the concept of mental toughness and its associated measure MTQ48 into the education sector in more than eighty countries by the end of 2013.

He is recognised as a leading authority on the application of mental toughness into just about every sector of society and the economy. He is in demand as a speaker at conferences and seminars all over the world.

He has authored, with Peter Clough, *Developing Mental Toughness* (Kogan Page, 2012) and co-authored a chapter in *Coaching in Education* (Karnac, 2011).

Doug holds a first class honours degree in economics. He is a fellow of the Chartered Institute of Personnel Development and a member of the Institute for Leadership and Management.

Contributors

Damian Allen is the director of children and families for the national children's charity, The Children's Society. Prior to this he was the director for children's services for seven years at Knowsley Council. Damian led the first educational application of mental toughness in secondary schools and is a strong advocate of innovation in the public and not for profit sectors. He is the UK representative on the CISCO Global Leaders In Education Programme (GELP) to which he has introduced MTQ48.

David Ayre is a transformation project analyst for The Children's Society. He has a BSc in politics with law (Aston), during which time he worked as a research assistant to a member of the UK Parliament, and an MA in political thought (Durham). He is also a budding 100 m and 200 m Olympic athlete, with his sights set on competing in the 2016 Olympic Games.

Andrea Berkeley has thirty years' experience in teaching and school leadership. Currently she is the education director at Teaching Leaders, a development programme for high potential middle leaders working in challenging schools, and an accredited executive coach and facilitator with wide experience developing teachers and school leaders at London's Institute of Education, the National College for School Leadership and Future Leaders.

Pauline Bowe has significant experience in education, health, local authority and, private sector organisations helping to develop young people and adults. Her varied career has spanned across the domains of teaching/training/lecturing, business psychology, coaching/ therapy and management. She holds an MSc in occupational psychology and is one of the UK's leading trainers in mental toughness development.

Sharon Bryan has worked as a consultant, facilitator and communications expert, specialising in change management projects. She has a wealth of experience in learning and development delivery to a wide variety of audiences including clients, staff, board, and senior executives. She specialises in the practical application of complex processes, making learning and understanding clear and straightforward for her audience. Sharon's focus and interest lies in change management, skills development, and transforming learning experiences.

Myfanwy Bugler is a chartered educational and developmental psychologist and works as a consultant specialising in education and child/adolescent development as well as being a lecturer at the University of Hull. Her research interests lie in adolescent development and wellbeing particularly the effects of educational success and failure on the psychological, physical, and mental health of the developing adolescent. She is interested in investigating cognitive strength variables such as mental toughness and grit that may act as protective measures to enable adolescents to deal with pressures and stresses in their everyday life.

Dr Fiona Earle is a chartered occupational psychologist and lecturer at University of Hull. Her research is broadly based in the area of stress, with particular interest in workload, fatigue and mental toughness. Specific areas of expertise include: psychometric measurement of fatigue and mental toughness; performance breakdown under stressful working conditions and the effects of working on-call. She also works in a variety of applied fields, in particular in the design of assessment centres for selection and development and the development of bespoke psychometric instruments.

Dr Keith Earle is a chartered sport and exercise psychologist working as a senior lecturer at the University of Hull. He is both an active researcher and an applied sport psychologist, working with athletes from a wide range of sports. Keith is the co-developer with Dr Peter Clough of the mental toughness model.

Anna Golawski is a postgraduate-qualified leadership coach and one of AQRs key associates delivering Mental Toughness programmes and is regularly invited to speak on the topic at conferences and events. She specialises in coaching for working parents to help them better manage the demands and pressures of raising a family and pursuing a fulfilling career. Her highly acclaimed book entitled *Swings and Roundabouts: A Self-Coaching Workbook for Parents and Those Considering Becoming Parents* was published in November 2013. She has also contributed to the book *Coaching in Education*, which was published in June 2011.

Kieran Gordon is CEO of GMCP Ltd, a leading provider of careers guidance in the UK. Kieran is a member of the National Careers Council advising Government on careers policy and is a past-president of the Institute of Careers Guidance. He has worked in the development of mental toughness programmes and the MTQ48 in the education and training sector.

Dr Suzy Green is a clinical and coaching psychologist based in Sydney. She is a leader in the complementary fields of Coaching Psychology and Positive Psychology having conducted a world-first study on evidence-based coaching as an Applied Positive Psychology. Suzy was the recipient of an International Positive Psychology Fellowship Award and has published in the *Journal of Positive Psychology*. Suzy lectured on Applied Positive Psychology as a senior adjunct lecturer in the Coaching Psychology Unit, University of Sydney for ten years. Suzy is also an honorary vice president of the International Society for Coaching Psychology, a visiting senior fellow of the Sydney Business School, University of Wollongong, an honorary fellow of the Melbourne Graduate School of Education, University of Melbourne. Suzy is the founder of The Positivity Institute, an organisation dedicated to the research and application of Positive Psychology for life, school, and work.

Bethan Greenall is a member of the AQR's team of psychologists. Bethan's core interest and expertise are in the area of mental toughness. Experienced in working with young people in primary, secondary, and further education Bethan also works with educational practitioners in the area of Not in Education, Employment or Training (NEETs), and youth services. Bethan holds an MSc in organisational psychology from Manchester Business School and a BSc (Hons) in psychology from the University of Leeds.

Liz Hall is editor of *Coaching at Work* magazine and author of *Mindful Coaching* (Kogan Page, 2013). She has a long-established mindfulness/ meditation practice, speaks and writes widely on mindfulness, and runs mindfulness programmes for individuals and for organisations including the NHS and the BBC. With trained .b teacher Ray Freeman, she has also developed mindfulness training and coaching for young adults, children, and teachers. Her mindfulness/meditation training has included a two-year foundation in Buddhist thought course; an eight-week mindfulness based cognitive therapy programme, and retreats with Zen master Thich Nhat Hanh. She completed mindfulness teacher training at the Centre for Mindfulness Research and Practice at Bangor University. She is a senior practitioner coach, whose clients include young adults and teachers.

Jen Lexmond is a social researcher and policy analyst, and the founder of CharacterCounts, a social enterprise that promotes, evaluates and designs public policy interventions that build character. Jen has worked at Nesta, the UK's innovation fund, and the think tank Demos, where she authored several major publications on early year's development and social mobility.

Dr Sarah McGeown is a deputy head of Institute for Education, Community and Society (ECS) and lecturer in developmental psychology at the University of Edinburgh. Her research concerns studying the relationship between mental toughness and attainment among primary and secondary school aged pupils and mental toughness among teachers as well as the influence of cognitive skills and motivation on children's reading development, and identifying ways to boost children's motivation to read.

Bethia McNeil has spent ten years working in youth policy, research and development, and training. Until recently, she was programme lead for young people, learning and work at the Young Foundation. In this role, she led work for the Department for Education, on behalf of the Catalyst consortium, to develop a framework of outcomes for young people. Bethia worked extensively with practitioners, commissioners, and investors to explore issues around defining outcomes in work with young people, understanding value, measurement, and evaluation. Bethia is a 2012 fellow of the Clore Social Leadership Programme. In early 2014, she will take up a new role at the Social Research Unit at Dartington.

John Perry is a senior lecturer in sport and exercise psychology at Leeds Trinity University. John is a chartered psychologist and an accredited sport and exercise scientist. His published research includes the development of a new model of sportspersonship, examining coping in sport, statistical methods in psychology, and mental toughness.

Paula Quinton-Jones has thirteen years' experience in career development and recruitment. Starting her career with the University of London, Paula moved to graduate and MBA recruitment at Allen & Overy, Deloitte, Standard Chartered Bank and Clyde & Co. Paula then joined Hult International Business School as the director of career services where she has embedded MTQ into the careers programme and this has now been adopted school wide as part of the core academic offering.

Claudine Rowlands is the support services director at AQR. Claudine is responsible for much of the support needed for the whole range of applications of the MTQ48 measure. This gives Claudine a unique perspective on practical issues in making the applications work. Claudine is a (ILM Level 7) qualified coach.

Dr Helen St Clair-Thompson is a lecturer in psychology at the University of Hull, but will soon be moving to the University of Newcastle. Her research is mainly concerned with psychological constructs that are important in educational settings, including mental toughness and cognitive constructs such as working memory. She is therefore particularly interested in mental toughness in young people.

Dr Christian van Nieuwerburgh is a leading international expert in the field of evidence-based coaching. He enjoys a number of rewarding professional roles: Executive coach working with leaders in the UK; senior lecturer in coaching psychology at the University of East London (UEL); chief executive of the International Centre for Coaching in Education (ICCE); and head of coaching programmes for AQR (TCA Consultants).

FOREWORD

Yvonne Roberts

Education in Britain, for the past couple of centuries, had a relatively simple task. Learning was seen as customising children and young people for their future role in a fixed, class-conscious Christian society, "the rich man in his castle, and the poor man at his gate" (Leavis, 1968, p. 134). H G Wells called the 1870 Education Act as not so much an "Act for a common universal education [but] an Act to educate the lower classes … [for employment] on lower class lines." (Dobson, 2009, p. 147) Later, the 1944 Education Act intended to provide a workforce for the post-war industrial economy. It was estimated that the country would need eighty per cent manual workers and twenty per cent clerical and professional staff. That narrow, static, insular world is no more.

As this book makes clear, we live in a globalised fast changing society. Children in school today will be employed in not one but several careers, many yet to be invented. Too often, however, the continuing strong focus on targets and league tables—most easily achieved by drilled exam technique, learning by rote and very little opportunity to exercise critical thinking—means that in the UK and in much of the rest of the world, what education systems provide is not what the majority of children require.

A small but growing group of innovators in education, business, and related fields, (some featured in this book) are beginning to develop tools and methods to equip each and every child, irrespective of background, to make the most of their potential. Mental toughness, resilience, self-control, confidence, and drive (we know from research) can take a person a lot further than a peer with a higher IQ but few of these capabilities.

A foundation of self belief and persistence or grit plays a part in encouraging a child to think creatively for him or herself; to collaborate with others; to use initiative; to turn setbacks into opportunities and to have the kind of adaptability that means change is not feared but embraced as a chance to flourish further.

A recent academic paper by Richard E. Nisbett, James Flynn and colleagues endorses the findings of psychologists Martin Seligman and Carole Dweck (referred to in this book), that self-regulatory skills and other non-cognitive traits including delayed gratification and self-discipline married to a positive attitude of mind, "contributes not only to life outcomes but to IQ scores themselves". Non-cognitive capabilities can improve IQ. In addition, mindset counts. If we tell ourselves a story of achievement and progress, we improve the chances that we will become that story. However, too often today, education fails to foster this frame of mind. On the contrary it breaks a prime rule of learning—first do no harm.

We can't afford to lose the untapped talent and abilities of all those thousands of children whom, too early, become dispirited and disengaged, written off instead of sparked so they perform well. At the same time, employers repeatedly say that even high flyers emerge from university lacking employability—the capacity to show initiative, work well with others, bounce back from disappointment and act maturely enough to see failure as an opportunity to learn.

How and why does mental toughness matter? Over the past thirty years or so, mental toughness has been given a number of definitions, Most include, to a greater or lesser degree, the non-cognitive capabilities of self-belief, resilience, a sense of agency, self-control and drive discussed here. This book endeavours to inject more clarity into what mental toughness means and to measure its impact when children and young people are taught how to acquire it not as a "chalk and talk" didactic exercise but experientially.

In building an education system fit for the twenty-first century, we still have a very long way to go. But there are pioneers both in this book and in a growing number of classrooms, lecture halls and workplaces, across the globe, who are creating different and important methods to provide learning for the many not just the few. Literacy, numeracy, and academic qualifications are vital but they are only a part of this endeavour. Hugely innovative and enterprising and constantly evolving holistic partnerships are developing between educators and pupils that can and will provide a schooling for life. Understanding how that happens is providing invaluable lessons for us all.

Why the twenty-first century is different and why developing young people to prosper is different

Doug Strycharczyk

One of the greatest challenges facing society today, at the start of the twenty-first century, is that of developing young people ensuring that they can play a full and productive part in the economic and social development of the world.

An important sub-theme is the need to take a long-term view of the way society develops and how those who make up society shape it. So the challenge is not just to develop young people so that they can secure their own futures but also to educate them in the importance of passing that continuous development message on to their children. Each successive generation must do better than what its predecessors have done. It's always been this way and always will be.

So ... what is special about now?

The need for change has always been there. That's the nature of things. As Darwin pointed out, adaptability is the key to survival. The ability to embrace change is the key to growth and development.

If we look back at history there have been changes, for those in their time, which will have seemed to have been every bit as big and dramatic as the changes we now face. The Industrial Revolution changed the ground rules for society in almost every way, as did the move from serfdom to individual freedom. If you look closely at these changes, it has generally been the most adaptable who have survived and thrived. Survival alone can be an achievement but thriving is a much more important and valuable aspiration.

What is different about now: Blink and it has moved on! It's simply that someone has stepped on the gas pedal.

Firstly there is a technological revolution which, although very accessible, is impacting on change in a very dramatic way. It has accelerated the rate of change to what now feels like a breathtaking pace. Fifty years ago, my father would have sat down at the end of the day and read his newspaper and would have watched the daily news on TV. Most of that "news" was already several days old. He was a scientist. Learning about new developments in other parts of the world often took months if not years to get to him. If he wanted to communicate with people in another part of the same country, let alone another country or continent, he would have written or typed a letter which would have been carried physically to its recipient. The person at the other end would then have to do the same to respond.

I am sitting here at my PC with an iPhone and iPad alongside me. Every so often they go "ping!". In the last hour I have received messages from colleagues in Australia, Canada, and the Arabian Gulf, and I am keeping an eye on text updates on how my football team is doing.

I no longer have a camera—it's in my phone …. Which I carry round with me wherever I go. My phone also doubles as a computer. I can carry out lots of tasks on it.

Only ten years ago this wouldn't have been possible. It's just over twenty years ago that I learned to email. But I didn't know anyone to whom I could send an email!

I am sure my father would have marveled at all of this but we no longer do. It's the way we live our lives now.

If I want to know something, I Google it and it's there—superfast. If I want to know something about a troubled part of the world I "search for it" and I see what is happening right now because someone will almost certainly be capturing it on the camera phone, uploading it onto the world wide web and relaying it around the world.

In another ten years we'll look back at this and think "how quaint!". I will speak to the screen which will be wall paper thin and carried rolled up so that I can stick to any convenient flat surface. Not only will it respond to my commands but it will speak to me to guide me in my work and suggest where I can find better information.

We are on the whole better educated, better informed, and much more knowledgeable than any of our ancestors. That too will continue into the future, and it is accelerating for a whole variety of reasons.

One of the most important factors to be considered in the context of a young person's development is the pace of change itself. We have already spoken about how fast technology changes. There are other changes coming through which are equally impactful.

Once upon a time (it does now feel like an old time story) you were encouraged to see a career as something you did through finding an employer and a job for life. Once again my father, typical of his genera-tion, only ever worked for two employers in his whole working life.

If we pay attention to the YouTube clip, Shift Happens,[1] we learn that forty per cent of graduates will, at the age of thirty be doing jobs that didn't exist when they were twenty-one! In North America it is thought that a person working today will have typically ten to fourteen jobs by the time they are thirty-eight and twenty-five per cent of all employees will have less than twelve months service with their current employer.

Simply standing still today will mean moving at a completely differ-ent pace to that taken by previous generations.

And what about those jobs? We operate in a genuinely global econ-omy. Those jobs can arise anywhere as the world order changes, and the competition for the job you seek can come from anywhere.

Is this a good or bad thing? The answer will be "yes" and "no" depending on your personal perspective. Those who are up for this level of change and challenge will relish it. Those who aren't will find this intimidating. As time goes by, the answer for more and more will be a positive one. Attitudes towards employment are changing along with everything else.

No-one can keep the promise of "a job for life" anymore. Employers have long restructured and reorganised as they face the challenge of responding to market forces. Measuring staff turnover used to be a key metric in organisations—the lower figure the better. It's not possible to expect unwavering commitment if the employer cannot honestly recip-rocate. The old norms no longer apply.

Furthermore people do not necessarily want to do the same job for their entire working life. The employment bargain seems to be shifting to one based on "I don't expect you to guarantee me a job for life. But whilst I am working for you I will give you my loyalty and commit-ment. In return I expect to have a purposeful job, to develop myself, to earn a reasonable wage and to be treated with a significant degree of respect and trust".

This is a key part of the mindset of those that we are beginning to know as Generation Y.

Other elements include the motivation for work. Generation Y people aren't necessarily money orientated. Self actualisation and doing something worthwhile are emerging as important motivators. This brings ideas like Maslow's hierarchy of needs back into vogue.

There is an important consequence to all of this. Lifelong learning and continuous professional development must become a permanent and consistent facet of a person's life. One's education cannot stop in your early twenties with only the occasional top up through attendance at a rare course or conference. Moreover the learner has to take responsibility for this. An important part of a young person's development will therefore consist of learning how to learn. That is a transferable life skill. It will determine employability—particularly in an environment where individuals may have to consider several jobs in their lifetime.

Another is realisation that learning to work hard is a necessity … not an option. Dweck (2012) in the US shows that developing a work ethic is more effective than developing a talent or ability ethic. The mantra of "work smarter not harder" is being replaced by "work harder and smarter".

One of the most interesting and most important of the changes we are seeing is the closing of the gap between aspiration and expectation in the minds of the young. At one time the young would have dreams and aspirations but only a few would dare to believe that these aspirations could be realised. So they would settle for something less. This generation and the generations that follow appear to see things in a more positive light. Their vision of the future is one where they can live their dreams to a much greater extent than before.

Shift Happens tells us that the ten most popular jobs in the US didn't exist ten years ago! If true, and it seems it is correct, how do you prepare young people to manage themselves in the world that they will inhabit?

What we are seeing is change, change and yet more change. Some of this change is already within view. We see it coming and we can at least try to understand it. Some of it is still unclear and appears only as a question.

How will all of this affect key issues such as social mobility? Can we really afford to have sections of society believing they cannot aspire, never mind expecting never to improve their lot because of some twist of fate means they are disadvantaged in some way—whether it is socio-economic, physical, or mental.

If one group of people in society believe that they can aspire and also achieve their aspirations but another significantly large group believes the opposite, what will this mean for developing the capability of all young people to fulfill their potential; to be productive engaged citizens; to believe they live in a fair and equitable world and to contribute to the wealth creating processes which will meet society's needs.

And therein lies the purpose of this book. At least that explains our interest in it.

Peter is a noted psychologist. He is concerned with performance in adverse conditions. He works in organisations, educations, and in sport. In all these areas he is interested in how to ensure all individuals can meet their potential. This is not necessarily about coming top or winning an award. It's essentially about identifying what matters to a person and helping them achieve this. There is no simple target for everyone to aspire to, but everyone can set a worthwhile and personally satisfying target. As the work discussed in this book has developed so has the concept of mental toughness. It is undoubtedly an advantage in many, if not most, circumstances, but not necessarily all.

All characteristics of personality have two ends, we speak about mental toughness at one end and mental sensitivity as the opposite of mental toughness. This is not a weakness—it's just another way of being. It offers challenges, but like all things in life, it offers advantages as well. At the core of all of our work are two things: First, a way of understanding and assessing toughness. Second, a set of skills, techniques, and approaches that might be drawn upon to allow a person to deal effectively in many pressure situations. This doesn't necessarily mean about changing the person. Rather it is about providing choice. It is about knowing yourself and doing all you can to help yourself through the bad times and allowing you to thrive in the good times.

Doug trained as an economist. Economics is the study of how wealth, in the widest sense of the word, is created and how it is distributed to those who need or want it (the two are not the same). If the population of the world is to double over the next thirty years and we are to improve the standard of living for all without reducing the standard of living significantly for anyone, society has massive challenges ahead of it. It's a challenge that will be faced not only by our generation but by future generations.

If they are not educated and developed to understand this and to adopt and apply solutions which are identified but, most importantly, to learn how to solve problems for themselves then the future will be a dull and difficult one.

We can however shape, support, and influence that from here by doing our best to foresee what those challenges are, what might be solutions and proposing ways of applying those solutions.

Some things we can begin to anticipate with an increasing sense of confidence that we have in our ability to grasp of the issues and in our ideas for their resolution. In some instances we are only beginning to ask the questions because we don't yet understand what the issues are. We'll raise those nevertheless to provoke thinking.

Some of the best solutions may be difficult to develop and implement. Some will cost money, often a lot of money, and will require political will to accomplish. Many will be capable of being implemented at the micro level—by committed practitioners who will hopefully become role models for others and inspire their engagement.

Both, Peter and I are united by a shared interest and passion. We are products of what we now know to be poor socio-economically disadvantaged backgrounds. Although neither of us knew that at the time because everyone else we knew was in the same position and that seemed to be the norm. Both of us have risen in their professions and lead a fulfilling life. Both of us talk about those with whom we grew up who didn't get this opportunity and experience. Both of us are determined to make a difference.

Together we have worked for twenty years on a concept called "mental toughness" which is now well established as an aspect of personality. It exists in all of us. What is also emerging is that it is a significant factor in performance, wellbeing and positive behaviour. It determines to a large extent how we, as individuals, respond to stressors, pressure, change, and challenge, and that pretty much describes life and the world we know. It describes the quality which enabled us to move from a background of disadvantage to our present state.

We believe that now, in the twenty-first century, those factors are more significant and more relevant than ever before because of the pace of change and the intensity of change. Those who possess and develop mental toughness will, as Darwin suggested and we would argue, be more likely to prosper.

The mentally sensitive (this being the opposite of mental toughness) may find it much more difficult to deal with this level of change and challenge. Our challenge is to point the way so that they too can survive and thrive, and many do.

This book will look at several factors and elements which are significant in the development of young people and will examine what should be usefully considered and what can be done to ensure that effective development takes place. Some are perennial issues. The role of the parent or guardian is one. Others, like social mobility are issues which have grown steadily in importance. A fair and efficient society cannot accept that the less privileged and disadvantaged should be provided with vastly different and fewer opportunities because of some accident of birth. Morally it's not right and economically it is a huge waste of talent.

We'll see that mental toughness is not actually a new concept. Sports coaches and sports psychologists have been well aware of its existence for a long time and of the value of working on an individual's mental toughness. However for a long time the concept was closely linked to the idea of winning and losing and was often too strongly linked to aggressive and highly competitive behaviour. That has been unfortunate. Mental toughness is about maximising your own potential, and through doing this, hopefully maximising the potential of others.

Our work on mental toughness has taken us on a fascinating journey. We have adjusted and developed the model throughout, and working with other colleagues has allowed us to incorporate new ideas, methods and philosophies. Mental toughness provides a firm foundation and we have found that practitioners and academics have used this to build a whole array of dazzling psychological strategies and tactics which are being shown to benefit their recipient. It applies everywhere where we need to act, behave, or perform as human beings.

In 2012 the Olympic Games were held in London. In the UK we were extremely fortunate to have Michael Johnson commentating for the BBC on many sports. A remarkable athlete in his own right, he spoke about mental toughness repeatedly. He seemed to mention it every ten minutes. However he did something else which was refreshing.

Most sports commentators talk about the winner, the gold medalist as if that was the only winner. Anyone else, even a silver medalist, could easily be perceived and even described as a loser. That often happens in sport. However Johnson focused much of his time on the athlete who has reached a semi-final or for whom the accomplishment had been qualifying for a final knowing that they weren't going to win the gold medal. He spoke about that athlete's mental toughness even though that athlete might not go any further in the competition.

He linked mental toughness with the notion of being the best that you can be. That semi-finalist was often someone who had achieved a personal best. They had optimised their own performance and had made the most of their abilities. Johnson reasoned convincingly that they were also winners.

This neatly describes a major challenge for education and the development of young people. Everyone has potential and everyone has some form of ability and knowledge. How can each of us optimise these, so that the challenges of living and working in the twenty-first century can be met head on? Can we support everyone "to be the best that they can be".

We strongly believe that developing mental toughness has a major role to play in creating a society not just of Darwin's survivors but of winners who are people who enjoy life and are a force for good.

Many of the chapters which follow are provided by contributing authors who add their own perspectives to this book. We have learned from each of these, and hope you do too. If we are to talk about mental toughness we need to demonstrate that in our own behaviour and practice and deal positively and willingly with a whole range of comments and feedback.

Some won't like our idea. That's fine. That is what diversity is about. If we provoke thinking then we have achieved something. We are finding that many do like what we are setting out and often become expert at finding applications for this in their work. That is extremely rewarding. We would be very pleased to receive your thoughts ideas and comments whatever they are.

There are two main goals for this book. One is to provoke thinking and start the debate. The other is to offer our ideas and the ideas of colleagues and co-workers, in the hope that some or even all of them prove to be of real value to the reader. They differ in tone, perspective, and methodology, but are united by an interest in the term "mental toughness".

On then, to those ideas and experiences …

Note

1. http://www.youtube.com/watch?v=czQXbv7jqKk

PART I

BACKGROUND

CHAPTER ONE

What is mental toughness?

Doug Strycharczyk

T he working definition of mental toughness is:

> It's a *personality trait* which determines, *in large part*, how individuals respond to stress, pressure, challenge, and change ... *irrespective of prevailing circumstances.*

It sounds a little like it's a definition of resilience. It shares some ground with the notion of resilience but there are subtle and important differences which we will explain in a moment.

From the minute you get up in the morning to the time you go to sleep your life is full of events which will represent, to one extent or another, some form of stressor, challenge, or pressure. If an individual responds poorly to this, they will often become what is commonly described as stressed.

However, many people respond differently to the same events and they will often achieve a very different set of outcomes. They will perform and behave exceptionally well and will appear to deal effortlessly with problems and setbacks which derail others.

This difference is both interesting and important. Firstly we see that it is possible to have two people who are of equal skills and ability, in receipt of the same training, receive the same education and who have equivalent backgrounds find themselves in the same situation but they will respond quite differently.

One will see a testing situation, like sitting an important exam or completing a challenging assignment as an exciting opportunity to prove to someone what they are capable of doing. The other will see the same situation as threatening. The situation they face is to be feared because in their mind there is a risk present which is likely to "find them out" and reveal to themselves or others how poorly they can perform.

Similarly with facing setbacks. One individual, when getting poor marks for an assignment sees that as a wake up call, a learning opportunity which drives them onto doing better next time. The other sees that as a "fatal blow" confirming that they can't do better.

That difference can be substantially explained by the difference in the individual's mental toughness. Mental toughness describes mindset. Faced with identical situations we will respond differently because of the attitude of mind.

Is a young person's life full of stress, pressure, change, and challenge? Of course it is. That is pretty much what a lot of education and development is about. Anyone involved in the development of young people will know that they see very bright people underperform and people with lesser abilities outperform their more talented brothers and sisters.

Some parts of the above definition are in italics. These highlight important elements of the definition.

First we now know that mental toughness is a "narrow" *personality trait*. That simply means that it is a part of each and every one of us. Our personality determines how we respond each time we are expected to do something. It applies in almost every situation we find ourselves— at work, in school, in play. In study, etc.

We also know that mental toughness is something called a "plastic" personality trait. It was generally thought at one time that past a certain point in a person's development that most aspects of personality were, to a large extent, fixed.

We now know that most of these are in fact "plastic". They can change and be changed. People can also learn to adopt behaviours which are not their first preference. Some do so more easily than others.

This is good news. It means we can train and develop people to see and do things differently when it is appropriate or beneficial for them to do so.

That does not mean that this is always automatically desirable. Mental sensitivity is the other end of the scale from mental toughness. There is nothing wrong essentially with being mentally sensitive. We know that mentally sensitive people can and do lead fulfilling and productive lives. What we do know statistically is that the more mental toughness you possess the more likely you are to perform better in a variety of settings and you are likely to experience better wellbeing. Therefore there may be benefits to developing a degree of mental toughness or learning what a more mentally tough person would do in a given situation and doing it.

The term *"in large part"* is also significant. Mental toughness can often explain much of the reason why people behave differently (and more effectively) when dealing with stressors. But it's not the only factor and it won't always be the most important factor. But it emerges consistently as a significant factor and for many in some circumstances as the most important factor. For instance, two large studies on young people preparing for tests and examinations, one in the UK and one in the Netherlands, shows that around twenty-five per cent of an individual's test performance can be explained by differences in their mental toughness (as assessed by the MTQ48 measure).

We therefore believe that understanding mental toughness is a part of the solution to many of the issues with dealing a young person's achievements, wellbeing and (positive) behaviour but it is only part of the solution. Often it will be a key part of the solution. It's not the whole of the solution.

Other aspects of personality will play a part, as will things like abilities, skills, environment, resources, interest etc. As will the support available from people like parents, guardians, teachers, and youth workers amongst others.

Finally we highlighted the term *"irrespective of prevailing circumstances"*. In a sense, this is a statement about accountability. But it's an important aspect of the concept. The mentally tough will more readily accept that they are largely responsible for their successes and failures. They won't point to a disadvantaged background or lack of a particular resource or support as reason for not doing something. They will generally accept that these are just life's hurdles they must handle—and will believe they can do it. Mentally tough people will achieve in most environments. They may feel let down by others—parents, teachers etc.—but they will still possess that inner drive and belief that it's down to them.

Others, who will often be found at the mentally sensitive end of the scale, will feel that some or all of the "blame" for their inability to achieve or perform satisfactorily can be laid at the feet of others. Their sense of "can do" is much less. They don't possess the same level of self belief or of commitment. They are sensitive to their circumstances.

Peter's work, and the work of his colleagues, has enabled us to identify what are the components of mental toughness. An extremely important aspect of that work has been the emergence of a high quality psychometric test called the MTQ48. This is described in more detail later in the book. It provides practitioners of all types a tool for assessing more accurately and more reliably the mindset of a young person (or indeed any person).

The four components are described in the MTQ48 measure through four scales called the four C's—Control; Challenge; Commitment and Confidence. Each one has subscales. The subscales for confidence and control are described below and can be measured through the MTQ48 psychometric test.

Control

This describes the extent to which young people feel they are in control of their lives and their work. This is where the sense of "can do" sits. If you ask a person who scores highly on this scale to do something which may be out of their comfort zone then their default response would typically be "Give it to me. I can do it". They are more likely to volunteer and more likely to be prepared to handle several things at once.

Young people at the other end of the scale are likely to hold back, to prefer to do one thing at a time and are likely to show (e.g., dismay and discomfort) what they feel to others.

Research has shown that there are two subscales here:

- **(Emotional) control**—Individuals scoring highly on this scale are better able to manage their emotions. They are able to keep anxieties in check and are less likely to reveal their emotional state to other people sometimes revealing only what they want to show.

- **Life control (sometimes called self-efficacy)**—Individuals scoring higher on this scale are more likely to believe that they control their lives. They feel that their plans will not be thwarted by outside factors and that they can make a difference.

Commitment

Sometimes described as "stickability", this describes the ability for an individual to carry out tasks successfully despite any problems or obstacles that arise whilst achieving the goal. It has two elements. One is the extent to which the young person is goal orientated. This is about the extent to which they will make promises, to themselves and to others. The other element is the extent to which they do what it takes to keep that promise. One implication is that a mentally tough young person will often be naturally hard working. They are also likely to persevere with difficult tasks. Someone with a low commitment score would avoid making promises and shy away from anything that carries a sense of measurement.

Mental toughness is often mistaken for resilience. Resilience is often defined as a function of control and commitment. Resilience represents the ability to deal with an adverse situation and still complete some or all of what you had set out to do. It is to some extent a passive quality. A resilient person won't necessarily be positive about it.

Mental toughness broadens this concept by adding two more components—Challenge and Confidence. This introduces a more proactive element.

Challenge

This describes the extent to which individuals see problems, setbacks, and challenges as opportunities. Those who see them as opportunities will actively seek them out and will identify problems as ways for self-development. Those at the other end of the scale see problems as threats. It determines to some extent how young persons deal with change and with new situations. It emerges as a significant factor in transition in education.

Confidence (self belief or self-esteem)

This assesses the extent to which individuals *believe* they have the capability to do what they need to do. On its own that is not enough either. Confident individuals must also be able to stand their ground when needed and have the confidence to present their views and ideas to others.

Individuals who are high in confidence have the self belief to successfully complete tasks, which may be considered too difficult by individuals with similar abilities but with lower confidence. They may also allow themselves to be talked out of doing something. Less confident individuals are also likely to be less persistent and to make more errors.

Confident young people are better able to deal with setbacks and mistakes. These don't disrupt their sense of self-confidence.

Again research show there are two sub-scales here.

- **Confidence (in abilities)**—Individuals scoring highly on this scale are more likely to believe that they are worthwhile and capable. They are less dependent on external validation and tend to be more optimistic about life in general.
- **Interpersonal confidence**—Individuals scoring highly on this scale tend to be less likely to be intimidated in social settings and are more likely to push themselves forward in groups. They are also better able to cope with difficult or awkward people. They will also respond more fully to examine questions and in completing assignments.

Each of these will be examined in much greater detail later in this book.

There is an important point to be made here. We find that confidence is the most misdiagnosed factor. People who work with young people will often observe negative behaviour and underperformance and attribute that to the young person's confidence (or lack of it). Close examination shows that in many cases this is wrong and in fact it's one of the other mental toughness factors at play. In which case the wrong interventions are chosen which have no impact and sometimes make a situation worse.

The four C's—a summary

If a mentally tough individual was asked to do something that most people saw as challenging, their default response would be to do it and these would be the thoughts that would typically be running through their heads

- **Control**   – I really believe I can do it
                    – I can keep my emotions in check when doing it

- **Commitment**   – I promise to do it
                    – I'll do what it takes to deliver it (hard work)

- **Challenge**   – I am motivated to do it—I can see the benefit
                    – Setbacks make me stronger

- **Confidence**   – I believe I have the ability to do it
                    – I can stand my ground if I need to

Together these give rise to a picture of **mental toughness**.

Finally, mental toughness is not a new concept. It is known by many names and is nearly always poorly defined. We have already seen that it is commonly confused with resilience. Other incarnations include mindset. If you look at the excellent work of Carol Dweck (2012) you will see that she has identified two poles for mindset—a fixed mindset and a flexible mindset. These equate to mental sensitivity and mental toughness. The same applies to the work of Seligman (2006), who writes of learned optimism and learned helplessness in the development of young people. The ideas overlap. Similarly with terms such as character, attitude, and tenacity, they all describe mental toughness or an aspect of mental toughness.

Some may not like the term but it is the correct term for what we are describing here. Coined originally by Loehr in 1983 he defined it as the ability to consistently perform towards the upper range of your talent and skill regardless of competitive circumstances. Although focused on the athlete it is still a definition we like. It essentially says that mental toughness is a significant factor in becoming the best that each of us can be. Surely one of the goals for those involved in developing young people.

CHAPTER TWO

The four C's model

Keith Earle and Peter Clough

Introduction

In developing the MTQ48, and the four C's model, we attempted to provide both an overall measure of toughness and also provide a more thorough assessment of the elements that underpin this overall score.

In our extensive development work it became apparent that a four-factor model best represented the mental toughness universe. The model of hardiness put forward by Kobasa (1979) seemed to incorporate most of the elements generated by the existing literature at the time. This provided the starting point for three of the four C's: control, commitment, and challenge. The final C, confidence, emerged from extensive interviews and practical experience.

In this Chapter the four C's will be briefly described and discussed in relation to a wider context of related psychological models and theories.

A summary of the four C's

Mental toughness is represented in our model by four scales: first, challenge, this refers to the extent to which individuals see problems as opportunities for self-development rather than threats. Second, commitment, which concerns deep involvement with whatever one is doing. Third, confidence (in abilities and interpersonal), reflecting a high sense of self belief and an unshakeable faith in having the ability to achieve success while not being intimidated and fourth, control (emotional and life), which reflects a tendency to feel and act as if one is influential.

Challenge

This component of mental toughness addresses how we, as individuals, respond to challenge. A challenge represents any activity (or event) which we see as out of the ordinary and which involves doing something that is stretching. It, like the other components, can be viewed as a mindset. Some will see opportunity—others will see threat. It's the same situation but a different outcome. How we perceive challenge is key to how we cope and deal with challenge.

For students, exams and coursework perhaps represent the most obvious challenge. We are in a competitive world and children can become obsessed with the need for success. Unfortunately some children are less able to deal with exam stress than others. They tend to see an assessment as a way of making them look bad rather than seeing it as an opportunity to show how good they are.

The most dominant factor relating to the challenge dimension is change. Change is inevitable, especially in education. For the children

Some descriptors and behaviours which may associated with extreme positions on the challenge scale.	
Lower scores	*Higher scores*
Don't like sudden changes	Like challenge
Don't like shocks	Easily bored—will seek change
Fear of failure	Provoke change
Avoid effort	Like problem solving
Intimidated by challenges	Work hard
Tend to achieve minimum standards	Volunteer for projects
Respond poorly to competitive	Enjoy competition and show it
situations	May not always be content with
Dislike being in new situations	daily life and routines
Prefer routine	"Addicted" to adrenalin
Avoid risk (particularly, of failure)	
May get things out of perspective	

they are constantly experiencing transitions, perhaps the most stressful type of events we have to deal with. For the educator the rules and regulations change at a bewildering pace, often necessitating huge alterations in a very short period of time.

THE BROADER PSYCHOLOGICAL CONTEXT OF CHALLENGE

Achievement motivation

There are a number of psychological theories and models that relate to the challenge dimension. Arguably the most well-known is achievement motivation. Murray (1938) developed his model in the 1930s and argued that we all have a set of significant motivators and, to some extent at least, these are learnt from our environment. This offers a powerful idea to those of us interested in mental toughness. If achievement motivation is learnt, can mental toughness also be developed in this way? Those high on achievement motivation will actively seek domains that will allow them to express this. They will be drawn to challenging situations to show they can succeed.

Fear of failure

The term "fear of failure" is often used, but rarely is it dealt with in any sort of depth. Fear of failure has been suggested as a reason why people don't put themselves forward to be challenged. Most explanations tend to be psychoanalytic and are generally based on the idea that people try to protect their psychological integrity. Therefore those dominated by the idea of failure will avoid any situations that might threaten their confidence and self-esteem. Sadly, there are few positive challenging experiences that do not have an element of risk. It is hard to succeed without risking failure. In a practical educational setting, fear of failure may be responsible for educational underachievement or for stalled career development pathways.

Competitiveness

Competitiveness is often a very observable trait. It also gets the classic "poor press", often being related to a "macho" approach to the world. Whilst it is clear that some people do get a great deal of satisfaction by beating people, there are many others who express their competiveness in a different way. They gain a huge satisfaction from a "job well done" and a sense of completion. They are internally referent and have no real desire to compete against others, but a strong desire to compete against themselves. Our challenge component tries to take a broad perspective, ensuring it incorporates all aspects of achievement and competition.

Commitment

Putting things off when we know we shouldn't is part of the human condition. However, some people do this infrequently, some do it all the time. In a nutshell, this scale reflects the extent to which we make promises, particularly those that are tangible and measurable, and the extent to which we commit to keeping them. Procrastination can be seen as a coping mechanism to reduce stress. However, whilst it can certainly help in the short-term, in the longer term it makes the situation much worse. This component of our model is the best predictor of academic performance in students.

But our approach to goals and targets (and indeed the same goal or target) can vary. It is clear that commitment is closely linked to goals. Goal setting is one of the great success stories of psychological research. Mento, Steel and Karren (1987) write:

> If there is ever to be a viable candidate from the organisational sciences for elevation to the lofty status of a scientific law of nature, then the relationship between goal difficulty, specificity, commitment & task performance are serious contenders. (Mento, Steel & Karren, 1987, p. 74)

Individuals scoring highly on the commitment scale are usually avid users of goal setting techniques. Unfortunately, those people who would benefit from goal setting probably use them least. Those individuals reporting lower commitment would certainly benefit from employing some of the classic planning techniques but are either uninterested in them or rather intimidated by them. This potential "catch 22" is evident in much of the personal development work relating to mental toughness interventions. Few people needing help will actively seek it out, so we need to bring it to them.

Some descriptors and behaviours which may be associated with extreme positions on the commitment scale.	
Lower scores	*Higher scores*
Intimidated by goals and measures—they induce paralysis	Like goals and measures—these describe what success looks like
May lack a sense of purpose—they can think "win-lose"	Goals are translated into something which is achievable
Goals become something which appears overpowering	Will break things down into manageable chunks
May resent the imposition of goals and targets	Prepared to do what it takes—Will work hard (and long hours if necessary)
May respond emotionally when given tasks	Maintain focus
Allow themselves to be easily distracted	Like the repeated opportunity to measure and prove themselves
Will avoid targets	Will prioritise effort and activities
Will skip meetings or classes	Will attend meetings/classes even if the don't like the people/topic
More likely to be late for thing	Set high standards for self and others
Find reasons to miss the target	Won't let others down
"I can't do ... Maths"	May deliver too quickly at times
Will default to a life experience which provides an excuse to blame someone else for failure— "I couldn't do this because my parents ..."	Can inconvenience others with their focus on KPI's (Key Performance Indicator)
Can feel unlucky—its not my day	

THE BROADER PSYCHOLOGICAL CONTEXT OF COMMITMENT

Goals revisited

Commitment is clearly related to setting goals. However it is much more than that. Setting the goal is perhaps the easy bit. Meeting them is much harder. The complexity of actually delivering a desired behaviour is well illustrated by the theory of reasoned action developed by Fishbein and Ajzen (1977). They described a complex decision making process that is common to us all. First they said you need to consider someone's attitude to the behaviour—do they value it? Second, they discussed subjective norms. These relate to your perceptions of the views of significant others. Finally, consider if you have control over the behaviours you want to exhibit. Clearly this reasoning process is more than commitment. All aspects of mental toughness play a part. Where commitment is dominant is at the final stage. Fishbein and Ajzen differentiated between intention to behave and the behaviour itself. It is easier to think you should finish that essay than it is to actually do it. Commitment really operates between the intention and the behaviour—basically making it happen. This has obvious implication for students as regards their study habits and staff members as regards their career development and general health and wellbeing.

The trait of conscientiousness

Conscientiousness has been linked to a myriad of positive outcomes across educational, health, and personnel psychology. It is a broad trait covering a number of aspects. Some of these are: orderliness, responsibility, conscientiousness, perseverance, conventionality, fussiness, tidiness, responsibility, and scrupulousness. Commitment encompasses this broad church, providing a simple and straightforward overarching entity. The commitment scale therefore offers an excellent tool with which to both explain and predict classroom behaviours.

Confidence

Confidence is a notoriously fuzzy term. It is widely discussed but rarely fully understood. From our initial research it became obvious that confidence was the "missing" component of mental toughness. It was clearly apparent from our applied work that clients felt their performance issues were down to a lack of confidence. Clearly we believe that this sort of attribution would be overly simplistic but it was also clear that confidence had a significant role. Using statistical models we found there were two distinct elements of confidence: confidence in abilities and interpersonal confidence.

For students confidence is key. Believing you can do something is important. However, belief needs to be backed up by real ability and excellent teaching. Lack of confidence is a potential killer. It prevents people developing to their full potential. Much of the classroom experience is dominated by relationships with other people. Students with high levels of interpersonal confidence can form better relationships and are more comfortable talking to classmates and teachers.

Most educators recognise that teaching has a clear performance element. It is important that a teacher is comfortable communicating with others. Anxiety cripples creativity and spontaneity, reducing the efficacy of the message. In addition, confidence is at the core of good networking skills. A solid and vibrant network is a huge resource for the professional educator.

The confident individual has little need for external validation. All of us like positive feedback but individuals who are low on confidence need it. The confident person can accept they have good days and bad days and their view of themselves is not based on this day-to-day variation. Basically they believe they are ok really, but sometimes get it wrong.

As previously mentioned we believe there are two distinct aspects of confidence.

Confidence in abilities

Low scores	High scores
Low self belief	Can believe they are right ... even when they are wrong
Not confident that they know their subject matter even when they do	Little or no need for external validation
Produce minimal responses when asked	Happy to ask questions
Will be reluctant to ask questions "in case it makes me look stupid"	Happy to provide full responses to questions and in exams
Inner belief missing—need others to build that	See critical feedback as feedback (no more and no less)
Unsure whether they have grasped a subject or not—feel they are still missing something	See competence and excellence in others as a motivator " I can aspire to that"
Can be inhibited by competence or excellence in others—feel they don't measure up	Happy to draw in their experiences into what they do
May underestimate their own capabilities	

Interpersonal confidence

Low scores	High scores
Easily intimidated. Won't express themselves in class/debate even when they know they are right Won't ask questions—low engagement Will accept criticism and ridicule even when not warranted Will back down quickly when challenged Will have difficulty dealing with assertive people Not good with negative situations Can be shy or self-effacing Will seek to avoid risk or making mistakes Will miss out on opportunities	Will stand their ground Will face down criticism etc Will easily engage in class and group activity Will use this quality to argue down others more knowledgeable Can be aggressive Not easily embarrassed Comfortable with negative situations—can deal with the fall out Comfortable working in a group and making a contribution More likely to be involved in lots of things "wont be shy coming forward"

THE BROADER PSYCHOLOGICAL CONTEXT OF CONFIDENCE

Self-efficacy

Self-efficacy has a central place in the history of psychology. It is often used interchangeably with confidence, but in fact they are different. Confidence relates to the strength of belief whereas self-efficacy is more focused on what that belief is directed at. So you can be too confident in some situations, but you can never be too self-efficacious.

Bandura (1986), who developed the self-efficacy model, was convinced that people learn through observing other people. Again suggesting that these core psychological skills can be developed. Some of Bandura's key techniques for learning and developing are:

• Vicarious experiences—seeing other people succeed. The closer these individuals are to the type of the person the observer is, the more powerful the impact

- Verbal persuasion—this is the basis of many of the cognitive behavioral therapies available and is the bedrock of coaching
- Techniques that reduce emotional arousal. Dispersing the emotional fog can allow an individual to more rapidly develop.

These techniques are very valuable and form the core of the many of the mental toughness interventions we regularly use.

Self-esteem

A major theoretical construct that can be linked to confidence is self-esteem. The key to self-esteem is pride. This pride is related to oneself and is based on both individuals' strengths and an acceptance of their weaknesses. Pride, like so many things, can be enhanced or destroyed by parents and teachers.

Optimism

It is clear that mental toughness and optimism go hand in hand. Greater levels of optimism have been found to be associated with better mental health, a greater striving for personal growth, better moods, academic and job success, popularity, and better all round coping. It is clear that pessimism is associated with neuroticism and negative moods whereas optimism is principally linked to extraversion, positive moods, and happiness.

Control

Control refers to the extent that we feel that we control our world or believe the world controls us. Control is a key concept in stress management. The seminal work of Karasek has shown us that it is not simply the amount of work we are expected to do that is important, it is the control we have over it. High demands with high control lead to a positive experience. High demands and low control lead to stress and unhappiness. Clearly there is a lesson for educators here, both in their teaching and in their working lives.

The control scale is split into two distinct but related categories: Life control and emotional control. The life control component is linked to controlling one's own future. It is especially important in understanding, and trying to break down, barriers in the educational system. It is still sadly the case that your socioeconomic status is a major predictor of academic success. It is important that we try to move on the mindset of individuals so that they recognise that they can achieve excellence no matter what their background. Clearly some people have resource advantages, but this cannot be left to be the whole story.

The emotional control component is very important in the class-room or lecture theatre. First, less controlled children are far more likely to act out their emotions than others. Whilst this has a posi-tive side when thinking about positive emotions, there is clearly an issue when dealing with the more negative aspects of the emotional continuum.

For the educator emotional control is an important skill. Again the expression of positive feelings is always welcome, however showing signs of stress and anxiety can unsettle a class and set in train a negative spiral. Emotional openness is often seen as an appropriate end goal, but those on the educational frontline usually recognise the importance of holding in the negatives—biting the proverbial tongue.

Emotional control

Lower scores	Higher scores
Feel things happen to them	Good at controlling emotions
See issues as "my problem"	Understand other people's
See things in terms of guilt and blame	emotions/feeling and know how to manage these
Internalise problems and the feelings that arise from them	Difficult to provoke or annoy
Show emotions when provoked or challenged	Does not appear anxious
Anxious	Impassive when others make comments which could upset or annoy
Show a reaction when criticized	Can be insensitive to others remarks
Deal poorly with provocation	Stays calm in a crisis
Respond poorly to poor marks or the prospect of poor performance	Direct their energy to their choices
Can create a sense of fear and avoidance in others	Better at helping others to manage their emotions

Life control

Lower scores	Higher scores
Believe things happen to them	Believe they can make a difference
Often believe "I can't do this because of my ... beliefs/ religion/upbringing etc."	Generally believe "they can"
	Comfortable when asked to do several things at a time
Will readily find excuses for not getting things done	Good at planning and time management
Tends to wait for things to happen rather than take the initiative	Good at prioritising
Freezes when overloaded	Prepared to work hard to clear blockages
Can feel stretched with modest workloads—poor at time management	Happy to take on multiple commitments and know how to deal with them
Comparatively unresourceful	Will feel they have more choices in life "If this doesn't work I'll do something else"
	See the solution rather than the problem

THE WIDER PSYCHOLOGICAL PERSPECTIVE

Learned helplessness

The control dimension of mental toughness is closely related to learned helplessness. Learned helplessness refers to the expectation, based on previous experience, where one's actions cannot possibly lead to success. This important idea was proposed by Seligman (1975). When under pressure learned helplessness individuals tend to experience performance decrements. For example Peterson and Barrett (1987), reported that college students with helplessness beliefs obtained lower marks. They tended to be more passive learners, for example seeking out less help from their academic advisors.

The power of attributions

Weiner and Sierad (1975) produced a model of attributions, which is still very relevant today. In this model ability and effort are seen as existing within the person. Ability is relatively fixed in nature, but effort is very malleable. An individual who believes they control their destiny will attribute success and failure down to these two internal factors. In other words they will succeed because they have talent and worked hard. They fail because they did not have the skills or they simply did not try enough. One of the core philosophies of mental toughness is just that. We are becoming an intensely blame dominated society. Anybody dealing with the public is exposed to the constant threat of complaints. Failure in educational terms is often attributed to the educator, rarely to the student. Clearly it is a combination of the two, and we cannot argue that there is not some bad teaching, but personal responsibility seems to have become rather lost in a cloud of potential litigation. The mentally tough individual is willing to accept the consequences of their actions: both good and bad.

CHAPTER THREE

Mental toughness: its relevance to teaching

Fiona Earle and Peter Clough

Is mental toughness useful in the world of education? Obviously we feel that is. In this chapter we will discuss some of the challenges in the real world and how an understanding of mental toughness might help. It is not meant to suggest that mental toughness is the answer. It is one tool in a vast array of useful options.

Areas that relate to mental toughness include:

• Dealing with stress
• Optimising and understanding the learning environment
• Dealing with change.

Dealing with stress

I am a teacher, working in higher education. I think therefore that I have some understanding of the demands of this role. Through my research work I have discovered that in all the teaching related professions there is a shared set of challenges and rewards that impact on us all.

Teaching is widely recognised as being one of the most stressful jobs. HSE research in 2000 found teaching to be the most stressful profession in the UK, with forty-one and a half per cent of teachers reporting themselves as "highly stressed". However, that is not the whole story. Many are attracted to the profession precisely because it is challenging. The demands are matched by the potential rewards. Many professional people would choose "burnout" against "brown out" any day. Mental toughness offers one way of hopefully avoiding both!

The stressors for teachers are many and varied, but include:

- Workload
- The behaviour of students
- Parents
- Lack of control over their work
- Role conflict and role ambiguity
- Lack of support
- Organisational change
- Poor resources.

It is important that these issues are addressed rather than simply trying to toughen the teachers. However, it is unlikely that all of these will be reduced in the foreseeable future. It will remain a challenging, and potentially rewarding, environment.

The stressful nature of the role is clearly recognised by the UK government who have insisted that a measure of resilience is included in the selection systems for those entering teacher training. At the University of Hull we are working with Peter Wiiliams and other teacher training colleagues at the Scarborough campus. We are trialling the MTQ48 as a selection tool. We are not using it to select, rather we run it in parallel to establish its potential usefulness. Only preliminary evidence is available at the moment but it is certainly interesting. The sensitive candidates do not, on the whole, pass the selection procedure. The very tough are very positively perceived by the existing teachers and are viewed as acceptable by the children. Those candidates, who had average toughness scores, are viewed as competent by the teachers and are often viewed very positively by the children. Whilst this project is in its very early days, it clearly suggests that the relationship between mental toughness and teaching is a rather complex one.

Obviously the students may also have issues dealing with stress. This could be viewed as creating a "perfect storm" with a stressed teacher dealing with a stressed cohort under the leadership of a stressed manager. Again stressors should be minimised wherever possible.

However the stresses related to assessments cannot be removed completely. Some students deal with these better than others. This provides educators with a real problem. In assessments we are really interested in the "true" ability of the student, but this is contaminated by test anxiety. Mental toughness assessment and development can certainly help. It is useful to know which students might be "under-performing" and also provide these vulnerable individuals with tools and techniques to keep their anxieties in check. In the UK we are moving towards a more exam-based system that will surely increase the problem. We would suggest that a child with average intellectual abilities with sound mental toughness will achieve their potential; a child with stronger abilities but with less mental toughness may not.

The learning environment

There are many excellent ideas and techniques to help maximise the learning experience. However many of these share a central problem—they fail to fully take into account individual difference. No technique works equally well for everyone. We believe that mental toughness is one of the key individual differences we should consider.

To illustrate this I will briefly describe an unpublished study we carried out at Hull as part of the initial development work for our model. Students were asked to do two independent tasks. Firstly they did a shooting task. We controlled how successful they were, ensuring that they did badly or well. They then completed a standard written exercise. The performance on these two distinct tasks should have been unrelated. However for the sensitive students failure of the first task led to failing the second one; success on the first task led to success on the second. For the mentally tough the two performances were indeed independent. This sheds new light on the old adage "we learn more from our mistakes than our successes". Clearly this is true for the mentally tough, less so for the sensitive. Much experiential learning involves making your own mistakes and finding your own solutions. This may be less effective for some students. Two basic solutions exist. Either tailor the teaching or enhance the toughness of all the class members so that they can deal more effectively with failure.

Our mental toughness model allows us to dig a little deeper than providing an over arching "general" relationship between it and performance. For example, the commitment scale is a clear predictor of academic success. Highly committed individuals simply stick to things. So a committed child will normally do their homework. They will set goals and try to meet these. Children scoring lower may not. In our opinion, this is not a result of not knowing how to schedule work but reflects a deeper issue. From our experience most people know how to manage their time, some people just don't do it. Skills training is important, but without an appropriate psychological foundation the information will often fail to become embedded.

Overall mentally tough individuals do better in performance tasks. It is possible therefore to generate some general rules of thumb on how to maximise performance in education. The mentally tough pupils will tend to follow these naturally; the sensitive may need greater coaching.

- We should help students establish a sincere belief that they are competent and that occasional imperfections or failures are the norm.
- It is not beneficial for students to attribute their successes entirely to ability. They need to recognise the impact of effort.
- When students perceive themselves as unsuccessful teachers can help them develop the conviction that they can still succeed if they try their best.
- It is important to arrange tasks so that students who work hard are able to perceive themselves as successful. There should not be too many possibilities to fail. Failure can spur on the tough but cripple the sensitive.
- Students should be made aware that just trying harder or spending more time doing ineffective activities does not constitute useful effort. The effort has to be correctly applied.

Bullying and being bullied are major issues in any educational environment. There is a significant problem and schools are working hard to deal with these issues.

We have found that there is a significant correlation between mental toughness and the extent to which an individual feels they are being bullied. Let us be very clear here. We do not endorse the existence of the victim personality. That somehow the bullying victims bring it on themselves. It is simply some individuals are more likely to see bullying in a behaviour than others do. Understanding this helps us understand what is going on. It does not mean that a sensitive person's view that they are being bullied is any less valid. It simply provides another level of explanation. One student may find a teacher to be aggressive towards them whilst another viewing the same behaviour may see it as simply a necessary behaviour to control the classroom. One possible practical benefit of understanding the mental toughness profiles of those reporting bullying is that it might give an insight into upskilling them to deal more effectively with the issues.

Mental toughness has something to say about the bully themselves. It might be suggested as an initial starting point that the mentally tough individual is more likely to bully, as they are certainly more competitive and driven. Whilst it might be the case that they can be a little careless about "bruising other people" it can be argued that most bullying behaviour is carried out by people who need to score points to bolster their psychological wellbeing. Mentally tough individuals are more self-referent, and therefore need less external validation. In other words they have no desire or need to build their esteem at the cost of others.

Change

Change is ever present in education. Mentally tough individuals tend to crave change and can become easily bored with routine. Embracing the opportunities that change and, sometimes, even chaos provide is at the heart of a mentally tough individual.

Often people are surprised at the failure of their new initiatives. However they tend to spend all their effort on expounding its virtues whereas we believe you need to prepare the ground for seeding. Anxiety and doubt are the killers of innovation. If an individual is focused on the "what if" rather than the "why not" even the best idea will not grow.

When operating at an individual level, openness to change has a slightly different flavour. The educator's role is to develop, or change an individual and this can only be achieved effectively with someone who wants to change. This is illustrated by the classic joke "How many psychologists does it take to change a light bulb?" The answer is "Only one—but they have to want to change". Mentally tough individuals are always looking for a new way forward and are not threatened by new ideas. They may robustly disagree with some of them, but only after proper consideration.

Kurt Lewin (1951) the "Godfather" of change theory talked about the need to unfreeze behaviours to allow change to happen. This can be done by either inspiring or by frightening. The former is ideal, but is perhaps less common. Both the approaches are about moving an individual outside their comfort zone. The mentally tough have a much bigger zone to start with and are only too willing to expand his empire of change tolerance.

So what of the sensitive?

Throughout this chapter we have talked about the mental toughness advantage. We believe that this is both real and tangible. But, and it's a big but, we are not advocating that everyone needs to be mentally tough. It is clear that senior positions and good grades are held by the tougher individuals in most instances. We do not believe that this reflects any greater abilities; rather it shows that these individuals are best at jumping the hurdles they have faced. These can be transitions, exams, interviews, and many other life obstacles.

The sensitive amongst us have a harder road to travel, but they have potentially very valuable things to offer the world. We need different thinkers and quickly. It's rather depressing that without help and guidance they may never be able to be in a position to put these ideas into practice. Most of us are averagely tough. This seems to be of little hindrance to progression. Whilst the very tough may have a slight advantage, their very nature may bring into play the downsides of being tough. The real challenge lies with the sensitive—about twenty per cent of the population.

Some of us are born tough, some of us become tough and all of us can behave tough (at least at times).

There are simply two approaches. These are complimentary and can be run together. First, we can provide the sensitive with a toughness toolkit. This does not necessarily mean that their fundamental approach to the world changes; rather it provides them with an operating system for the "real world". It's a stepladder model. If you can't reach the top shelf you can wait until you get taller (which might not happen) or work on getting taller (better nutrition, better posture etc). Or you could just stand on a tool box. We are entering an exciting time with our research. We believe we can help people "behave tough" but we are investigating if this is a skill set enhancement or a fundamental personality change. To the end user it probably does not matter. They can deal more effectively with pressure.

Another very important aspect when discussing the sensitive is identifying them early. Tough and sensitive are fundamentally different. The sensitive are "of the clouds" the tough are "of the earth". They require different support models and different educational practices. The tough prosper despite their environment, but the sensitive are perhaps less lucky. They are easily setback by poor and/or inappropriate teaching. Our research has shown they have a greater need for emotional support and a caring attitude. We need to provide a truly egalitarian environment where the sensitive and tough have an equal opportunity to become the decision makers of the future.

CHAPTER FOUR

Research using the MTQ48

Peter Clough

Introduction

There has been a huge amount of research using the MTQ48 and the model it measures. This is an ongoing process and there is a developing dialogue with researchers across the world.

In this chapter I will summarise some of this research. Most of this has been published in refereed scientific journals, but I have also included some very recent studies that are still in their development phase.

The research will be clustered into three main categories

- Research looking at potential benefits of being mentally tough
- Research looking at why mentally tough individuals may have an advantage
- Research looking at the biological precursors of mental toughness.

The benefits of mental toughness

Mental toughness, as measured by the MTQ48, has shown to be related to a number of psychological advantages. For example, to pain tolerance (Crust & Clough, 2005), injury rehabilitation (Levy, Polman, Clough,

Marchant & Earle, 2006), managerial success (Marchant, Polman, Clough, Jackson & Nicholls, 2009), and recovery from setbacks (Clough, Earle & Sewell, 2002). In addition to these general benefits, two areas of special interest can be identified: potential health benefits and potential educational benefits.

Benefits to health

Veselka and colleagues (2010) showed that both positive and negative humour styles do exist, and that these are differentially associated with mental toughness. Individuals exhibiting either affiliative or self-enhancing humour are more likely to also yield high scores on mental toughness, thereby demonstrating greater resistance against life's adversities. In contrast, those habitually employing aggressive or self-defeating humour show reduced mental toughness, and therefore a vulnerability to stress and the potential health issues associated with this.

A research group based at the University of Basle have carried out a number of interesting studies relating mental toughness to health. Gerber and colleagues (2012) examined whether mentally tough participants exhibit resilience against stress using secondary school students and undergraduates. Participants provided information about their level of perceived stress (10-item Perceived Stress Scale), mental toughness (48-item Mental Toughness Questionnaire) and depressive symptoms (Beck Depression Inventory). Consistent across the two samples, mental toughness mitigated the relationship between high stress and depressive symptoms.

Gerber and colleagues (2012) compared the mental toughness of adolescents and young adults with self-reported exercise using a sample of 284 secondary school students. Participants with higher exercise and physical activity levels scored higher in most MTQ48 subscales. Individuals who fulfilled current physical activity recommendations also reported elevated mental toughness scores compared to those who did not. They concluded that acquiring a mindset of mental toughness might be one way that physical activity and exercise can impact an individuals' mental health.

Gerber and colleagues (2012) using a sample of 284 adolescents (mean age: 18.4 years) investigated sleep, a key aspect of mental and physical wellbeing, to mental toughness and psychological functioning. Increased mental toughness was highly associated with favourable sleep, decreased perceived stress, favourable coping strategies, increased curiosity and optimism.

Gerber et al. (2013) carried out the first longitudinal study using the MTQ48. Their ten-month study prospectively examined the association between mental toughness and stress resilience in 865 students from two vocational schools. Within each school, separate cluster analyses identified groups with different profiles of risk. Four clusters emerged characterising students with well-adjusted (low risk, good adaptation), maladjusted (elevated risk, bad adaptation), deteriorated (low initial risk, worsening adaptation) and resilient profiles (elevated initial risk, improving adaptation). The latter two clusters reported similar levels of mental toughness at baseline, but resilient adolescents scored significantly higher on mental toughness at follow-up. After controlling for possible confounds, baseline toughness levels predicted depressive symptoms and life satisfaction over time.

Benefits in education

Up until now there has been limited research into the direct academic advantages of mental toughness. At the University of Hull a number of researchers are actively investigating this area. Some of these are reported in more detail elsewhere in this book. A few highlights of this research stream are described below.

Myfanwy Bugler and colleagues have looked at the relationships between mental toughness, academic motivation, and negative classroom behaviour. One hundred and eighty one adolescents (93 females and 88 males) aged fifteen to sixteen years completed two questionnaires, one examining academic motivation and the other examining mental toughness. Teachers completed assessments of the students' classroom behaviour. Both motivation and mental toughness were significant predictors of classroom behaviour. However, mental toughness was more significantly negatively associated with behaviour.

Helen St Clair-Thompson and her team carried out a series of three exploratory studies, examing the relationship between mental toughness and different aspects of educational performance in adolescents aged between eleven and sixteen. They found a significant association between several aspects of mental toughness and academic attainment and attendance, significant associations between mental toughness and classroom behaviour, and finally they demonstrated significant associations between mental toughness and peer relationships.

Peter Clough and colleagues looked at the relationship of mental toughness with performance in higher education. The participants were 161 first year university students (105 men, 56 women) enrolled on three different sports-related degree programmes at a large UK university in the north of England. The sample consisted of sport and exercise science students ($n = 46$), sport coaching students ($n = 65$) and sport rehabilitation students ($n = 50$). Two measures concerning academic progress (i.e., credits) and achievement (i.e., end of year grade) were calculated.

The results of the study supported predictions concerning the role of mental toughness in higher educational, as students who passed compared to those that failed their first year of study were found to have significantly higher levels of mental toughness. In addition, the actual academic performance of students with high mental toughness was found to be significantly higher (i.e., mean year grade) than those with low levels of mental toughness. In combination, these results indicate that students with high levels of mental toughness are more likely to pass and proceed (rather than fail and dropout) and achieve higher grades than students with low mental toughness.

Explaining the advantages

Work has begun into trying to identify the underlying mechanisms behind the obvious mental toughness advantage found in many people.

Nicholls, Polman, Levy, and Backhouse (2008) found significant relationships between mental toughness and the use of coping strategies. Consistent with expectations, mental toughness was found to be associated with more problem or approach coping strategies (i.e., reducing or eliminating the stressor) such as mental imagery, effort expenditure, thought control, and logical analysis; but less use of avoidance coping strategies such as distancing, mental distraction, or resignation. This finding suggests mentally tough individuals prefer to tackle problems head-on by actively seeking solutions. Building on this work, Kaiseler, Polman and Nicholls (2009) assessed stress appraisal, coping, and coping effectiveness in a study where 482 athletes reported how they coped with a self-selected intense stressor experienced within a two-week period. Higher mental toughness was associated with more problem-focused coping strategies and less emotion-focused coping strategies.

Using the MTQ48, Crust and Azadi (2010) found mental toughness was related to the use of performance strategies in competition; namely activation, relaxation, self-talk, emotional control, and goal setting. Furthermore, Crust (2009) investigated whether or not mentally tough individuals experienced different levels of affect intensity (e.g., response to emotional stimuli) than more sensitive individuals. However, mental toughness and affect intensity were found to be unrelated, Crust argued that there is no evidence to suggest that mentally tough individuals are less affected by pressure; they may simply deal with pressure more adaptively.

Dewhurst and colleagues (2012) carried out the first ever study to directly examine the cognitive underpinning of the mental toughness advantage. They did this by using the directed forgetting paradigm, in which participants are given a surprise memory test for material they were previously instructed to forget. Participants with high mental toughness showed better recall of a to-be-remembered list following instructions to forget the previous list. The superior recall of the to-be-remembered list suggests that mentally tough individuals have an enhanced ability to prevent unwanted information from interfering with current goals. These findings support the proposal that cognitive inhibition is one of the mechanisms underpinning mental toughness.

The possible biological base of mental toughness

This new area of research is necessarily speculative but we are beginning to accumulate evidence relating to the biological basis of mental toughness. It is clear that mental toughness can be developed, but is also probable that people are born with a different starting point of mental toughness.

There appears to be a significant biological component as suggested by a study of monozygotic (identical) and dizygotic (non-identical) twins (Horsburgh, Schermer, Veselka & Vernon, 2009). The findings from this study have provided evidence in support of the heritability of this trait and suggested that the expression of mental toughness appears to be largely due to genetic and non-shared environmental factors. This supports the argument that mental toughness, like other personality traits, has a biological basis. The four subscales of mental toughness all showed a somewhat lower level of heritability than the overall mental toughness score, but individual differences in challenge, commitment, control, and confidence were nonetheless attributable to genetic and non-shared environmental factors.

Following on from this genetic research we were interested to see if there were correlates of mental toughness within the brain. Eighty young adult participants took part in a brain scanning study. All participants were recruited from the general public and from the staff and student populations at the University of Modena and Reggio Emilia, Italy where behavioural and scan data for this study were collected. They completed the mental toughness questionnaire and also had their brains scanned using MRI techniques.

Of great significance was the identification of a significant positive correlation between high total mental toughness scores and grey matter volume values in the precuneus. This structure plays an important role in multisensory integration, helping individuals deal with multiple stimuli with high levels of competence. In addition, this structure is also involved in taking a first person perspective and when interpreting an action as being controlled by oneself as the agent. This might be a major contributing factor to individual variance in mental toughness, leading to greater levels of life competence, more controlled and diligent actions, and consequently greater levels of efficacy and coping.

Summary

In the last fifteen years there has been considerable research interest in the MTQ48. This test is the most widely used measure of mental toughness in the world at the moment and the data generated by these research studies have provided a fascinating insight into the potential role of mental toughness in the real world. Mentally tough individuals appear to be happier, healthier, and perform better. We are beginning to understand the underpinnings of these advantages and this offers an opportunity to develop this aspect of peoples' lives. The biological basis of mental toughness offers some powerful support for the validity of the model. However, it does not mean that mental toughness is fixed, rather it simply says some people are born tougher than others.

CHAPTER FIVE

Assessing mental toughness—MTQ48

Peter Clough and Keith Earle

Establishing validity and reliability is considered to be an important ongoing process in our work on mental toughness. The various forms of testing we have carried out over the last ten years have provided good support for the MTQ48.

There are two technical aspects of test design that will be discussed in this chapter: reliability and validity.

Reliability

Reliability is the foundation of the usefulness of a test. If the reliability of a test is too low it cannot be used to explain or predict behaviour. The variation within the test simply swamps the variations between individuals. If a test had perfect reliability it would always give exactly the same score. This is never achieved. If the reliability was zero it would mean that test scores were simply random. In reality we need a test that falls somewhere between these two extremes.

The most common approach to assessing test reliability is internal consistency. This looks at the way the individual items relate to each other. Items written to measure one aspect of mental toughness, for example challenge, should relate to the other items in that scale more strongly than they relate to items written to assess other aspects of mental toughness. Perhaps the "gold standard" for this type of analysis is Cronbach's alpha. A score of 0.7 or above is widely accepted as the quality threshold.

Table 1 shows the initial reliabilities of the scales produced when the test was first developed.

It can be seen that all sub scales reached the minimum acceptable level. This supports the homogeneity of each sub scale and the MTQ48 as a whole.

Following on from this initial work the overall internal consistency of the MTQ48 has repeatedly been found to be satisfactory in a number of published research articles. (e.g., Kaiseler, Polman & Nicholls, 2009; Dewhurst, Anderson, Cotter, Crust & Clough, 2012). Although there is clearly some variations in the scale reliabilities in the published literature, especially in relation to the emotional control scale, taking them "in the round" it is clear that the test reaches satisfactory levels of reliability.

Data relating to test-retest is also positive, but less common. Test-retest reliability looks at changes in the test scores. It is clear that mental toughness scores can change, but it is important these changes are attributable to some form of intervention or identifiable action. Random fluctuations would reduce the predictive power

Table 1. Initial scale reliabilities of the Mental Toughness Questionnaire 48.

MTQ48 sub scales	No. of items	Cronbach's alpha
Challenge	8	0.71
Commitment	11	0.80
Control	14	0.74
Emotional control	7	0.70
Life control	7	0.72
Confidence	15	0.81
Confidence in abilities	9	0.75
Interpersonal confidence	6	0.76
Whole scale	**48**	**0.91**

of the questionnaire. In a study carried out with Hull 108 students the test-retest reliability as measured by Pearson's correlation coefficient, was high for all scales, with a range from 0.80 for challenge to 0.87 for emotional control. The sample was tested and retested at a six-week interval.

Validity

Basically validity relates to the usefulness of a test. There are many ways of doing this but four of the main forms of validity will be discussed in this chapter.

Face validity

Face validity relates to the "feel" of the questionnaire. Simply put—does it look right? A test of mental toughness should appear to be a test of mental toughness. The MTQ48 was carefully designed to have appropriate items, have a relatively low reading age and have a simple rating system. The MTQ48 is acceptable to a wide range of people and there are seldom any issues about its applicability. End users find it appropriate and can understand the items. Very young children find it difficult but we have found no issues using it with secondary school students and older. The questionnaire has been translated into many languages and few problems have been identified.

Content validity

This refers to the instruments ability to cover the full domain of the underlying concept. There is considerable debate about this at the moment. Whilst it is clearly possible to write a very short test that has excellent reliability, the usefulness of such a test can be questionable. There are a number of very short quick tests available, but because of their limited number of items they have some difficulty providing a useful differentiation between individuals. Conversely, if you make a test too long, ensuring it covers every possibly aspect and item, its usability declines rapidly and its psychometric integrity is severely challenged. We have therefore tried to design a test that has the complexity to reflect the nuances of mental toughness but short enough for the test to be both useful and useable.

Construct validity

This is a rather complex idea. It relates to the question of whether or not mental toughness is actually a valid concept. Does it exist as a discrete and useful entity? One approach is to ensure that the concept being measured relates to other concepts that are similar in nature. The results of our initial attempt to do this, which was carried out in the development phase of the test, are reported in Table 2.

These correlations are both in the expected direction and are obviously explainable. For example, mental toughness should be associated with lower levels of trait anxiety and it can be seen that it is.

The validation of the questionnaire and the model has continued apace since its initial development. For example, Horsburgh and colleagues (2009) found evidence that mental toughness was significantly related to the big five personality factors of extraversion, neuroticism (negatively), agreeableness, openness to experience, and conscientiousness.

In developing the MTQ48, Clough, Earle and Sewell (2002) found that mental toughness consisted of six components or factors. These factors were, first, challenge, the extent to which individuals see problems as opportunities for self-development. Second, commitment, which

Table 2. Correlations table for MTQ48 and various personality scales.

	Life orientation test	Satisfaction with life scale	Self-esteem scale	Self-efficacy scale	State trait anxiety inventory
Overall MT	0.48**	0.56**	0.42*	0.68**	−0.57**
Challenge	0.39*	0.59**	0.45*	0.66**	−0.54**
Commitment	0.45*	0.52**	0.40*	0.69**	−0.59**
Control	0.49**	0.55**	0.41*	0.64**	−0.61**
Control: life	0.53**	0.59**	0.49**	0.66**	−0.63**
Control: emotions	0.46*	0.56**	0.34*	0.59**	−0.61**
Confidence	0.47*	0.50**	0.39*	0.70**	−0.58**
Confidence: in abilities	0.49**	0.49**	0.45*	0.74**	−0.60**
Confidence: interpersonal	0.41*	0.56**	0.37*	0.69**	−0.61**

Note: ** $p < 0.01$, * $p < 0.05$.

reflects deep involvement with whatever one is doing; third, emotional control, the ability to keep anxieties in check and not reveal emotions to others. Fourth, life control, concerning a belief in being influential and not controlled by others. Fifth, confidence in abilities reflects belief in individual qualities with less dependence on external support, and sixth, interpersonal confidence, this is about being assertive and less likely to be intimidated in social contexts.

The second approach to establishing construct validity is more statistically based. Since the identification of the four C's model, independent researchers have tested the factor structure of the MTQ48 using a statistical procedure called confirmatory factor analysis. Horsburgh, Schermer, Veselka and Vernon (2009) provided support for the factor structure proposed by Clough and colleagues (2002) using a North American sample. There has since then been some vigorous academic debate around the structure of the model. We therefore decided to carry out a very large study to try and resolve the debate. A total of 8,207 participants took part in this study. The participants in this study consisted of 4,342 senior managers, 1,440 lower and middle managers, 1,004 clerical/administrative workers, 442 athletes, and 978 students. Model fit was assessed using confirmatory factor analysis (CFA) and exploratory structural equation modeling, in addition to the robust maximum likelihood estimator. Overall, the results support the factorial validity of the MTQ48 and indicate that the MTQ48 is a robust psychometric measure of mental toughness. It also supports the model itself.

Criterion validity

Finally there is criterion related validity. We feel this is the both the core and the key to the MTQ48. It is a measure of whether or not a score on the MTQ48 is associated with an external measure. Much of our work has concentrated on performance measures. This type of evidence is really at the core of this book. A number of case studies and published studies described in the other chapters reveal an impressive foundation of criterion validity. We believe that the test and model are truly useful and can help enhance both performance and provide an explanation of behaviours in a number of domains.

Summary

The MTQ48 and its associated model have proved themselves over a decade of research. The MTQ48 provides a reliable measure of mental toughness. The model of mental toughness it measures has clear theoretical roots and appears to offer a solid understanding of what mental toughness means. Although there are many models and theories of toughness, we feel ours has a proven track record. It is certainly not the only way of conceptualising this interesting concept, but we feel it offers a parsimonious and useful way forward.

CHAPTER SIX

MTQ48 report types and handling feedback

Bethan Greenall and Claudine Rowlands

MTQ48 report types

There are two basic versions of MTQ48 which each have their own set of reports available.

The standard version generates up to five different reports (briefly described below) which meets the needs of most users. Users and candidates should read the introduction to each report carefully to ensure that they use the report properly.

The young person's version generates a reduced range of reports. This version is most widely used with young persons within secondary education and FE (further education) where it is much more appropriate to provide feedback in oral rather than written form. The report text has been tailored to be more applicable to the young person, that is, references to the workplace have been replaced by terms used within schools or colleges or focused around study and examinations.

Reports

Development report (standard version and young person version)

This reports the individual's scores and an explanation of what they mean together with some potential implications for the workplace. The narrative is provided for the overall measure and for each of the four component scales. Generic development suggestions are offered to enable the candidate to think about modifying behaviour should this be required.

Assessor report (standard version only)

This report provides the individual's scores, a narrative description and potential implications for the workplace. In addition a list of suggested questions is provided to enable a manager to probe the area. The questions are designed to be open and to be behaviourally orientated to generate the fullest responses. They may need to be adapted by the coach or manager to ensure that they are appropriate to the specific situation.

Coaching report (standard version and young person version)

Like the other reports this provides individual's scores, a narrative description, and potential implications for the workplace. With each narrative comes a list of suggested coaching or development actions that the manager or coach can consider for application with the candidate. It is important that the candidate accepts and agrees with any action to be taken. It is a mirror report to the development report.

Distance travelled report (standard version and young person version)

This is a comparison report based on a current and a previous assessment for an individual. This will identify areas in which an individual's sten scores have changed or remained the same after a period of time and/or a period of training and development.

This report is widely used in training, development, and coaching programmes to assess differences arising from the intervention. Hence this is very valuable in ROI (return on investment) studies.

Organisation development report (the group analysis report in the young person option)

This report is created from data gathered from individuals who form a particular group. The report takes the form of histograms of the patterns of scores for individuals who form the selected group.

The grouping might be a specific team, or it could be the entire management cohort of an organisation or a year group in a school or college. It shows the pattern of results for each scale as a histogram of the total number of people who achieve a particular sten score within that group.

This report is useful in identifying trends and patterns within a group and may be an indicator of cultural issues within an organisation.

Handling feedback

Feedback can be a daunting prospect for the provider, but as with many things, full preparation helps to make the process a lot more effective. Good feedback is a powerful tool. Poor feedback can often make things a lot worse—leaving the recipient with a feeling of helplessness and having being judged.

Young people are especially vulnerable to poor feedback. They are developing and often don't have a clear self image. Information that's given to them is therefore often taken as objective and true, rather than as a start for discussion. When working with young people the adage "silence is assent" is rarely true. The person providing the feedback needs to work hard to ensure that the results are;

- Understood
- Discussed
- Agreed in an informed manner.

The importance of preparation

Good preparation begins with informing the test taker why they are being asked to complete the psychometric and in what way their results will be used. It is common for test takers to be resistant to the measure if they haven't been informed of its purpose. Young people often worry that the results may be used in a negative way, rather than to inform an individual's development. It is crucial that the young person is told a little bit about the concept of mental toughness, and that it is being used for their individual development. Remember to check understanding.

An example: using the MTQ48

The MTQ48 can produce three reports. Each report provides a narrative to accompany the test taker's scores on each of the mental toughness scales. Whilst each narrative provides a good description to accompany the result, these descriptions should be used as a guide only. In the most effective feedback sessions, the narratives are used as a prompt for discussion. Always think of a feedback session as a starting point—a foundation for discussion.

Below is an example of an MTQ48 profile. It provides an overview of the sten results for the young person on a ten point scale. The first result provided is the overall score followed by the underlying four scales and two sub scales that make up control and confidence.

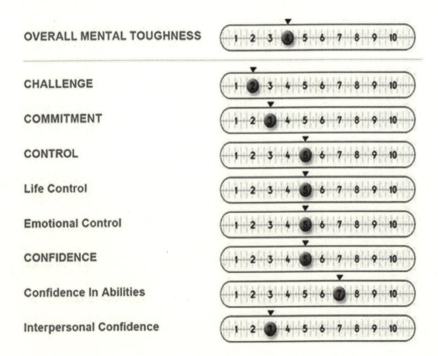

The protocol for interpretation can be set out in four distinct but related stages.

First, consider the overall mental toughness score for the young person.
There are three bandings of scores along the ten point scale indicated below.

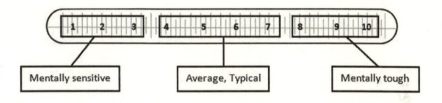

Are you working with a mentally tough scorer, a score typical of the general population or a more sensitive individual?

The key here is never be judgemental. There is not a right or wrong answer—just an answer. In the example above we can see this individual's overall mental toughness is a 4 suggesting they will fall at the lower end of a typical or average result. So this is the start. Is this result credible? Does the participant agree?

Second, consider the spread of scores on sub scales.
A good technique is to scan the sten graph from the overall mental toughness score to the bottom of the profile. Scores on the sub scales should be broadly in line with the overall score. Those that are out of line should be noted. These differences should be explored—they make the discussion come alive. Examine these results for outliers. Outliers are scores that are significantly away from the overall mental toughness score. These often indicate a distinguishing feature in the young person's make-up.

Finally, what are the key themes and issues that have emerged?
Having worked through the profile combining the various scores you will naturally have built a bigger and more thorough picture of the young person. By combining several results, you can pull out the broader themes and make note of any specific issues that emerge.

Billie Jean King once said "Champions keep playing until they get it right."[1] Understanding the distinctions between different profiles will not become clear until one has practised time and time again. Experience is helpful—but so is thoughtfulness. Always think about and question a profile.

Handling feedback—best practice

Any feedback session comes with a number of golden rules. The individual providing feedback should be mindful of these when using any form of psychometric test.

- It should be done
- It should be managed properly
- It should be a two-way process
- It should be open and nonjudgemental
- It should be flexible.

Handling feedback with young people

There are a number of issues to be aware of when handling any feedback with young people ...

1. Suggestibility—this refers to the susceptibility of the young person to take what the feedback provider says as gospel. It is explained by the level of experience the feedback provider has in comparison to the young person. By challenging any assumptions you prevent them from simply agreeing with what has been said.
2. Use of language—young people will relate to the feedback process more easily if it's delivered with the use of simple language. Language is a common barrier we face when working with young groups so information must be provided in a nontechnical way but also contextualised. Always be sure to draw on any situational information for the young person.
3. Social desirability—young people are as susceptible as they want to present a favourable image of themselves. This often manifests itself in the young person challenging more sensitive scores. Ask them why they disagree with it? What experiences can they provide which support the challenge?
4. Scoring out of ten—because results are provided as scores young people tend to see their results as a score out of ten where therefore

ten is the desirable result. This isn't the case. As with other personality instruments the results are an indicator of where someone "sits" on a particular characteristic.

General structure of any feedback discussion

Opening the discussion

The feedback provider should be mindful of exactly how the conversation is opened. Again, the young person should have been introduced to the concept prior to completing the questionnaire. The first point for discussion is a thorough explanation of the feedback process. This usually involves the following points:

- approximate duration of the session, for example, thirty minutes
- the feedback provider will be making brief notes throughout
- it will be a two-way discussion where the test taker should be encouraged to respond to the coaches observations as much as possible
- together actions will be set prior to the next discussion.

Psychometric tests are a mystery to younger individuals. Our experience of working with students at secondary level is that many have never heard of them, let alone know why they are used. We therefore take great care to explain that the MTQ48 is a psychometric measure and is used to help individuals understand and develop an aspect of their personality that is important for almost everything they do. Making reference to the norm group tells the young person that their results are being carefully considered against other individuals similar to themselves, and this is an important facet of the test.

The final part in opening the feedback discussion is to ask the young person for initial observations regarding their results. The young person will commonly respond by saying "That's me!" Or "That's not me at all!" You will often find that it's the extreme scores that provoke this response. The challenge is then to ask the individual what caused that response, why do they feel that way?

The discussion

The discussion needs a plan. When using the MTQ48 we normally examine each of the scales in turn. It is not advisable to simply jump in with an overall summary of the young person's mental toughness. The feedback provider's role is to probe each scale one at a time initially to decipher to what extent the young person is agreeable or not with that score. For example, with an interpersonal confidence score of nine, the coach, teacher, or advisor might say "This score suggests you feel confident getting your point across in a discussion or debate. Can you give me any examples at school where you've argued your point confidently?" The feedback provider has then described a trait that's illustrative of someone high on the interpersonal confidence scale, but also offered an open-ended question which offers the young person the opportunity to either agree or challenge the result.

One of the most important rules to bear in mind when handling feedback that we've previously made reference to is the language used. Psychometric tests are fallible and therefore their sole purpose is to probe for discussion around particular aspects of personality and abilities. Results are not black and white—they are open for interpretation. A great feedback session will encourage as much interpretation from both individuals as possible. When describing the score on a particular scale, the advisor should be careful to use softer language. Softer language might include phrases like "these results indicate you might have a tendency to." Here we have been careful not to suggest that the results "say" the young person is like this or like that. We have also used the word "tendency" suggesting the young person leans towards that particular behaviour but does not necessarily always demonstrate it. Describing the scales in the feedback provider's own language also avoids the discussion being a formal process and allows the young person to more easily recognise those behaviours in themselves, if in fact they agree with the score.

After having talked through a score on a scale you should check:

- "To what extent the young person feels this is a reasonable description of their ..."
- "Can they provide examples of behaviour which supports the score?"
- "Can they provide evidence which challenges the scores and interpretation?"

This process is repeated throughout the feedback session.

Moving forward

The feedback provider will now have identified any areas that the young person wishes to develop and any areas of particular strength that can be maximised for their development.

Using notes gathered during the discussion, the feedback provider together with the young person should spend the final part of the session actioning any development requirements. They should also agree at what time these are to be achieved if they are not ongoing. The table below provides a useful template for using the MTQ48. Obviously, a similar template can be produced for any test.

Scale	Action	What support will be needed?	When will this be achieved?
Life control *The extent to which you believe you control your own destiny*	For example, set smaller, more manageable goals to achieve a bigger one	For example, parental support to make sure that goals are achievable	For example, at the end of every week
Emotional control *The extent to which you can keep your emotions in check*			
Commitment *The extent to which you set goals and promises and the extent to which you are prepared to keep them*			
Challenge *The extent to which you see challenge and change as an opportunity or a threat*			

(Continued)

(Continued).

Scale	Action	What support will be needed?	When will this be achieved?
Confidence in abilities *The extent to which you have the inner belief to deal with setbacks and adversity and do well*			
Interpersonal confidence *The extent to which you are prepared to assert yourself and deal with verbal challenge from others*			

Summary

If done correctly, the feedback session is a learning experience for both parties. It is an intellectual exploration of a complex issue, leading to an agreed answer and action plan. It is a deeply satisfying experience for both the young person and the individual providing feedback when done with care, openness, flexibility, and planning.

Note

1. http://www.brainyquote.com/quotes/quotes/b/billiejean121917.html last accessed December 2013.

CHAPTER SEVEN

Mental toughness—its links to current thinking

Doug Strycharczyk

Mental toughness as a concept stands at the crossroads of some of the most important thinking about young people today. Not just young people either, it is important for the development of all people whatever their age. Like many positive psychological concepts, the earlier the development the better. But developing mental toughness or one of its apparent variants (and there are many) is arguably worthwhile at any time. In fact perhaps the biggest strength of mental toughness is to provide an overarching concept that links many of the recent initiatives with young people.

First, there are so many words and phrases that are used to describe what is essentially the same concept—resilience, character, confidence, grit, tenacity, mindset, optimism, purposefulness, heart, will, reliability, future-mindedness, hard working, and even entrepreneurial. Several models add other qualities for descriptors—creativity, forgiveness, generous, gratitude, honesty, humility, joy, thrift, awe, and even love.

Around the turn of the century we have seen the emergence of two similar pieces of work from North America—Carol Dweck's (2012) mindset concept and Martin Seligman's, (2006) learned optimism and learned helplessness concept. Both are described more fully in this chapter. In the UK Guy Claxton has led thinking around this area and although neither an academic nor an educator, Matthew Syed has added some very useful ideas in his book *Bounce: The Myth of Talent and the Power of Practice* (2011) which is a reflection on his experiences as an elite athlete. Yvonne Roberts in her work with the Young Foundation has also pulled together a good deal of the thinking in this area.

We like to think that our conceptualisation of mental toughness has done something similar.

We have, we think, one main advantage. Almost every other researcher has focused on their understanding of the concept from the specific perspective of their own discipline—whether it is sports or education. We operate (Doug through AQR and Peter through the University) with every major sector in the economy—occupational, social, health, sports, and education. AQR works in more than forty countries, soon to be almost ninety. Our perspective is very broad, but it is interesting and useful to spot the common themes which seem to apply everywhere. It is also helpful in connecting our thinking to other relevant models such as the theory of motivation. You only need to read Daniel Pink's book *Drive: The Surprising Truth About What Motivates Us* (2011), to see the relevance.

In 2011/12, the UK Department of Employment commissioned a paper entitled: "An education for the 21st century: A narrative for youth work today". Although the paper focused on youth work it spoke to the education community as a whole. Youth work is where non-vocational skills of young people are often developed.

One of its key observations was:

> Youth work is concerned with a holistic approach to development, which is fundamental to the emotional wellbeing of young people and promoting greater 'resilience' and 'mental toughness', the quality which determines in large part how individuals respond to stress, pressure and challenge such as change, irrespective of prevailing circumstances.
>
> Outcomes such as increased resilience or mental toughness are products of the capabilities in the logic model *described* below. Increasingly evidence highlights the link between the development of these capabilities and the achievement of 'harder' outcomes around employment, education and health. (UK Department of Employment, 2011/2012)

In 2012, the All Party Parliamentary Group on Social Mobility published a paper on social mobility called the "Seven key truths about social mobility". One of its key findings was personal resilience and emotional wellbeing are the missing link and added that one of the challenges for (social and educational) policy in the UK is to recognise that social/emotional skills underpin academic and other successes and that these can be taught.

Well we would mostly agree with that.

When they write about personal resilience and emotional wellbeing we would say they are talking about mental toughness. We would also argue that young people could be shown how to learn to be mentally tough or personally resilient and possess good emotional wellbeing. But it's not easy to teach them to do this. Like most important things in life—it requires hard work and a clear direction. As we'll see in the chapters on developing mental toughness most of the approaches that work are experiential in nature.

So in the UK we are seeing a groundswell of understanding that developing the whole person is vitally important in developing young people who are skilled and talented and hard working. Focusing on knowledge and abilities is too narrow an approach to be truly effective.

In the USA, there have been two key players in creating this kind of understanding and of creating models which have a good degree of accessibility. This is the work of Dweck and Seligman mentioned earlier. With careful thought they can be applied in most situations. The MTQ48, described elsewhere in this book, provides a truly effective assessment tool. Without a measure it becomes impossible to effectively evaluate a model and, perhaps most importantly, it is not possible to fully evaluate the effectiveness of any interventions.

Another issue is that, although the two sets of ideas are not competitive or particularly contradictory to one another, there has developed a curious tribalism amongst the supporter of either model. It's pointless. Both contribute to our understanding of this key aspect of young people's development.

We would like to think that the mental toughness model overarches both sets of thought and helps to explain how they come together. Take Dweck first.

Carol Dweck is a professor of psychology at Stanford University. She is primarily interested in motivation, personality, and how people develop. In 2006 she published a book *Mindset: The New Psychology of Success*. Anyone remotely involved in the development of young people should read it. She has introduced the notion of mindset which we will see shortly is very similar to mental toughness.

Within this idea she believes that individuals can be placed on a continuum according to their understanding of where intelligence comes from. At one end of this continuum there are those who think their success is based on innate ability. She described these as having a "fixed mindset". When you try to do something you can either do it or not do it, because you have the ability or you don't have the ability to do it.

Those at the other end of the continuum believe success is based on a different, opposite mindset. This she called a "growth mindset". This is based on notions of hard work, learning, training, and good old-fashioned doggedness. Whether or not you succeed when you set out to do something is down to how much effort you put in.

People aren't necessarily self-aware about this. An individual's mindset can often be inferred from their reaction to challenge, change, setback, and failure. Those with a fixed mindset will fear failure. It means (to them) that they are not able enough to do what they have been asked to do. It's a pretty disheartening conclusion to reach about one self.

If a young person takes this view when facing a setback or a rejection (like poor marks for a piece of work) they can damn themselves.

People with a growth mindset are much less sensitive to setback and challenge. They are more likely to see these as one of life's experiences and believe that they can learn from failure. She surmised that those with a growth mindset enjoy better wellbeing and are likely to achieve better performance in most things.

Dweck carried out several large studies which provided a good deal of support for this idea of mindset. Dweck argues that the growth mindset will allow a person to live a less stressful and more successful life.

One of the interesting things to emerge from her work is that when giving recognition to a young person for a piece of work well done, it is much better to praise the individual for their effort than it is to praise them for being clever. The former encourages a growth mindset. The latter promotes a fixed mindset.

The table below list a number of qualities Dweck has associated with having a growth or fixed mindset. Virtually all are commonly use descriptors in mental toughness too.

FIXED MINDSET—Risk avoidance; focus on ability rather than effort; effort is disagreeable; success should be effortless; failure can be attributed to others (blame); mistakes and setbacks are to be avoided, circumstances will influence my success, if I can't succeed it's because I don't have the ability.

GROWTH MINDSET—Challenge is good; risk oriented, confidence; learning from mistakes; hard work is important—more important than ability; practice develops ability; people can change; what one person can learn, everyone can learn, I can shape what happens to me, it's down to me.

Only a growth mindset delivers sustainable success. Growth mindset = mental toughness.

Seligman is a professor of psychology in the University of Pennsylvania's Department of Psychology. He is widely acknowledged as the "father of positive psychology" and has published many books on this subject. *Flourish*, one of his most recent, is to be recommended.

Like Dweck he developed a model about learned optimism and learned helplessness which also appear to have two points at either end of a continuum. His original work on learned helplessness led him to a view that it is a psychological condition where a person has learned to act or behave helplessly in given situations. These situations usually involve some exposure to a setback or adversity. However the significant thing here is that the person will often have the potential to deal with the adversity but will choose not to do so.

Like Dweck he argued that there were two types of people at the extremes of this continuum. Pessimists and optimists. Both learn to be their type.

Pessimists learn to be helpless in a number of ways—they cannot deal with failure and setback and accept their helplessness. They will learn to be helpless if others do things for them and be prevented from learning from their experience. Learned helplessness is a key concept in Psychology and has a significant place in the development of the discipline.

Optimists learn optimism as a result of dealing with events in a positive way—and learning from the experience. Learned optimism was important in creating a state of happiness. In that state it was also much easier to maintain a level of optimism. Again he argued the optimist got more out of life than pessimists—they achieved more and they enjoyed better health and wellbeing.

Once again the ideas correlate closely with the notions of mental toughness and mental sensitivity.

The table below list a number of qualities Seligman has associated with having a growth or fixed mindset. Once again most are commonly use descriptors in mental toughness too.

LEARNED HELPLESSNESS—Feeling out of control—things happen to you—avoid challenge and risk—lack confidence. Doing things for people teaches them to be helpless.

LEARNED OPTIMISM—Feel in control—visualise a world full of opportunity (happiness) irrespective of real surroundings—confidence. Learning develops optimism. Resilience.

Some of Seligman's ideas are challenged by other psychologists. His attention on subjective wellbeing is not universally popular. Others argue that psychological wellbeing is more important. Nevertheless much of his work is admired and it contributes to our understanding of how young people respond to life events.

In the UK, cognitive scientist, Guy Claxton's ideas on learning power have gained some traction. Learning power is described as the collection of psychological traits and skills that enable a person to engage effectively with a variety of learning challenges.

Claxton sees learning power as a form of intelligence which is rooted, not in abilities, but in personality variables such as emotional resilience. Moreover this power can be developed in most people.

To put it simply—improve your learning power and you learn more and ultimately you become more effective.

Guy Claxton[1] has developed a model for building learning power. He identifies a list of seventeen learning capacities grouped around four clusters called resilience, resourcefulness, reciprocity, and reflection.

- Resilience covers the emotional and attentional aspects of learning, and includes perseverance, absorption (or flow), concentration (or managing distraction), and perceptiveness (or attentive noticing).

- Resourcefulness focuses on the cognitive aspects of learning, including questioning, connecting (making links), imagining, reasoning, and capitalising (making smart use of resources).
- Reciprocity covers the social dimension of learning, and includes interdependence (balancing social and solitary learning), collaboration, listening and empathy, and imitation (receptivity to others' learning strengths).
- Reflection covers the aspects of learning that are to do with strategic management and self-awareness. They include planning, self-evaluating (revising), looking for further application (distilling) and fluency in the languages of learning (meta learning).

Once again the overlap with resilience and mental toughness is apparent.

In her book *GRIT: The Skills For Success and How They Are Grown* (Young Foundation), Yvonne Roberts puts forward a compelling argument that Britain's schools need to prioritise grit and self-discipline. Providing evidence from around the world she shows that these contribute as much to success at work and in life as ability (IQ) and academic qualifications.

Over emphasis on exams and academic qualifications has led to these life skills being pushed to the margins. With the UK facing a situation where over a million young people are not in employment, education, or training and tens of thousands of graduates are facing unemployment, she argues that a large proportion of young people have not been adequately prepared for a much tougher and much more challenging economic environment.

In 2011 Matthew Syed published an interesting book *Bounce: the Myth of Talent and the Power of Practice* which became an international bestseller. Syed is a former world champion table tennis player who experiences the high and the lows of elite sports performance. Now a lead writer for *the Times* newspaper he is a clear advocate of Carol Dweck's.

Drawing on his experience as an elite athlete, and extensive reading of other models of performance, he argues that for any significantly complex human activity (especially sports and games) natural talent is comparatively unimportance to "purposeful" practice. He believes the wiring of the brain required to succeed is best achieved through significant amounts of "purposeful" practice. This hard work and purposeful practice is often mistaken for natural talent. Although he is concerned with how young people develop, his writing widens the application of his ideas to other areas of life.

The high performer who appears to have appeared from nowhere will have often served an apprenticeship that no-one will have noticed. The reality is that what most high achievers have in common is a belief that working harder than their peers delivers better development and performance. A belief in their fixed superiority is not their driver.

Syed also draws attention to other factors that he sees as important in performance and wellbeing. None of these ideas are truly his and he acknowledges their provenance. What he does is look at the work of others and seeks to pull them together into some form of more complete picture. These factors include:

- Character and Attitude are important—mind over matter, self belief (even when it's not really there), look for citadels of excellence (work with stars to be a star)
- Choking—control, confidence, dealing with setback, fear
- Learning from mistakes—confidence, it's OK to choke if you do it once …
- Motivational jolts—where does inner drive come from, sustaining it, and "I can do that if he can do it".

Again all of this pretty much corresponds with what we know is described as mental toughness.

Finally we now see the concept appearing in other world's altogether. Jim Collins wrote *Good to Great* in 2001. This is one of the most influential books in management in the world. Looking at what are the characteristics of the most sustainably successful organisation over the previous thirty years, he noted that one of the key factors was something he called "hardiness". He observed that the truly successful didn't avoid difficulty and they faced setbacks as much as any business over the course of their existence. They confronted the brutal facts—they never lost faith.

The net effect is to see that, in recent years, the concepts of resilience, hardiness, and mental toughness have bubbled to the surface in every walk of life. It may not have been "politically correct" to suggest that working harder was a good thing. Being competitive and setting goals and targets has been derided. But these are characteristics of the real world. The world in which we all live is full of challenge, change, and opportunity. With that comes the potential for, and the reality of, failure, setback, and adversity.

It is what we have to prepare young people for.

Note

1. Claxton, G., Powell, G., & Chambers, M. R. (2005). *Building 101 Ways to Learning Power*. Bristol: TLO.

PART II

APPLIED PERSPECTIVES

CHAPTER EIGHT

Evaluation and Return On Investment (ROI)

Bethia Mcneil

Introduction

What matters more, the pleasure or the measure? Or is it in fact both? In working with young people, particularly in out of school or informal settings, measurement is often considered to come at the expense of something else; it is burdensome, and gets in the way of developing relationships. It can be felt to be at odds with a more intuitive perspective, which values individual experiences and stories, and the quality of interaction.

Services that focus on the personal and social development of young people have long collected and shared qualitative evidence about the difference they make to the lives of those they work with—through stories, journeys, and anecdotes. This evidence can be very powerful, but the youth sector has historically struggled to draw together quantitative evidence of value and impact. An important part of making the case for such services is showing that they can offer savings to the public purse, preventing the outcomes we know can represent high costs to society and the individual. Articulating value clearly is critical, particularly when resources are stretched. It can help build a case for investing in the most effective services which secure the best long-term

65

outcomes for young people. It can also help services evidence their role and impact.

But measurement is often seen to be someone else's agenda, usually imposed. It is not felt to be something which sits comfortably alongside the practice and processes of our work with young people, which would prioritise their voice and their individual journeys travelled.

Measurement is difficult, and resource intensive. Many organisations feel isolated when they think through the practical implications, and are struggling as they consider the path that lies ahead.

But measurement is not an agenda that can be ignored. More to the point, we should not want to ignore it.

This chapter focuses on the role of measurement in work with young people, and why it should be a shared agenda. It explores the wider context and the growing emphasis on evidencing impact. It looks at some of the challenges of "measuring" personal and social development, and offers some guidance on translating theory into practice.

Measurement in context: focusing on mental toughness

As a society, we tend to value what we measure, so the first step is to make sure that we are measuring what we value—the things that matter.

Young people are living, learning, and negotiating transitions to adulthood and independence in an increasingly complex and challenging world, in which they face greater levels of choice and opportunity, but also unprecedented uncertainty and risk. This calls for empowered, resilient young people, who play an active role in navigating these paths.

There is substantial and growing evidence that developing social and emotional capabilities supports the achievement of positive life outcomes, including in education, work, and health. Employers increasingly talk of capabilities such as resilience, communication, and negotiation as being the foundations of employability. These capabilities are important for their own merit and for their significance in achieving other outcomes. In other words, the services that support young people to develop social and emotional capabilities help them to achieve "personal change" in their lives, which itself can lead to "positional change" in their circumstances.

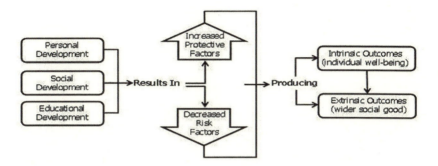

Figure 1. The factors that can affect young people's outcomes.[1]

Evidence suggests that approaches focusing on building social and emotional capabilities can have a greater long-term impact than ones that focus on directly seeking to reduce the "symptoms" of poor outcomes for young people. Yet, at the same time the very services that most explicitly focus on supporting young people to develop these capabilities are under unprecedented financial pressure. At a time of financial austerity, demonstrating how services improve outcomes, and reduce costs to the public purse, will be attractive to providers, funders, and commissioners alike.

Many services play a vital role in this picture, but while they have powerful examples of lives transformed, over time they have struggled to provide "harder" quantitative evidence of the difference that they make, and to articulate the value that they produce for young people and for society more broadly.

Historically, the evidence base for the significance of social and emotional capabilities has been hard to draw together. There has been a lack of consensus around language and definitions, and it has been widely assumed that the development of these capabilities is too difficult to measure or evidence. Providers have tended to depict the value of their work through the individual journeys of young people, and by measuring or monitoring the activities that are easiest to quantify. Often these are the tangible aspects of their work: "indicators" such as number of qualifications achieved, number of hours of services provided, or attendance, for example. These are activities where it is possible to capture externally verifiable and recognised inputs and outputs relatively easily. This focus on the "harder" outcomes often comes at the expense of so-called "softer" social and emotional capabilities. Self-esteem, resilience, and thinking skills, for instance, all underpin young people's progress but can be hard to assess. It can be difficult to make the case for such "softer" outcomes, even where young people need to develop these capabilities before they can go on to achieve "success" in other areas of their lives.

But just focusing on the aspects of services that are easier to measure has major weaknesses, and does not reflect their value. It fails to reflect a cornerstone of the value added by services for young people: the attainment of social and emotional capabilities.

Moreover, it has never been more important to reflect this value. In times of financial austerity, all public spending is under scrutiny. Every service funded with public money needs to be able to demonstrate the difference it makes, and its long-term value—its case for investment. As a consequence, there is increasing pressure to assess and articulate the value that services produce, both for the young people who use them and for society as a whole. Individuals and organisations involved in funding and/or commissioning, organising and delivering such services need to know the outcomes that matter and the difference services are making to the lives of young people.

However, measuring and isolating the impact of a particular service on the development of young people's social and emotional capabilities is not straightforward. The link between the impact of services and the achievement of these outcomes is hard to assess or demonstrate, because for many young people, these outcomes are some way ahead in the future. Part of the difficulty lies in the complexity of young people's lives: there are a huge range of influences on their development—from school and youth clubs to health professionals, alongside family and friends—and many services will touch on multiple aspects of a young person's life, across home, family, and community. The process of measuring outcomes is hard too—we do not always share the same language or terminology, and there are hundreds of different approaches in use.

The drive to measure

But where is the drive to measure coming from? And what does "measurement" really mean in practice?

There are a number of factors influencing theory and practice around measurement in work with young people.

- A growing need to demonstrate value for money, accountability, and transparency in all areas of public spending
- The rise of Payment by Results and outcomes-based commissioning
- The changing profile of philanthropists and the growth of social investment—leading to a greater interest in the impact of investments, and a more "business-like" approach
- An increasing need to address inequality, disadvantage, and exclusion
- The reduction in public spending, meaning services need to be better targeted.

This is unlikely to be a temporary departure from normal service—these shifts represent a fundamental reshaping of funding, commissioning and delivery in work with young people, the way we do business and the way that investment into our services is made. It is a development we need to embrace and to feel confident in—and part of this is about understanding the benefits of building the evidence base for our work.

So why should this matter to us? And what do all these terms mean? Where do outcomes and impact fit in? And how do we know whether we are measuring, monitoring, or evaluating?

The measurement and evaluation of the impact of services is an important part of the wider cycle of planning and commissioning. Findings about what has worked, for whom, and why, are a key output of the commissioning process and need to be fed back to inform future provision.

Outcomes can be defined as the changes your service or programme creates. Impact is the cumulative difference you make, to your target group, but also to the wider community. It is the change that you can attribute to your activities—not what would have happened anyway.

Outcomes and impact can be measured, monitored and/or evaluated. It is important to understand the difference.

Measurement refers to the gathering of data, using a standard unit of measurement, or a measure. This may be counting something (qualifications or accreditation for example) or, in our context, using a particular tool or approach to capture change or difference. Measurement may be for the purpose of monitoring, or for evaluation.

Monitoring involves collecting, analysing and learning from information. This might be tracking the numbers of young people attending a group or programme, exploring whether there are differences based on gender or age, for example, and changing the activities provided in response. It could also include seeking regular feedback from young people, and using this to inform the development of new programmes. It could also involve using a tool like the Mental Toughness Questionnaire, and recording young people's scores over time.

Evaluation involves making judgements about whether or not a project or programme "works"—whether it has had the impact you intended. Evaluation goes beyond monitoring, and is dependent on a number of other factors, such as being clear about what would have happened to the young people you work with if they had not been involved in your provision: the so-called "counterfactual".

So why do it? Monitoring and evaluation can be time consuming and challenging. They can reveal difficult facts/findings that you might not want to know, and pose even more questions. However, they should be a vital part of what we do. There are a number of reasons why measurement is critical, particularly in work with young people:

- The impact of negative outcomes on young people and communities: negative outcomes for young people, such as unemployment, poor mental health, early unplanned parenthood or debt have far reaching consequences, impacting on their lives well into adulthood, and in many cases, on their lives of their children too. Young people can bear the scars of these outcomes for a lifetime, and it is vital that we understand the services that can prevent and protect against these outcomes, and support them to grow their reach.
- The costs associated with poor outcomes: the financial cost of unemployment, poor health and family intervention are high, and the social costs can be higher. It is essential that available funds are spent on effective provision that offers value for money.
- The potential to improve outcomes and prevent harm: not all services for young people are beneficial, particularly to those who are most vulnerable or disadvantaged. Equally, we know that there are so many programmes and services that can have a transformative effect on young people's lives. Robust measurement can ensure that harmful interventions are recognised and stopped, and the potential to transform lives is realised.
- Reliance on public funding: many services working with young people are heavily reliant on public funding, and have been so historically. There is stiff competition to provide services to young people now, and commissioners and funders want robust evidence that the

services they are being asked to invest in make a difference and offer value for money.

- The importance of advocacy: many organisations working with young people do not just provide services for young people, but also advocate on their behalf. Many organisations seek to change society's perceptions of young people. better measurement could strengthen the case these organisations can make, and help to demonstrate the effectiveness of services in promoting positive outcomes for young people as positive members of our communities.
- The potential to influence policy and practice: if providers were able to evidence the effectiveness of their services, it could lead to a change in policy and practice, moving towards models of earlier intervention and support, and ultimately change policy where it impacts particularly on the most vulnerable and disadvantaged.

Stuart et al.[1] usefully summarise the benefits of monitoring and evaluation in work with young people:

- it links individual learning and its impact to both the programme's aims/objectives and the business' needs
- it is a natural part of review for individuals and organisations
- it can clarify what the programme is trying to achieve (content) and how (process)
- it establishes where the programme is working well and further improvements needed
- it closes the loop with feedback on progress against business needs.

But we know there are challenges—the evidence base for personal and social development, and indeed wider services for young people, is patchy and has not benefited from sustained focus or attention. Making causal links between the work we do and the impact and outcomes for young people is hard, and there is little agreement on the sources of value which correspond to our work, and the best way to assess them.

Facing the challenges—putting measurement into practice

Attribution and contribution

Making a judgement about whether or not a programme "works", and achieves its intended impact, involves making causal links between what we do and the outcomes for young people—that is, that the outcomes young people achieve are because of their involvement in our programme, and are not likely to have happened anyway. This is particularly challenging in work with young people, for two main reasons: first there is the problem of attribution—young people lead complex lives, and it is difficult to isolate the impact of one service or programme in amongst a range of other influences. Second, for many young people, the outcomes we want for them (and that they want for themselves) lie some way ahead in the future. This may be because of their age (for example, a ten-year-old will not find fulfilling and sustainable employment before he/she is at least sixteen) or because of their stage (a young person leaving custody, for example, will need intensive and long-term support to build new relationships, find somewhere safe and secure to live, and to re-enter learning or work).

So, how can a service or programme working "upstream" with young people demonstrate its impact? How can it show it is making a difference even when it cannot directly measure the numbers of young people achieving longer-term or "harder" outcomes like finding and sustaining a job, getting a degree, or settling into a healthy, happy relationship? Most services work to develop young people's social and emotional capabilities precisely because of their importance in achieving these longer-term outcomes, and much effort has gone into understanding the relationship between social and emotional capabilities and the achievement of such outcomes—for although important, this link is not straightforward.

There is a growing consensus around the role that social and emotional capabilities play in the achievement of "extrinsic" outcomes—those that can be measured and valued by other people. The evidence base which supports these connections is substantial and evolving, but more work is needed to strengthen our understanding.

One way to reflect on the challenge is to focus on contribution—where it is too difficult to prove cause and effect, contribution analysis[2] can help to make reasonable conclusions about the impact a programme is having on outcomes. Contribution analysis means taking into consideration all other influencing factors (for example, a young person's family, peer group, and teachers) and clearly articulating why you think the programme will play a part—what is its contribution and why might we logically expect it to make a difference?

Articulating return on investment

Alongside demonstrating the impact of the work they do with young people, many services are increasingly keen to show return on investment—that is, the positive "returns" that are generated, after the service has been paid for. This is usually calculated as savings—costs that are avoided as a result of a service. For example, this may be a service which aims to divert young people from prison, thus avoiding the high costs associated with custodial sentences. A key challenge for services for young people is that potential savings are spread among a variety of agencies: programmes that support young people to return to employment, education or training, for example, may provide savings for the local council, but also the Department of Work and Pensions in the future; similarly, work with young people to prevent drug and alcohol misuse may accrue savings for the Department of Health too. When savings are spread around like this, and sometimes over time, it can be difficult to make a strong case for investment into programmes—who should make the investment if the returns are shared? It is also important to understand the range of fixed costs and economies of scale to take into account: diverting a young person from custody, for example, will not close a unit in a Young Offenders Institution. Building positive mental health and wellbeing will not make the local CAMHS team redundant—in the short term at least, many more young people will be on the waiting list. Whilst we can hypothesise savings, we need to translate this into available hard cash in order to make the strongest case. Furthermore, the issue is made much more complex when focusing on social and emotional capabilities. The challenge here is to connect the development of these capabilities with outcomes where we can ascribe costs savings. The diagram below shows how we might begin to do this, but more work is needed to strengthen these connections.

"Good data": what counts as evidence?

When the impact of a service or programme is measured, we are effectively gathering data to grow an evidence base. There are two factors that must be considered when thinking about what counts as evidence: reliability and validity. This means that, through data gathering, consistently robust results are achieved over time, even when working with different groups of young people, and with different staff using the measure. It also means measuring the outcomes that matter, and that the programme intends to have an impact on. This is easier said than done—many services feel they should be measuring impact on long-term outcomes like employment, even when the programme itself focuses on social and emotional capabilities.

There are three key factors that are important in producing good evidence:

- well-defined outcomes—the difference you want to measure
- metrics that provide an accurate standard for measuring that outcome
- a robust methodology—the approach to measuring (or gathering data) fairly.

Making the case about the impact of a programme, and in particular, attributing savings means showing that the programme in question causes improvements in the lives of young people. This means, as far as possible, ruling out other possible causes for these improvements. The normal way to do this is to use a fair comparison. The comparison may be with outcomes for the same young people before they took part in the programme, or with another group of similar young people who

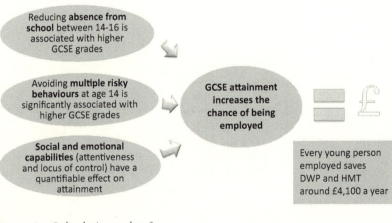

Figure 2. Calculating value.[3]

are not taking part in the programme. If the only significant difference between the two groups is the programme, then we can say the programme is very likely to have caused the difference. For example, with measures of social and emotional capability, testing using an externally validated score both before and after the programme would normally imply that the programme itself has caused an improvement.

To make robust statements about the difference a programme makes to the lives of young people, data on young people's social and emotional capabilities must be collected using a validated scoring tool and we must be able to compare it with a population average spread of scores.

This approach is not widespread in services for young people, and as a consequence, the evidence base for our work is not as strong as it could be. Traditionally, we have relied too much on before and after measures, with no comparison group (that is, asking young people what they think at the start and end of a programme, but not comparing results with young people who are not taking part), retrospective reports (for example, asking a young person to look back to the beginning of a programme and say what they think has changed), and unvalidated measures created for specific programme (such as in-house questionnaires).

Validated tools are based on extensive trialling and research which, over time, provides a sound evidence base that can substantiate claims about "average results" and produce similar scores for individuals in similar situations—a "population average". This means that if person A scores themselves a five out of ten, we know this indicates roughly the same as a five out of ten for person B. Without this, it is hard to add up scores for groups of individuals in a way that is meaningful.

Developing your approach: finding what works

Building confidence in the links between social and emotional capabilities and longer-term outcomes for young people is only part of the story. Consistently and robustly measuring the difference that services make to these capabilities—and why—is critical in developing the evidence base for the value of services for young people.

There are many measurement tools and techniques available, some well-known and widely used, and others less so. Different types of tools will produce very different types of evidence. Some tools can be used for evaluation and others for monitoring.

There will be a range of reasons for selecting certain tools or approaches: the time involved in using the tool, the level of expertise required, the demands placed on young people, cost and the standard of evidence achieved. Tools can be more appropriate for diagnosis (understanding the needs and wants of young people) than performance management (how well they were met), and it is important to exercise caution regarding the conditions under which the tool is used. Tools used in isolation may give restricted or narrow information, and do not always provide an objective picture. It can be beneficial to use tools alongside other approaches such as case studies or witness testimonies in order to triangulate, or verify, the information gathered.

Deciding on an approach to measurement involves thinking through a number of questions:[3]

- What is the question you are seeking to answer?
  Reflecting on the question you are seeking to answer will influence the evidence you will need to gather. Your question may be more about monitoring ("how can I understand the distance travelled by the young people we work with?") or evaluation ("what is the difference my service makes to young people who would otherwise not access such support?"). It is also useful to think through the questions that others might have—what would parents want know? What about teachers, funders, or commissioners? And young people themselves?

- What standards of evidence do you want to achieve?
  The approach to measurement also needs to be shaped by the standards of evidence you want to achieve. Different approaches such as case studies, or validated measures, will produce very different types of evidence. Different evidence enables you to draw different conclusions, such as the extent to which you can compare one service with another.

- What is proportionate?
  A provider working with a small group of young people over a short time scale may decide on a reduced level of measurement, which is proportionate to that cohort. Alternatively, if a provider wants to take a particularly rigorous approach, it may opt to work with a sample

of young people in the first instance, rather than a larger group or the whole cohort.

Proportionality also relates to how often you measure—beginning, middle, and end on a short programme might be burdensome, whereas this may be too infrequent on longer programmes. This also needs to be considered from the perspective of young people, in terms of what proportion of their time with you is taken up with measurement or evaluation.

- Who are you working with, and how?
  This involves thinking about both the young people you are working with, and your approach, alongside the agencies and individuals with whom you have relationships.

  The young people you work with, and how you work with them, will influence your practical approach to measurement. This may be because you work more in a group work setting than one to one, for example, or because the young people you work with have a disability such as a visual impairment or an autistic spectrum disorder.

  Similarly, thinking about who else you work with (schools, local authorities, funders, parents, and so on) can highlight who you need to communicate your impact to, and how. Different stakeholders will respond to different types and standards of evidence.

- What outcomes are you focused on?
  The priority outcomes for a programme will influence the approach to measurement. This closely relates to the tool chosen but also when and how often a tool is used, and in what setting. It is also useful to consider what other information might be helpful, and how others can assist. Asking a referral agency for information on next destinations, for example, can add colour or depth to your data, as can asking a school or other institution for wider information about a young person's progress.

- What resources are available?
  In practice, available resources often play a strong role in determining the approach to measurement. Resources can include funding to purchase tools and associated training, access to IT systems, or time to embed an approach across a service. Different approaches will make very different resource demands. This is also important

to consider in how data are used. A paper-based approach has little value, for example, if there is no capacity or process to feed the data into a wider system which enables learning from the findings.

Evaluating difference and what makes a difference

Being able to confidently say that a programme or service makes a difference to the lives of young people is important—but can we also say why? Knowing why a programme or service has the impact it has is vital in achieving the same positive outcomes consistently, spreading this learning to others, and replicating success more widely. It also helps to demonstrate what is unique about a service or programme: there may be many others who aim to—and do—develop young people's social and emotional capabilities. But approaches will differ. Why should your particular service or programme be continued, scaled up or invested in?

A key step in understanding why a programme or service has the impact it does is developing a theory of change. A theory of change is a causal pathway, which links what you do with your outcomes and impact. It explains the "how", by setting out the steps needed to make change happen. It also helps to check assumptions (for example, are you assuming that all young people respond to IT, which is why they engage with your programme, or is it really the lunch you provide?) and the evidence behind a programme (for example, how do you know that young people learn effectively using IT? Is there evidence to suggest that this is the case?). This can assist in focusing measurement— making sure what is being measured is what matters, and that the methodology is robust and appropriate. Developing a theory of change can be a positive transformative experience for those involved, and is also very effective at bringing together different stakeholders—face to face practitioners, managers, funders, parents, and young people themselves.

Conclusion

This chapter has looked at the importance of measurement in work with young people. Measuring our impact is critical in demonstrating not only the difference we make directly to longer-term outcomes around learning, work, and health for example, but also how we contribute indirectly through the development of social and emotional capabilities—the outcomes we know that matter to young people as they navigate risk and opportunity.

We know that there are no easy answers, and the size of the challenge we face: we have thousands of individuals and organisations working with young people, who provide vital services that change lives and offer good value for money—but who are struggling to prove it. Even when we can begin to show where we are making a difference, we cannot always show how.

We also have funders, investors and commissioners who are struggling to identify effective programmes, services and approaches, and risk making uninformed decisions about where best to put their money.

At sector level, the evidence base for social and emotional capabilities is not growing, the difference in language and terminology remains, and there are no common platforms that allow for knowledge sharing or comparison.

Ultimately, perhaps the biggest and as yet unspoken problem of all—young people lose out. The best services are not always sustained, decision-making processes are not transparent, leading to a loss of trust, and young people—as service users—cannot always explain the value they take from services.

So what is the solution? A useful way to think about this is in the context of a change agenda for the whole sector—a journey we are travelling on together, rather than an individual path.

In previous work, New Philanthropy Capital NPC[4] has set out a series of steps that we might follow:

1. What is the outcome to be measured? Do organisations in the sector agree on a single outcome or set of outcome measures?
2. How is that outcome defined? Has it been defined by a measurement tool or set of criteria?
3. How should the outcome be captured? Are the right systems in place to enable services to capture it?
4. How can the outcome be attributed to an intervention? Can services explain what would have happened to young people without their intervention?
5. How can the outcome be valued? Are there good financial proxies that can be used to estimate value?

A clearer focus on the outcomes that matter, and why, alongside greater consensus and consistency in use of language, is the first vital step. This will allow a clearer focus on measuring these outcomes, and understanding how our work makes a difference. More robust measurement will also enable us to grow more confident in showing where we contribute to cost savings.

We also need to remind ourselves of the benefits to our sector:

- The development of a common language—transparent, comparable, and consistent
- A growing evidence base, which testifies to the role and contribution of services for young people
- A virtuous circle where providers grow in confidence as do investors, commissioners, and funders
- Clarity about your role to communities, schools, and business, forging links and creating partnership opportunities
- A better understanding of value, and parameters for assessment
- Support for reflective practice, professionalisation, and growth
- Better service design and hence better outcomes
- A stronger case for the most effective services.

Notes

1. Stuart, K. et al. (2011). *Literature review 5: Research and evaluation methods with children and young people*. Ambleside: Brathay Trust.
2. For more information, see Mayne, J. (2008). Contribution Analysis: an approach to exploring cause and effect. In: *ILAC Brief*, 16.
3. These questions are taken from McNeil, B. *et al.* (2012). *A Framework of Outcomes for Young People*, produced for the Catalyst Consortium, available at www.youngfoundation.org
4. NPC. (2011). *Measuring together—impact measurement in the youth justice sector*.

CHAPTER NINE

Developing mental toughness in young people: coaching as an applied positive psychology

Christian van Nieuwerburgh and Suzy Green

Coaching in education

Whilst coaching has been used in the corporate setting for decades, coaching in education did not make a real presence until the early part of this century. During the last decade, coaching in education has flourished in the UK, Australia, and the US (van Nieuwerburgh, 2012b). Within the UK, a landmark document written in 2005 (National Framework for Mentoring and Coaching) encouraged educators to broaden their interventions to include non-directive coaching. This was followed by an influential workbook entitled *Leading Coaching in Schools* which provided a rationale for the use of coaching in educational settings and offered "structured support for leaders who wish to embed coaching practices throughout the school" (Creasy & Paterson, 2005, p. 2).

Coaching in the education sector is an increasingly popular approach to the enhancement of staff and student performance and wellbeing. Whilst research is embryonic and further research is required, the results of scientific studies so far are encouraging and suggest that it is a promising approach for educators to consider (Green, Oades & Grant, 2006; Green, Grant & Rynsaardt, 2007; Spence & Grant,

2007; Passmore & Brown, 2009; Grant, Green & Rynsaardt, 2010; van Nieuwerburgh & Tong, 2013). In addition, coaching is increasingly being used as part of whole-school Positive Education Programmes that successfully integrate coaching with positive psychology interventions (Green, Oades & Robinson, 2011). There has also been a recent interest in exploring the use of coaching approaches and skills in primary schools (Briggs & van Nieuwerburgh, 2010–2011; Adams, 2012).

Through research and practice, it has been proposed that student performance and wellbeing can be improved through a number of coaching related interventions, including coaching of teachers (Ross, 1992; Shidler, 2009) and coaching students directly (Campbell & Gardner, 2005; Green, Grant & Rynsaardt, 2007, Passmore & Brown, 2009). This chapter aims to introduce the reader to the research and practice of coaching (as an applied positive psychology) for both students and teachers, with a particular emphasis on coaching for mental toughness.

What is coaching?

Whilst the term "coaching" has many definitions and uses, it is popularly referred to as sustained cognitive, emotional, and behavioural change that facilitates goal attainment and performance enhancement, either in one's work or personal life (Douglas & McCauley, 1999). A definition that is particularly resonant in the education sector is "unlocking people's potential to maximize their own performance" (Whitmore, 2009, p. 10).

The term "evidence-based coaching", coined by Grant (2003), is also increasingly being utilised. It is defined as an applied discipline and is informed by knowledge drawn from multiple disciplines (e.g., psychology, sociology, adult learning, education, organisational behaviour, business management) (Green & Spence, in press).

It is also important, at this stage, to make a distinction between "coaching" and "mentoring". In a new definition of coaching in education, van Nieuwerburgh highlights the non-directive nature of coaching, proposing that it is "a one-to-one conversation focused on the enhancement of learning and development through increasing self-awareness and a sense of personal responsibility, where the coach facilitates the self-directed learning of the coachee through questioning, active listening, and appropriate challenge in a supportive and encouraging climate" (van Nieuwerburgh, 2012b, p. 17). Coaching is more about facilitation than providing answers. Green and Spence (in press) describe coaching as a collaborative relationship formed between a coach and a coachee for the purpose of attaining valued outcomes. Central to the coaching process is the clarification and articulation of personal and professional goals, goals that are generally set to stretch an individual's current capacities (Spence & Grant, 2007). Whilst the coaching process occurs within a supportive, collaborative relationship, it is action-oriented and focused on creating purposeful, positive change. It involves talking, reflecting and most importantly, planning for action. The coach does not assume control of the coachee's change process (by telling them what to do), rather she uses questioning to build self-responsibility for change in order to discover (or rediscover) the latent strengths and tacit knowledge needed to create the solutions required for goal attainment to occur (Berg & Szabo, 2005).

Green and Spence (in press) state coaching assists individuals to enhance goal striving by: first, developing a positive or preferred future vision, second, identifying desired outcomes, third, establishing specific personal goals, fourth, enhancing motivation by identifying strengths and building self-efficacy, fifth, identifying resources and formulating action plans, sixth, regularly monitoring and evaluating progress, and seventh the modification of action plans (based on an ongoing evaluation of progress) (Grant, 2003). The use of simple coaching models such as the Goal, Reality, Options, Will (GROW; Whitmore, 2009) encourages coachees to take ownership of their goal striving and behaviour change by inviting them to set the agenda for each coaching conversation. The GROW model also forms part of an ongoing iterative process that includes the Review and Evaluation (RE-GROW) of goal-directed action over multiple coaching sessions, which permits modifications to goals or action plans as needed. This review-evaluate-modification component of the coaching process creates a "cycle" of self-regulation (see Figure 1) that is important for successful behaviour change (Grant, 2003).

Coaching in education: the evidence

As noted earlier, there is increasing interest in the use of coaching in education, both for students and staff. For example, the University

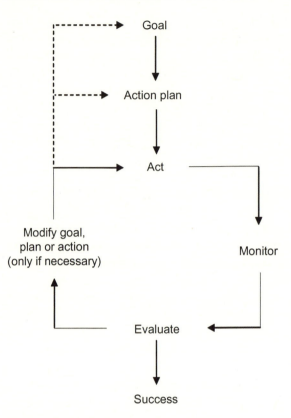

Figure 1. Generic model of self-regulation.

of East London's (UEL) Coaching Psychology programmes include a dedicated optional module on "Coaching in Education" and UEL hosted an international conference on coaching and positive psychology in education in July 2010. However there is currently limited research on evidence-based coaching in the education sector.

Research conducted at the University of Sydney has given prelimi-nary support for the use of evidence-based coaching in educational settings for students and staff. Green, Grant and Rynsaardt (2007) con-ducted a randomised waitlist control group study of evidence-based life coaching with an adolescent population. Participants were randomly assigned to receive either a ten-week cognitive-behavioural solution-focused life coaching programme or a waitlist control. They found that the 28 female senior high school students in the coaching programme experienced a significant increase in levels of cognitive hardiness, hope, and a significant decrease in levels of depression, compared to the wait-list control group.

Furthermore, a pilot study was conducted by Madden, Green and Grant (2011) utilising strengths-based coaching for primary school boys in a within-subject design study. Thirty-eight year five (aged ten to eleven) male students participated in a strengths-based coaching programme as part of their personal development/health programme at an independent, private primary school in Sydney, Australia. Participants were randomly allocated to groups of four or five with each group receiving eight coaching sessions over two school terms. The Youth Values in Action survey was used to highlight participants' character strengths, and the participants were coached in identifying personally meaningful goals, and in being persistent in their goal striving, as well as finding novel ways to use their signature strengths. They also completed a "letter from the future" activity that involved writing about themselves at their best. The strengths-based coaching pilot programme was associated with significant increases in the students' self-reported levels of engagement and hope. The authors concluded that strengths-based coaching programmes may be considered as a potential mental health prevention and promotion intervention in a primary school setting to increase students' wellbeing and may also form an important part of an overall positive education program.

In another study, Grant, Green and Rynsaardt (2010) studied the impact of "developmental coaching" on teachers. A randomised controlled (pre-post) design was used to explore the impact of coaching on goal attainment, workplace wellbeing, resilience, and leadership styles. Participants were forty-four high school teachers who were randomly assigned to either a twenty-week cognitive-behavioural, solution-focused coaching intervention or a waitlist control group. Participants in the coaching group received multi-rater (i.e., 360-degree) feedback on their leadership behaviours and with the help of a qualified coach, attempted to use that feedback to develop a more positive, constructive leadership style. The findings indicated that the coaching participants reported significant increases in goal attainment, wellbeing and resilience, and also significant reduction in stress. Coaching also appeared to enhance dimensions of constructive leadership whilst reducing self-reported aggressive/defensive and passive/defensive styles. These findings suggest that coaching, as a professional development methodology, has great potential to contribute to the professional development and wellbeing of teachers in an educational setting.

In the UK, van Nieuwerburgh & Tong (2013) undertook a mixed methods study on the impact of training secondary school students to become coaches. Being trained to become a coach and then coaching other students was found to lead to improved attitudes towards learning. Participants reported improved study skills, as well as increased levels of emotional intelligence and better relationships in schools. These findings suggest that training students to become coaches can help to improve their performance in school. Whilst these studies provide promising support for the ongoing use of evidence-based coaching in educational settings, further research is required.

Positive psychology, coaching and mental toughness

Gable and Haidt define positive psychology as "the study of the conditions and processes that contribute to the flourishing (well-being) or optimal functioning of people, groups, and institutions" (Gable & Haidt, 2005, p. 103). It has been noted that many of the components of positive psychology are not new (Noble & McGrath, 2008), but Peterson (2006) and Linley and Joseph (2004) believe that it is a useful umbrella term that has the potential to unite a range of related but disparate directions in theory and research. Whilst much of the research in positive psychology has been focused on the understanding and development of wellbeing there is increasing recognition that the research and development of resilience also falls under the positive psychology umbrella. Resilience has been a topic of broader psychology for a long time although more recently topics such as "post-traumatic growth" and "mental toughness" have been included and focus on resilience as a crucial part of a flourishing life.

Green and Spence (in press) suggest the link between positive psychology and coaching is clear as both disciplines are focused on the cultivation of optimal functioning and wellbeing. As noted above, positive psychology dedicates itself primarily to the scientific study of wellbeing and resilience which includes the identification of intentional activities designed to increase both aspects. Coaching however focuses primarily on the application of methods that encourage individuals to set and strive for personally meaningful goals within the framework of a collaborative relationship. Whilst goals may be varied, we would suggest that the goals of coaching are often broadly related to the goals of positive psychology (i.e., to "increase wellbeing", "increase resilience", "develop mental toughness") and hence coaching can be used a methodology to apply the science of positive psychology.

There are increasing discussions on the integration and implementation of positive psychology research within coaching (e.g., Kauffman & Scoular, 2004). The term "Positive Psychology Coaching" (PPC) has become popular in the last few years as a result of some influential publications (Biswas-Diener, 2010; Biswas-Diener & Dean, 2007). Whilst there are no known scientific studies conducted on PPC, some evidence-based coaching studies have been published using positive psychological constructs as dependent variables. These include the first published randomised controlled trial of cognitive-behavioural, solution-focused life coaching for the enhancement of goal striving, wellbeing and hope (Green, Oades & Grant, 2006) and a subsequent study that compared professional and peer life coaching for the enhancement of goal striving and wellbeing (Spence & Grant, 2007). Whilst the evidence-based coaching methodologies used in these studies did not specifically include positive psychology techniques (i.e., "gratitude visits" or "random acts of kindness"), their aim was to increase both goal striving and wellbeing.

Whilst the term "mental toughness" has not yet been consistently linked to the umbrella term of positive psychology, we would argue that it does indeed fall under that umbrella. Clough and Strycharczyk make the connection when they propose that mental toughness is about "providing every individual with the opportunity to reach his or her full potential" (Clough & Strycharczyk, 2012a, p. 226). We would suggest that this definition is consistent with the aims of coaching and the definition of positive psychology (i.e., the scientific study of the conditions and process that lead to optimal human functioning) (Gable & Haidt, 2005).

As such we would encourage coaches to introduce the concept of mental toughness and utilise the MTQ48 in a Positive Psychology Coaching scenario whether the goals of coaching relate to "increasing resilience" or "enhancing wellbeing".

Mental health considerations?

It is broadly acknowledged that evidence-based coaching interventions are primarily aimed at a "normal population" rather than a "clinical population" (Grant, 2003). However this often leads to broad sweeping assumptions about the mental health of those presenting for coaching or positive psychology interventions. Coaches may falsely assume that those presenting for coaching fall within the "normal population". This assumption has been challenged by three scientific studies showing that twenty-five to fifty-two per cent of people attending for coaching interventions present with significantly high levels of psychological distress (Green, Oades & Grant, 2006; Spence & Grant, 2007; Kemp & Green, 2010). Green, Oades and Robinson (2012) also highlight this issue and provide the example of a school student who may undertake a "strengths-based coaching intervention", fail to apply their strengths sufficiently or achieve their goals, due to an underlying clinical disorder such as depression, potentially worsening the clinical disorder, rather than improving the child's wellbeing. As such, mental health is an important consideration when introducing coaching in an educational setting. Coaches should also have a strategy for the identification of psychological distress and mental disorder, particularly in the context of coaching where most coaches will not be mental health professionals. We would also encourage those offering coaching in the education sector to be trained in the identification of psychological distress and mental disorder, in order to make appropriate referrals for professional treatment (e.g., to the school counsellor).

Coaching students for mental toughness

Mental toughness is seen as an increasingly necessary attribute for young people (Clough & Strycharczyk, 2012b). Through the introduction to the concept of mental toughness and the use of the Mental Toughness Questionnaire (MTQ48) within a coaching context, it is possible to identify ways in which young people can increase their mental toughness in the face of examination pressures and the challenges of the workplace. Coaching can then be used to support young people to build their levels of mental toughness, if required. Broadly speaking, the introduction and use of the Mental Toughness Questionnaire in schools requires a number of stages:

Introduction of concept	The concept of mental toughness should be shared with the organisation and the young people within it
Use of MTQ48 questionnaire	Young people should be asked to complete the questionnaire
Discussion of results	Young people should have an opportunity to consider the results in a one-to-one conversation
Opportunities to develop particular mental toughness scales should be offered	Young people should have access to a range of skills sessions or one-to-one coaching in order to develop their mental toughness
Use of MTQ48 questionnaire	Young people should be asked to complete the questionnaire again, to measure the impact of the interventions above
Discussion of learning	Young people should have an opportunity to discuss the entire process and their ongoing development in a one-to-one conversation
Celebration of achievements	Young people and the organisation should reflect on the process and celebrate positive outcomes

As seen in the table above, the first stage of introduction requires an explanation of the concept of mental toughness within an educational setting. A clear understanding of the terminology and a discussion of the importance of mental toughness are needed before any intervention can take place. In a school, this could be delivered through an assembly or in a "mentor group" or "pastoral care class".

The next stage involves creating an opportunity for the young people to complete the questionnaire. This should take no longer than twenty to thirty minutes. This can be done as a supervised large group, or by allowing individuals to complete the questionnaire online over a relatively short timescale (e.g., one week).

A very important element of the process is the one-to-one facilitated dialogue to discuss the reports generated. This can cause logistical and practical difficulties but is essential in order to gain the most out of the process. The purpose of the dialogue is to focus on what the young person has learned about their mental toughness and what they will do about it. In some schools it may be possible to arrange these discussions over a week or two after completion of the questionnaire. The report should be handed to the young person for her to read for herself. The coach's role is to discuss the report with the young person as she considers her results.

The school can offer some optional group activities focusing on the different scales of the mental toughness measure (control; challenge; commitment; confidence). These activities might include workshops on anxiety control, positive thinking, relaxation, attentional control, and goal setting (Clough & Strycharczyk, 2012a). The workshops could be offered in-house by school staff. In addition, it is recommended that coaching is offered to everyone who has completed the mental toughness measure. It is important that any follow-up coaching (following the one-to-one facilitated dialogue) is optional and not mandated. The young person concerned should not feel that she is obliged to be coached about her mental toughness.

An integrated, person-centred coaching approach has been proposed as particularly appropriate to support the development of young people (van Nieuwerburgh, 2012a). This approach will encourage people to "thoughtfully consider potential areas for development and take personal responsibility for pursuing these" (van Nieuwerburgh, 2012a, p. 179). When coaching young people about their mental toughness, it is recommended that the following stages be followed (adapted from van Nieuwerburgh, 2012a).

Pre-coaching stage: Young person should request coaching. Coach should be given access to the young person's report and bring it to the session.

1. The coach should build rapport with the young person, building the foundation for a coaching relationship to discuss the topic of mental toughness.
2. The coach should discuss the way in which the coaching will be delivered, agreeing how often they are likely to meet. The sessions should be confidential, although the coach may want to be explicit

about any situations in which this would not apply. With young people, it is necessary to explain that confidentiality will be broken if the coach believes that the young person is at risk of harm.

3. It is important that the young person chooses the area for discussion. As the discussion is about mental toughness development, the young person can decide whether she would like to talk about confidence, commitment, challenge, or control. In some situations, the coachee may prefer to talk about a particular situation in school that she is finding difficult.

4. The young person is asked to share her overall goal with the coach. What is it that she would like to achieve? This helps to highlight the importance of improving the young person's mental toughness. For example, if her goal was to improve her grades in Mathematics, linking the development of mental toughness to this goal will assist in making the coaching a more meaningful endeavour to the young person.

5. In addition to the overall goal, the young person should be asked to think about what she would like as an outcome for the coaching session. This should be an achievable target for the coaching conversation. One important element of mental toughness is the sense that the young person can achieve targets that she sets herself, so the coach should ensure that the proposed outcome of the session is likely to be met.

6. The young person should then reflect on the results of her MTQ48 report, thinking about how the findings relate to her everyday experiences in school. It is helpful for the coach to explain that the results are not 100 per cent accurate, and that the young person can challenge or question some of the results. The coach can ask her to talk about how the results on the various scales affect her academic performance and social relationships in school.

7. To support the young person with her mental toughness, it is doubly important that the coach does not provide advice or suggestions. The purpose of the coaching sessions is to build the young person's confidence and self-reliance. The coach's role is to encourage the young person to generate as many ideas as possible for working towards optimal results.

8. Once the young person has proposed a number of ways of improving her MTQ48 results, the coach can support her to select the ideas that are most likely to make a difference.

9. The coach should then support the young person to sketch out an action plan for the time in between coaching sessions.
10. Finally, the coach and the young person should reflect on the outcome of the session. Have they achieved what they set out to achieve? When will they meet for the next coaching session?

Training students to peer coach for mental toughness

Many schools and colleges would argue that they do not have the resources to offer coaching to every young person who has completed the mental toughness questionnaire. A powerfully effective way of making this type of support available is to develop a coaching resource within schools and colleges. A number of studies have been conducted on the training of secondary school students to become coaches in order to support peers (van Nieuwerburgh & Passmore, 2012; van Nieuwerburgh, Zacharia, Luckham, Prebble & Browne, 2012; van Nieuwerburgh & Tong, 2013). Initial results point to increases in emotional intelligence levels in those students trained to be coaches. It seems that when these students support their peers in study skills, their own ability in this area also increases. One study showed that training students to become coaches improved their attitudes to learning (van Nieuwerburgh & Tong, 2013). Once trained, these student coaches could provide the additional resource needed to support their peers on their mental toughness. Based on the findings above, it is possible that there will be a positive effect on the mental toughness results of both the coaches and the coachees. This requires further research.

Coaching teachers for mental toughness

As noted in the introduction, one of the approaches to improving student performance and wellbeing is to directly target teachers through professional or peer coaching. The development of mental toughness for teachers is particularly important and necessary given statistics highlighting the significant levels of teacher stress (Kyriacou, 1987; Wiley, 2000; Kyriacou, 2001).

Grant, Green and Rynsaardt (2010) suggest some of the key challenges facing secondary school teachers in particular include stress, lack of resources, increased scrutiny and evaluation from key stakeholders, dealing with cumbersome bureaucratic systems, dealing constructively with diverse student populations, and the need to display positive leadership behaviours while under pressure (MacKenzie & Marnik, 2008). In addition, a key challenge facing the secondary school sector is the retention of teaching staff (Quartz, 2003).

Given one of the key tasks of coaching is to assist individuals in their ability to cope effectively with challenges, it becomes clear as to why the development of mental toughness in a coaching setting can be a relevant and important initiative when it comes to teacher development and wellbeing. It is also noted that secondary school teachers can wield considerable influence over their students. Grant, Green and Rynsaardt suggest teachers are, in a very real sense, the embodiment of leadership (Grant, Green & Rynsaardt, 2010, p. 151). Not only do they provide direction, guidance, and feedback to their students, they also act as role models as they are often in front of their students for up to six hours daily (Grant, Green & Rynsaardt, 2010).

As mentioned earlier, research has shown that coaching can increase hardiness (Green, Grant & Rysaardt, 2006) in student populations and maintain hardiness in teacher populations who have undergone coaching (Grant, Green & Rynsaardt 2010). Grant, Green & Rynsaardt (2010) suggest that coaching may have a protective or preventative effect, as teacher coachees commit to engaging in the goal striving process over time, they overcome inevitable obstacles and challenges. They further suggest that overcoming such difficulties within the context of a supportive, goal-focused relationship with a coach is likely to develop one's self-regulation abilities and that the processes inherent in a cognitive-behavioural, solution-focused executive coaching approach are similar to interventions that have been formulated to build resilience (e.g., Maddi, Kahn & Maddi, 1998).

Whilst the provision of coaching for teachers can be delivered by external professional coaches, a school may also consider creating a team of "coaching champions" who have been trained in evidence-based coaching and provide in-house coaching to staff who request it. Coaching for teachers may be offered as a leadership development intervention, a broader professional development intervention or specifically utilised to enhance resilience and wellbeing. In any of these coaching scenarios, the MTQ48 can be utilised to assist with achieving the outcomes of coaching.

As noted previously (van Nieuwerburgh, 2012a) the MTQ report is a good basis for a coaching conversation or a more structured coaching engagement. Van Nieuwerburgh (2012a) suggests that the introduction of the MTQ48 and the concept of mental toughness provide an opportunity for careful self-reflection and exploration and raise coachee self-awareness.

Three components of coaching

Whilst coaching is often viewed as a systematic process relying on the use of a coaching model such as GROW, there are two other elements that are crucial to the successful outcomes of coaching: the skills of coaching and a particular "way of being" (van Nieuwerburgh, 2014).

Skills of coaching

The key skills of coaching include effective listening, asking questions, clarifying, and giving feedback (Bresser & Wilson, 2010). Many teachers will already have these skills and it is useful to hone these given they are the foundation of good coaching.

Way of being

In implementing the skills and process of coaching it is important that a coach reflects on the "self" she is bringing to the coaching relationship. This "way of being" may be difficult to teach in a traditional sense (van Nieuwerburgh, 2014) and requires a commitment to self-awareness and self-management. Carl Rogers (1957) suggests that in a therapeutic setting, and we would argue similarly in a coaching setting, that there are three elements for success: congruence, unconditional positive regard for the coachee, and empathy. In a school setting, this would translate into the following:

- Congruence: In their coaching interactions, teachers (coaches and coachees) should be genuine, being open and honest about their feelings and thoughts.
- Unconditional positive regard: The coach should maintain a positive attitude to her coachee, remaining non-judgemental about what is raised during the coaching conversation.
- Empathy: Teachers must demonstrate empathy, trying their best to understand the situation from their coachees' perspective.

For us, the "way of being" is the most important, foundational element needed for a mutually respectful, trusting relationship. When it comes to the coaching process, the GROW model or the ten-stage integrated, person-centred coaching approach proposed earlier in this chapter can be used. If we can combine the right coaching skills, an appropriate coaching process and the "way of being" discussed above, we will be able to create the ideal environment in which to address topics related to mental toughness and wellbeing.

It is acknowledged that there may well be a number of practical difficulties in bringing professional coaching into educational settings on a large-scale basis including the cost of such engagements. For this reason, schools should be encouraged to consider their particular unique needs and priorities. We would argue, however, that given the high levels of stress frequently associated with the teaching profession (van Dick & Wagner, 2001) that a priority is given to the provision of one-to-one coaching for staff in leadership positions. We would also suggest that further consideration be given to the widespread application of coaching for teachers and school staff more broadly. Evidence-based coaching that enhances mental toughness may also have the potential to reduce stress-related sick leave, increase motivation, and enhance the performance of teachers.

If external professional engagement is not possible, then another approach may be to invest in professional coaching training offered to a small group of coaching champions who can then provide in-house coaching to their peers. Whilst there are potential issues associated with this approach (i.e., lack of objectivity that an external coach can provide, lack of high level of coaching expertise etc.), this may be a viable option for many schools. In-house coaches may then provide one-to-one coaching and/or support teams within the school. Such champions would also be required to maintain their own professional development in coaching. Coaching champions can also assist with the creation of coaching cultures within schools. There is a growing body of evidence that coaching not only improves results for individuals but for organisations more broadly (e.g., Evans, 2011; Mukherjee, 2012). At an organisational level, resilience and wellbeing have been found to be related to positive organisational citizenship behaviours (Avey, Wernsing & Luthans, 2008). These are important factors in building healthy, efficient, and high-performing organisations (Luthans, Youssef & Avolio, 2007), and as such have direct relevance for school cultures that play a significant role in shaping the citizens of the future. The UK's National College for Teaching and Leadership also concurs that "there is strong evidence that coaching promotes learning and builds capacity for change in schools" (Creasy & Paterson, 2005, p. 4). Van Nieuwerburgh & Passmore suggest that "successful implementation of coaching cultures within schools (based on proven coaching principles) can lead to improved environments for learning and conclude that this will mean better results for students, staff and the wider community" (van Nieuwerburgh & Passmore, 2012, p. 153).

Conclusion

Given the increasing research showing that mental toughness is a crucial factor in achieving academic outcomes and enhanced wellbeing (Clough & Strycharczyk, 2012b), it is important that schools and educational institutions more broadly identify evidence-based approaches to support the development of mental toughness in young people. The use of coaching as an applied positive psychology is one powerful intervention that research has shown to be effective. Coaching can be provided directly to young people via professional coaches, teacher-coaches or by their own peer-coaches. We have also suggested that a young person's mental toughness and wellbeing may be impacted on and enhanced by her teacher's own mental toughness and wellbeing. The investment in teacher development, resilience, and wellbeing is likely to positively impact on student development, resilience, and wellbeing.

This chapter has provided an up-to-date review of current research and practice in coaching in education, particularly relating to coaching for mental toughness, resilience, and wellbeing. We have made explicit the links between mental toughness and positive psychology and believe that this connection will be more broadly acknowledged over time and that mental toughness will be viewed as a key construct in positive psychology and a core component of a positive education programme in schools. We have argued that the aim of positive education is to not only enhance wellbeing but to increase mental toughness and wellbeing of both students and staff.

We have also provided an introduction to the coaching process with a step-by-step approach to providing coaching for mental toughness to both students and teachers. We have highlighted the importance of identifying the unique needs of a school and prioritising coaching initiatives, which could range from the engagement of external professional coaches, to the training of a small group of coaching champions who then become in-house coaches within a school. We have also proposed that it may be helpful to train students as coaches, which can have both beneficial effects for the students they coach and the student-coaches themselves.

In conclusion it is our hope that coaching in education (for wellbeing and mental toughness) becomes more widespread in schools globally and ideally becomes part of larger scale positive education programme that integrates positive psychology and coaching (Green, Oades & Robinson, 2012). The overall aim of such programmes is to create flourishing students, staff, and schools.

CHAPTER TEN

Social mobility and managing shift

Kieran Gordon and Jen Lexmond

Understanding social mobility

Social mobility is a measure of how free people are to improve their position in society. It matters for both fairness and for economic growth. A great many factors shape the social mobility of societies—from the size of the gap between the richest and poorest, to the level and quality of welfare, health, and educational provision from the state, to the prevailing political, cultural, and civil rights discourses of the day. These external factors play a huge role in determining the relative life chances of each child in each generation.

But it is not the whole story.

Getting on and getting ahead in life is as much about what we possess inside ourselves—our will to succeed, our creativity in solving problems and seeking opportunities, our ability to take on new challenges, our commitment to seeing things through even in the face of adversity, our ability to manage our emotional responses and get on with others.

Today the gap between rich and poor is growing. The recession marches on. The welfare state is undergoing its biggest cuts since its creation.

This backdrop makes acquiring and developing inner aspiration and drive ever more important.

The foundations of mental toughness, character and resilience, are set in the earliest years, forged through the unconditional love, care, and attention provided to babies by their parents and carers. This is where trust is developed, and from it the confidence that baby requires as it grows up to begin to try things out for herself, to explore the world and not give up when things don't quite go according to plan. This is where the mental toughness qualities of control, commitment, challenge, and confidence are derived. When the conditions of a safe, warm home environment, and a loving, consistent adult carer are not in place, the foundations for these capabilities don't develop—and insecurity grows in its place.

It comes as no surprise that factors faced by many families such as poverty, crime and domestic violence, poor housing, illiteracy, and social isolation, hinder the efforts of even the most committed and loving parents and have adverse affects on their children's development.

We see this statistically through observing the sizeable gap in "school readiness" (in large part a measure of attention, social, and emotional development) between children from affluent and poor backgrounds at age five. We also see how this gap leads to even larger gaps in educational attainment as children grow up, and hence to the major markers of social mobility, like the acquisition of vocational qualifications or a sustainable job, or acceptance into university. This is the beginning of the intergenerational cycle of immobility. Parents, then, are some of the primary architects of social mobility. Breaking that cycle is possible, but it gets harder and more resource intensive as children grow up.

So mental toughness is a key factor that helps people get on and get ahead in life. But it is harder to develop mental toughness when certain basic conditions are not in place. This amounts to a double disadvantage for those starting out at the bottom rung of society. The growing research base revealing these unhappy truths is the reason why character and resilience has shot up the policy agenda in recent years, and why addressing mental toughness is becoming a key priority in public policies designed to build social mobility.

What is social mobility

Social and economic disadvantage is a pervasive and disabling factor globally, from nations to entire communities, families to individual family members. It creates conditions in which peoples' day-to-day lives become a constant struggle against poverty, lack of opportunity, ill-health and, even hope. On a global and a national scale it is a major concern for all governments, even so-called developed wealthy nations manage significant pockets of deprivation caused by economic and social disadvantage. This chapter focuses on social disadvantage and social mobility in the UK and how people, particularly young people, can be helped to overcome the immediate and apparent constraints of income, educational achievement, upbringing, and place.

The term social mobility describes how individuals can get on in life through raising aspirations and accessing opportunities; it is often viewed in terms of progression and advancement in learning and employment, particularly professional levels of employment.

It is a contested idea.

For example, looking at the extent to which an individual improves their position across their adult working life will produce a different picture to looking at the extent to which a child's future outcomes differs from that of their parents. This is the difference between "intragenerational" and "intergenerational" mobility. Both are important, but liberal government's will be primarily interested in tackling intergenerational mobility—ensuring that one's family background does not determine or consign them to a particular future.

Equally, examining the relative chances that different ethnic groups or genders have in reaching certain social or income groups will produce a different picture to the more straightforward measure of whether one generation ends up in better positions than their parents' generation. This describes the distinction between "relative" and "absolute" social mobility. Again, liberal governments will be primarily concerned with relative social mobility because it is an important barometer of equality within society.

Whatever measure is examined, the general consensus is that social mobility has, at best, stagnated in the post-war period, although it is a myth that social mobility has stopped completely: many children move up the income or social scale compared to their parents.

That said, who your parents are matters a great deal: those from more advantaged backgrounds tend to do significantly better as adults. It's also important to note that the UK has relatively low social mobility compared to other countries:

> the association between parental income and child income is one and a half times higher than in Canada, Germany, Sweden or Australia.

The drivers of the current squeeze on social mobility in the UK today are laid bare in David Willets' 2011 book *The Pinch*. In it he describes how absolute social mobility is declining. He examines how the baby boom of 1945–1965 has produced the richest, biggest generation that the UK has ever seen, and how this generation has succeeded in fashioning the world around them to prioritise their own needs. The baby boomers hold a monopoly on political power, financial, and asset wealth. As this big generation approaches retirement and begins to draw down their pensions as well as health and medical support from the NHS, it is the next, smaller generation Y that is footing the bill—inheriting a hollowed out welfare state, higher taxes and fees for education, and an environment brought to its knees through over-consumption and waste. Here is the world that Generation Y is emerging into as adults. Willet's tries to convince baby boomers to address this state of affairs, for the sake of their children, focusing on macro-economic policies. Building inner drive and aspiration is also an essential component of preparing the next generation for the world they are inheriting.

The roots of social mobility

Economic and social disadvantage, as well as advantage, is self-perpetuating. People are socialised into particular outlooks and modes of behaviour from an early age, shaped by what they see around them, taking their leads from parents, siblings, other family members and friends, and what happens to them. They are limited or liberated by their surroundings, whether physical in terms of the fabric and levels of prosperity of their immediate environment, or social in the way that they learn behaviours and develop a sense of hope and expectation from their closest relationships.

There is clear evidence that what happens in the first few years of a child's life will have a profound influence on their future choices and outcomes. Some of this "conditioning", or learned behaviour, can be explained by the fact that a child's brain is particularly plastic, or responsive to its environment, in the first few years of life. This means that young children are both more sensitive to bad influences, but also able to recover from them more quickly.

But plasticity—the way experience configures the brain through forging synaptic connections—continues through the whole of life.[1] This process continues through different phases of childhood into adolescence, in the teenage years many brain functions become more automatic allowing the young person to perform more complex tasks.[2] In later adolescence the propensity for planning and managing risk is more developed, a critical factor in recognising and responding to opportunities that present.

These early years are, therefore, when we are at our most impressionable. That is not to say that because early child development has a significant bearing on what happens in later life there is certain predictability to how things will turn out for an individual. Because behaviours are learned they can also be "un-learned" and new behaviours adopted to positive effect.

Importantly, this is a relatively new scientific finding. Up until the 1990s, it was presumed that the brain was essentially static or "hard-wired" after an initial development period in early years when neural pathways are being formed very quickly. But as neuro-scientific research has developed, and particularly as social scientists have taken these biological findings into the realm of behavioural studies, we have learned that this not the case.

The study of how environment impacts on gene expression and brain development is called epigenetics, and is one of the most exciting and fast developing areas of research today. It is telling us that the brain can change and adapt throughout life; that environment can shape biology. Suddenly, the nature *vs.* nurture debate becomes far less interesting and important.

Of course, forging new neural pathways becomes more difficult the more well worn existing ones are. In this way, neural pathways are like streams: water takes the path of least resistance, unless it is actively, forcefully rerouted elsewhere. To throw some more metaphors into the mix, it's not true that "an old dog can't learn new tricks"—just that it's harder to, and takes more time and practice.

This is where the principle of early intervention comes from, and why prevention is so much more cost effective and time effective than treating symptoms.

The next section will explore how more can be done to help individuals take greater control of their destiny even when it means overcoming what may appear to be immovable objects in the way of achievement.

Identifying social mobility

There has been a great deal of focus on social mobility and how it has declined in recent decades. Successive Governments have commissioned studies into why social mobility has declined and what needs to be done to remedy this fact. The UK's Coalition Government quickly identified with the work undertaken by Alan Milburn, MP, who produced the report "Fair Access to the Professions: Unleashing Aspiration".

Research undertaken on behalf the Sutton Trust indicates that improving levels of social mobility for future generations in the UK would boost the economy by up to £140 billion a year by 2050.[3] As this chapter will go on to say, there are more immediate interventions that can be applied to ensure that any large scale strategic investment in future generations do not leave behind today's young people, avoiding another lost generation in the public policy response to what is a widely accepted social injustice.

So, how does social mobility manifest itself and how is it measured?

Educational attainment

In the context of young people, an early indicator for social mobility is attainment, in particular academic attainment whilst at school, and how this prepares individuals for higher education and higher levels of employment. It is also referenced in connection with levels of affluence or deprivation in terms of income and social class. Evidence shows there to be wide variances between the academic achievement of children from more "well-off" families and children from poorer backgrounds. Young people from well–off backgrounds are twice as likely to achieve good GCSE's (Grades A*-C) in key subjects by age sixteen than young people who are eligible for free school meals.[4]

The disparity in attainment continues beyond age sixteen; only three per cent of the lowest socioeconomic group achieve higher than three Grade Bs at A Level compared to twenty-five per cent of the highest group and this has profound implications for entry to University, particularly those Universities that are held in higher esteem.

Approximately seven per cent of state school pupils go to an "elite" university, only two per cent of those on free school meals do the same. At the most privileged end of the spectrum, ninety-six per cent of those young people educated in independent schools progress to university, compared to one third of students overall.[5] The top 100 elite schools (almost all independent schools) accounted for a third of Oxbridge admissions between 2003–2008.[6] Of course, social class or income of a family is not the determinant of achievement, but the correlation between class and income and educational attainment is strong.

These figures must be understood in the light of the numbers and ratio of young people from different socioeconomic backgrounds who actually apply to university, where it is clear that proportionally far fewer young people from disadvantaged background do so, partly a product of attainment levels and partly of aspiration; surveys of young people from differing backgrounds show the gap in aspiration and expectation. It is not just academic attainment that shape individual aspirations, but the wider attitude and character of individuals, whose outlook is shaped by their experience and that of their elders and peers.

Research undertaken by The Prince's Trust, RBS, and YouGov[7] show the disparity in expectation between young people from different social and economic backgrounds:

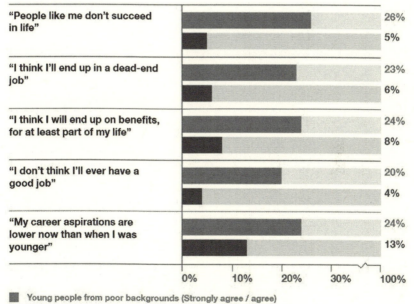

Work and career

Although academic attainment is a strong indicator for future success and describes success itself to some extent, social mobility is primarily measured by changes in employment status and individual or family income. A university education is essential for many careers, particularly professional careers and an increasing number of professional careers have graduate entry minimum criteria which hitherto was not the case. There is still a considerable way to go to open up these professional routes to wider sections of society in achieving greater social mobility. The economics of university tuition fees, which have tripled in recent times, may make this even more difficult to achieve. It should be the case therefore that professional bodies will need to look beyond universities to source the talent they will need in the future? However, it is the case that there are many young people who have the talent and the ability to pursue professional careers, but don't because university entry routes are not attractive, or simply because university education is considered to be not for people like them; particularly where there is no history of family members having had the benefit of a university education. Yet, a core requirement for many of these careers goes beyond academic qualifications and highlights the importance of personal and interpersonal skills. In preparing young people for working life and to open up the range of possibilities before them it is necessary to help them to aspire, which may mean challenging them to think and act in ways that have not felt comfortable or confident.

Social mobility is not just about the move from one strata of society to another, but the ability, for example, to move from unemployment into employment or to progress in employment to higher level occupations. Here again, education and academic achievement is important, but it is not the only, nor necessarily the main, prerequisite to be successful in career terms. The employment market is changing at a rate that has not been witnessed before, with a greater impact for wealth creation and productivity than the industrial revolution of its time in the nineteenth century. It is estimated that young people leaving school today can expect up to fourteen changes of career by the age of thirty-eight, such is the pace of technology and the way in which industries are having to adapt to a global and competitive economy. Enabling young people and adults to operate in this volatile environment will require them to be able to manage change and demonstrate resilience, to keep pace with change and where they can keep one step ahead.

Managing transitions

Young people from disadvantaged backgrounds are less likely to make a successful transition to adulthood and work; they are more likely to not be in employment, education, or training and are less likely to progress to higher education, especially in the most selective universities as described above. In the UK, Special Educational Needs (SEN) impact around twenty per cent of the school population, a significant majority will go on to be disadvantaged in adult life if they do not get the educational support and opportunities they need. The kind of support required will need to address life-skills and work skills; these are not mutually exclusive.

Around 1.36 million young people aged between sixteen and twenty-four years are not engaging in any form of education, employment, or training; these are described as NEET. Despite a small fall in 2012, this still represents a quarter of all young people in the job market in England. There are significant increases in the number of young people becoming long-term NEET and disengaged among sixteen to twenty-four year olds, which has doubled from 110,000 in 2008 to around 260,000 in 2012 and often these are concentrated in communities where economic and social deprivation as well as limited opportunity is prevalent. Many NEET young people suffer from a lack of hope, which in turn manifests itself as inaction or poorly managed actions in the attempt to find employment. Such young people cite a number of barriers to engaging in learning and work, though very few indicate an unwillingness to do so. Amongst the top reasons cited are:

- Family members and peers can be a significant obstacle to engaging in learning. (This can be due to a number of reasons such as low family expectations and aspirations, a lack of value placed on education, the impact of young people's choices on family welfare benefits, alcohol and substance misuse, and instances of chaotic family life)
- Young people often find academic styles of learning to be repetitive and uninteresting, resulting in a lack of motivation and a cynical view of the value of learning.
- Financial barriers to learning, associated directly with the cost of the course and the wider costs of being in learning, including travel.
- Behavioural problems or low attendance at school or college resulted in them being asked to leave courses.
- A lack of information, advice, and guidance support, either when looking for opportunities, or when on-course, acted as a barrier to learning, including where advice and information received did not match the eventual experience of the course.

- A lack of skills, particularly literacy and numeracy, or formal qualifications often acts as a barrier to engaging in education and training.[8]

Young people from lower income backgrounds are more likely to face the multiple barriers described above, although not exclusively so. The traditional response to such issues has been to provide new or reconstructed learning opportunities to engage them on their terms. Whilst this has some success it is not sufficient to increase social mobility. We must also build the personal capacity of young people to make the most of their opportunities by being able to deal with challenge and overcome barriers. It is tempting to treat the symptoms by restructuring the opportunities or the ways in which these opportunities are presented, but this misses the point. Of course more can be done to attract and engage young people in learning and work, but unless we help them to turn disadvantage into something positive by challenging perceptions and preconceptions we will not go far enough in equipping them with the skills to take control of their lives.

Increasing social mobility through individual development and opportunity awareness

By listening to the problem (or, put another way, the need) from the viewpoint of the individual it is possible to help them to see how best they should approach it and how to adapt to different challenges. For some there will be multiple issues at play and for others these may boil down to one or two obstacles only. One area highlighted above is the need for supportive information, advice, and guidance in managing one's career. Young people are citing the lack of access to such help and it is true that the area of careers learning, advice, and guidance is undergoing a major upheaval, particularly for young people in England and many of the support structures that existed previously are either reducing, fragmenting, or disappearing altogether. The severe reduction in funding for young people's support services since 2010 and the removal of services such as Connexions in many areas of England has had a profound impact on the way in which young people can access help. Nationally more than £200 million of funding for careers advice and guidance services to schools has been withdrawn and the availability of wider information, advice, and guidance services for young people outside school has become fragmented and something of a postcode lottery. The decision to create a statutory duty for schools to provide access to impartial and independent careers services has not been matched with the resources for schools to ensure this is done adequately.

For many years the aim of careers advice and guidance services has been the ability to help young people understand themselves and what they have to offer when it comes to employment. Raising self-awareness as well as opportunity awareness is essential if individuals are expected to manage their careers in a dynamic and constantly changing job market. Career development support addresses the personal qualities and skills that people need to make decisions, become more mobile and gain sustainable work. This often includes:

- Developing self-awareness—what interests, aptitudes, and abilities an individual possesses
- Developing self-confidence—increasing an individual's self-esteem and how they can apply themselves to succeed
- Developing career decision-making skills—utilising relevant and up-to-date labour market information and assimilating this information to suit personal needs
- Developing motivation—creating a momentum for change
- Career goal setting—understanding routes into work and setting targets to achieve
- Career planning—breaking down "big" career goals into measurable and achievable steps, with clear timelines
- Taking action—following through on the career plan and adjusting steps to overcome barriers or changes to circumstances
- Reflecting on decisions and the actions taken to put these decisions or choices into practice—understanding the journey and being able to navigate unforeseen or unsuitable outcomes.

For unemployed young people the opportunity to access support from trained careers personnel can be instrumental in helping them on this journey. Having access to trained and knowledgeable professionals can help them to understand their strengths and weaknesses and address these in ways which helps them make learning and work choices that best suit.

Evidence shows that young people in Britain spend much less time with adults during their teenage years than contemporaries in other developed countries. Probably, as a result of this disengagement, British teenagers are more likely to to be influenced by their peers. This results in a lack of guidance and support for young people at what is a crucial time for character development.[9] Nuffield/Rathbone[10] found that many young people suffer from a lack of belonging and of failed relationships and need someone they can trust and rely on, to help them re-engage.

This support need extends beyond that of the help of a careers adviser as young people are making career plans. When in employment many young people benefit from a guiding hand from their employer, be this through a formal career development plan or appraisal function, where this exists, to the experience and support of an experienced and, often older, work colleague who can provide instruction and support. This "trusted adult" relationship should not create a situation where a young person becomes dependant on others, rather its unique benefit is in providing a role model from which to learn important behaviours and skills, in the case of workplace colleagues or supervisors.

Developing self reliance and resilience in enabling social mobility

It is the behaviours and skills of self-regulation and self-management that will be critical in individuals being able to make the most of their careers in a constantly changing labour market. The careers profession has branched out beyond the perceived traditional role of providing information and advice to individuals in helping them to make informed decisions about learning and work. Increasingly it has come to terms with the fact that "career" is no longer a choice made early in life and pursued for the remainder of one's working life; this concept, if it was ever the norm, has given way to the realisation that a career is a varied journey that will have many changes in direction, even U-turns, and individuals need to learn the skills to adapt. For most people career is viewed as being on a vertical trajectory; the acquisition of skills, qualifications, and experience all go to enabling people to move up the career ladder. This aspect has not changed, but the concept of a ladder can usefully be replaced by a climbing frame in the modern labour market, where individuals can advance through lateral as well as through vertical career progression.

The best laid plans of mice and men often go astray.[11]

One of the ways the careers profession has broadened its approach in the way it supports individuals to manage change is the adoption of tools designed to assess, and then help to develop, a young person's character and capacity to adapt. The "traditional" components of successful career management, such as access to good careers and labour market information and analysis of abilities and aptitudes are important in making choices, but the careers adviser must be increasingly aware of the personal capacity of the individual to use these to their advantage; this includes relating career planning to personality factors that can enhance personal effectiveness. It is not necessarily sufficient to enable informed planning; we must also equip individuals with the skills and awareness they will need to see the plans through. Key to this is supporting the development of internal drive and determination to succeed.

One way this is being tackled is through the application of mental toughness and, in particular, the use of the MTQ48 psychometric test as a complementary measure in helping individuals to increase their effectiveness when making career decisions and following career plans.

The MTQ48 psychometric measure

Commitment and challenge

When it comes to helping people succeed there is a clear correlation between the mental toughness of individuals and their subsequent performance. Mentally tough people demonstrate greater tenacity in setting and achieving goals; this is measured in MTQ48 on the commitment scale. They have the confidence to make plans and to navigate their way forward even when they face obstacles to progression or setbacks. Commitment is something that young people who are faced with choices must master as they learn to discriminate between those opportunities that have a long-term benefit over those that may bring more immediate satisfaction or reward, but are short-lived. Where goals or rewards are distant it is often more challenging to stick at a plan or a task.

Putting the timeless nature of handwringing and angsting about feckless youth aside, there may be some legitimacy to contemporary anxieties that our instant-gratification culture is having an adverse affect on young people's ability to defer gratification and develop an ability to work towards goals over longer periods. Certainly, it is the case that they are socialised into a more immediate results lifestyle, whether through the interactive and spectacular returns from online and modern gaming technology or the ability to use search engines for instant answers to questions or problems. Learning the benefits of long-term commitment and its rewards and how to achieve this can be the key to success in managing one's career. MTQ48 has been used to identify levels of commitment in individuals as they start to think about and plan their careers. One way that the results have been used has been to undertake goal setting. Individuals low on commitment often find goal setting difficult, which induces behaviours that avoid this. It is commonly found to be associated with a lack of ability to focus or concentrate for any length of time, which is another aspect of low commitment on the MTQ measure. By showing individuals how to concentrate longer and to break down goals in to measurable tasks with timescales it is possible to help them to become effective planners. This in turn helps to motivate individuals who can see the steps to be taken and as they are achieved to benefit from the sense of wellbeing and achievement. Young people who have taken part in exercises using MTQ48 have commented positively on its effect on them:

'I thought the mental toughness sessions were very good. It taught me to think about how I organise my time better. I told my friend about it because I think it will help her'—Danielle, aged fifteen.

'I liked learning how to get more organised with my time'—Kirstie, aged fifteen.

'The mental toughness programme helped to improve my confidence—it made me feel stronger. I really enjoyed the brain training activities and learnt to do things step by step. My friends should do it too'.—Scott, aged fifteen.

Challenge

The same is true for venturing into the unknown or the unfamiliar, where some young people who when faced with a difficult set of circumstances decide to walk away from rather than persevere with tackling the situation. It is the case that young people are more likely to change their minds and their choices more frequently than adults, particularly where this is related to career choice. This is partly a function of maturity; as the theories on character development indicate young people show a greater propensity for managing risk, planning, and decision-making as they get older. Hence, they are more likely to have assessed their options and understood the consequences of their choices.

Employers will often discriminate between employing older people in favour of young people and will cite the fact that young people are likely to be less reliable than adult employees. Employing adults with experience is associated with productivity as they are familiar with the workplace disciplines and character that is required to work effectively. Employers see "dependability" as critical in employees where the employer is more confident in their investment of time and resources for someone who will stay and grow with the organisation rather than see their investment dissipate as young people change their minds and leave. On the other hand, employing older workers can have downsides as they will normally expect a higher rate of pay than a young person just starting out and in training. Retention rates in apprenticeships for example are a cause for concern and more can be done to develop the resilience of apprentices by developing the way that they commit to the longer term, when the acquisition of skills and relevant qualification bring reward in salary levels, promotion, and advancement. In 2008–2009 the overall success rate for apprenticeship completion was 72.2 per cent[12] and whilst that is an improvement on the 2005–2006 rate at 46.9 per cent there is still some way to go to achieve a level that could be considered to give maximum return on investment. Evidence points to non-completion occurring as a consequence of the apprentice first, leaving one employer to join another (either in the same occupation or a different one); second, returning to school, college, or university (depending upon qualification level); or third, dropping out of the education and training system to enter unskilled work, unemployment, or inactivity.[13]

When it comes to challenge people can react in very different ways. Some see challenge as an opportunity to grow and progress, whereas others see it as a threat and may recoil to a safer option. Challenge, as captured in the MTQ48, assesses how people react when they are faced with change. Therefore it will have a bearing on how people make career choices, with some preferring to "play it safe" and look for stability, with others being positively turned off by the safe option in the search for new and varied experiences. Using the MTQ48 therefore to measure an individual's capacity to deal with challenge can inform their reaction to certain types of career. The use of the measure can also be used as a challenge to individuals, to show them that it is possible to develop appetite for dealing with new and changing situations, or at least to manage these eventualities better. Applying for a place in university, or applying for a job inevitably brings an element of competition into people's lives, a fact which will be repeated throughout one's working life. Therefore helping individuals to develop strategies and techniques designed to deal with challenge is a precursor to helping them to manage their careers. This can be done by getting people to identify success in others, from celebrities and cultural or sports icons to people in their own walk of life who they have know to be successful. By identifying what makes these people successful it is possible to design steps that can be translated into the life of the individual in question.

Control and confidence

It is also the case that in promoting social mobility careers professionals realise the importance of overcoming a range of limiting factors. These range from individual to individual, but often appear for whole groups of individuals, whether through stereotypes in the case of gender, race, social class, or lack of positive extended family role models. Thus, when identifying opportunities individuals must be helped to overcome artificial or imposed boundaries, this will only be achieved if they are equipped to see the opportunity behind the challenge and deal with it. In moving into new areas of experience, whether this may be a woman choosing a job in a male dominated profession or workplace, or a young person from a family background of no university or professional experience choosing a career in medicine or law, the stakes will be high. The fear of failure can be daunting if not overwhelming and the lack of an informed support structure heightens the anxiety.

In such cases MTQ48 can be used to build a more positive mindset that enables individuals to go beyond their norms and to develop the confidence and resources to explore careers which are outside of their immediate considerations and which may not feature in their education, both formally through school influences and less formally through family and friendship perceptions and experiences. Stepping outside of the norm is not easy, young people are more likely to conform to self or externally imposed norms, even to the point of conforming by choosing options that their immediate friendship groups choose. The element of control is important in the choices we make, people will make life choices they are either comfortable with or where they believe they can exercise sufficient control to be able to be successful through the choice they make. For individuals to step outside of imposed norms they must feel able to take or maintain control of the situation.

The MTQ48 test measures the degree of "control" an individual possesses in their make up. This is broken down into "life control", the ability to take control of their circumstances, and "emotional control", the ability to manage or control their emotions, particularly when faced with a seemingly threatening situation. The act of measurement itself is illustrative of an individual's strengths, and hence can reinforce them. Where there are weaknesses, assessment identifies these through lower scores, and can help clarify where support is needed. The careers adviser or "trusted adult" will interpret the MTQ48 results and work with the individual to determine those strategies that suit best in enhancing control and provide exercises designed to achieve this, which can be practiced over time. Although not a causal relationship, higher levels of control are correlated with higher levels of self-confidence.

All of these inner capacities that make up mental toughness—commitment and challenge, control and confidence are linked to increased performance and achievement. The use of the MTQ48, as an assessment and development programme, has demonstrated positive changes in the levels of mental toughness for the majority of individuals who have used it. This is verified by re-testing individuals after applying interventions designed .to address levels of commitment, challenge, control and confidence. This is particularly valuable when addressing external deficits for individuals. It is the case that young people from higher socioeconomic groups generally have a more positive outlook and belief in their ability to achieve and succeed as the research by the Prince's Trust, RBS and YouGov attests. It is more common for people from advantaged backgrounds to have a "good" support network which they are more likely to draw upon seeking to succeed.

Individuals from disadvantaged backgrounds often lack the lack the social and cultural capital, the business contacts, and the financial means that set more affluent young people on a positive trajectory in life, which insulate them in the face of adversity and set back. For young people without these insulating factors, inner capacities of mental toughness, resilience, and strength of character are arguably even more important in helping them get on and get ahead.

Notes

1. Lexmond, J., & Grist, M. (Eds.). (2011). *The Character Inquiry*. London: Demos.
2. ibid.
3. The Mobility Manifesto, The Sutton Trust, March 2010.
4. Free school meals are used as a proxy for identifying relative poverty, when assessing the social backgrounds of students in education.
5. The Mobility Manifesto, The Sutton Trust, March 2010. http://www.suttontrust.com/public/documents/20100312_mobility_manifesto20102.pdf last accessed 3 December 2013.
6. For more information visit http://www.suttontrust.com/research/university-admissions-by-individual-schools/ last accessed 1 July 2013.
7. Broke Not Broken: Tackling Youth Poverty and the Aspiration Gap, (Prince's Trust: 2011) London. http://www.princes-trust.org.uk/pdf/PovertyReport_170511.pdf last accessed 3 December 2013.
8. Motivation and Barriers to Learning for Young People not in Education, Employment or Training, Department for Business Innovation and Skills. February 2013.
9. Lexmond, J., & Grist, M. (Eds.). (2011). *The Character Inquiry*. London: Demos.
10. Nuffield Review/Rathbone, (2008). Engaging youth Enquiry: Final consultation report, London: The Nuffield 14–19 Review.
11. Burns, R. (1785). To a Mouse. In: *Kilmarnock volume*. Kilmarnock: John Wilson.
12. Taken from The Data Service All, March 2010. SFR Files, Table 4 and Table 6.2.
13. Maximising Apprenticeship Completion Rates. University of Warwick Institute for Employment Research (IER), 2010.

CHAPTER ELEVEN

Employability and young people

Kieran Gordon

What is employability?

In its most simple form "employability" is the ability to get employment and maintain it. Increasingly, sustaining gainful employment is becoming as challenging as the act of getting employment in the first place. This is due to the short and long-term trends in the employment market where jobs are threatened by economic downturns (cyclical unemployment) and by the fast changing skill needs of businesses in a global and technology driven marketplace (structural unemployment). It is right to include here the importance of progression or promotion in and through employment, as this is a great individual motivator and motivation is an important dimension of employability.

Defining employability skills is not straightforward as they are broad ranging and can vary according to the needs of different employers and employment sectors. They are inclusive of core components such as numeracy, literacy, and use of IT, which are measurable through the national qualifications framework, and extend beyond to encompass what are termed "soft skills" for which there is no set curriculum or qualifications infrastructure.

Employability skills deal with behavioural aspects of a person's readiness for work, this includes attitude, motivation, enthusiasm, self-discipline, commitment, confidence, and timekeeping. These are frequently cited by employers as the essential ingredients of what makes a "good employee", particularly when referenced to young people. A recent survey of employers undertaken by reachfor[1] and AQR[2] in developing a new psychometric careers assessment tool elicited similar responses from respondents and added others such as: the ability to focus on customer needs, which may be interpreted as emotional intelligence; adaptability, the ability to deal with changing circumstances or resilience; creativity, the ability to suggest and believe in new ways of working; and responsibility, the preparedness to be accountable for one's actions at work.

Employer representatives are often critical of the lack of these skills in school leavers, which begs the question as to whether these are skills which we expect to be acquired at school as part of the curriculum or are they acquired through other social influences such as effective parenting and family life? The answer to this is probably both, but what is certain is that there is no normative measure that embraces all of these attributes and for the most part there hasn't been a valid, consistent, and reliable measure of the individual skills that go to improve one's employability. However, as this chapter will go on to explain there has been a significant development in relation to measurement of a number of these attributes, which has come to be known as mental toughness.

The case for employability

The cost of youth unemployment in the United Kingdom in the next decade is estimated to be £28 billion,[3] a figure arrived at when the full cost of the loss of economic productivity, coupled with the welfare and health costs associated with unemployment and the wider social impact of large numbers of young people disengaged from mainstream society. Apart from the economic costs, youth unemployment has a personal cost to those who experience it, and for young people in the transition from education to the world of work even short periods of unemployment can leave an indelible mark on their outlook and their wellbeing; what has been termed the "scarring effects" of youth unemployment.

Young people unemployed on leaving school will spend an average of an additional two months per year out of work between the ages twenty-six and twenty-nine, according to research. They will also suffer a thirteen per cent to twenty-one per cent wage penalty by the age of forty-two[4] when compared with those who make a "smoother" transition from education to work, due to lower earnings potential and the levels of work they are able to secure and sustain.

The "scarring", referred to above, involves psychological scarring with increased potential for illness, mental stress, helplessness and damaged self-esteem, all of which can lead to depression. Stress levels and recorded cases of mental illness amongst young people are on the increase and this is exacerbated by the alienation felt by those not in education, employment, or training (NEET).

So, in making a case for employability we must go beyond the skills demands of the workplace and look at the whole person when seeking to adequately prepare people for the demands and rigours of the working world. These demands and the challenges they bring are ever more complex and numerous due to the pace and scale of change in the modern economy. Increasing competition through the globalisation of markets, technological advancements, and changes to organisational structures all have implications for the future nature of work and therefore for employment. Employability skills will change with time and with greater frequency than has been the case thus far.

Developing the skills to enhance employability for young people

The task of preparing young people for work will involve different inputs and different professional applications, from teacher to careers adviser, to employer. This will begin for many in the home with parental guidance and will continue through education, particularly as young people get closer to leaving school and through further and higher education, where applicable. It will not end there however, employers will need new employees to develop a range of on-the-job skills and knowledge and to keep on top of these as they change over time. So, developing employability becomes a lifelong process, it evolves over time and circumstances. It will include the acquisition of cognitive skills, the knowledge needed to become and remain employable/employed; technical skills, the specific skills needed to do a job or series of jobs; and the "softer" skills which are more to do with behavioural competencies, attitudinal outlook and expression, and the ability to deal with challenges and manage change.

Until recently (2012) secondary schools in England had a statutory responsibility to provide programmes of careers education, designed to raise aspiration and develop the motivation to make decisions about future learning and work options. Amongst the key components of such learning programmes are:

- Helping individuals to know their strengths and development needs
- Raising awareness of how they behave and interact with others
- Being self aware in an emotional intelligence sense, how they are perceived by others
- Taking control of their choices
- Demonstrating resilience throughout life and career.

This aspect of school learning has traditionally sat outside the National Curriculum in England and Wales and as it was a non-examined subject it had less importance, squeezed out by the pressure on schools to perform against a series of academic examination results whose value determined where a school is ranked in league tables of school effectiveness. Furthermore the statutory requirement for schools to manage a programme of careers education has ceased as a result of the 2011 Education Act, suggesting that this is no longer seen as a national priority in the development of young people; a belief not shared by many engaged in the business of preparing young people for the world of work.

For some time there has been recognition of the need for young people to acquire "life skills" and there have been many different iterations of life skills programmes in operation, particularly in the realm of further education and work related training. Their aim is to engage, energise, and equip young people to become responsible and adaptable individuals and employees. The evidence of their impact is variable and this has been hampered by the lack of a consistent and robust methodology of measurement, resulting in there being no defined and universal qualification.

Against this backdrop there are a number of bespoke developments designed to address how young people can be helped to become more employable and successful citizens. One such example is the Right

Track project operated by the joint venture social enterprise, reachfor Limited. The Right Track project has trialled an innovative approach using seedcorn funding from the Department for Education to develop models of early intervention to increase participation by, and improve the achievements of, disadvantaged young people. Reachfor designed the Right Track project to provide an evidence-based method of building the personal resilience of young people, considered to be at risk of becoming NEET on leaving school. Through this they aim to equip young people with the skills that will help them make the most of their other achievements whether measured by educational attainment or skill acquisition; the realisation being that qualifications alone are not reliable predictors of success in finding or keeping a job.

The Right Track project adopted as the cornerstone of its innovative project the application of mental toughness utilising the MTQ48 psychometric tool (both mental toughness and MTQ48 are described in detail elsewhere in this publication). It targeted young people who were disadvantaged by their diagnosis of having behavioural, emotional, or learning difficulties whilst at school with a view to building their resilience to enable them to manage smooth transitions through key phases of their lives, including the transition from school to adult and working life. For these young people to make a successful transition into employment will ultimately depend on their ability to manage the conditions that are deemed to make them vulnerable and their behaviours.

The basic hypothesis underpinning the project was the view that particular interventions can be applied that can help young people assess their challenges and understand the personal resources available in overcoming them. It set out to help young people identify the consequences of some of their negative behaviours, such as poor school attendance, behavioural problems whilst at school, and the way in which these can hinder their chances of finding and keeping a job in later life. The project worked with more than 4,000 young people in eight areas across England and at different stages of education from year six (aged ten to eleven) to year ten (aged fourteen to fifteen). The work was carried out through individual face-to-face sessions as well as through group work activity with the young people. Central to the project's design was the application of the MTQ48 mental toughness measure, which was used with each participant along with the application of a series of development workshops designed to increase their resilience and develop their sense of self. This was overwhelmingly a positive experience for the individual participants, who expressed the benefits of looking at aspects of their personality and having a measurable value placed on these attributes. These benefits were further enhanced where young people could be shown to have increased their levels of mental toughness from the start to the end of the project by re-testing individuals following the adoption of new approaches and techniques to improving personal effectiveness.

The project's outcomes focused on three areas of individual progress:

1. Changes in mental toughness
2. Changes in attitudes to school, behaviour, and work
3. Attendance at school.

Mental toughness increased in all areas of the country where the Right Track project independently operated and in six of the eight areas this change was statistically significant. For those participants who completed two MTQ48 tests:

- Forty-nine per cent increased their mental toughness
- Twenty-three per cent decreased their mental toughness
- Twenty-eight per cent stayed the same.

However, these initial results may be even more significant as the measurement of movement was based on where individuals' scores moved sten ranges. A sten range represents a range of raw scores, therefore it is possible that participants' raw scores may have increased, or decreased, within that range and not shown up in the analysis to have changed. Further analysis when the project evaluation has been completed, will look at this. Because almost as half of the participants' scores showed an increase in mental toughness, it is conceivable that more of them may have had an increase in mental toughness raw scores than the forty-nine per cent measured by sten changes alone.

The measure of the young people's progress included the use of attitude surveys at the beginning and the end of the project to determine whether the young people could articulate the personal benefits to them. The overall attitudes expressed were positive at the beginning and the end of the project, with individuals indicating that they saw misbehaviour and poor school attendance as wrong and potentially harmful to their chances of entering further study or employment after school, which for the majority was their goal. Where the differences in attitude were evident between the beginning and the end of Right Track, these tended to be related to school: seven per cent more agreed that they liked being at school after Right Track than before they began the project; Eleven per cent fewer young people agreed that teachers were always "getting at them" and eleven per cent more young people wanted to study full time when they were eligible to leave school at sixteen by the end of Right Track. This concurred with teacher assessments and perceptions of the young people involved. The feedback from teachers was positive, they indicated that forty-three per cent of participants improved their behaviour, thirty-three per cent had improved attendance and forty-six per cent had improved their work in class.[5]

At the time of writing, the independent evaluation of the Right Track project has yet to be completed and this will be done in the next few months, with the results here representing the independent evaluator's emerging findings in the last quarter of the project. The results are positive and have provided both quantitative and qualitative evidence of the improvement in young people's outlook, attitude, and behaviour when they understand the benefits of working on their character and have objective and reliable measurements to rely on. The motivational benefits as well as the actual benefits to young people of developing their mental toughness can be significant in improving their outlook and improving their employability skills as they enter the working world.

The use of mental toughness measurement with young people in an employability context has enabled the young people, their teachers, and their careers advisers to enhance their preparation for adult and working life. As individuals learn to understand the importance of being able to make plans (take control of their lives) and to stick to them (demonstrate commitment to a goal) they raise their personal self esteem (confidence) and ultimately develop the ability to deal with changing opportunities and challenges. Overlaying these characteristics with the ability to perform work based functions, improve technical skills and navigate change will be the key to their future employability.

Notes

1. Reachfor is a joint venture social enterprise of eight career advice and guidance organisations in England working predominantly with young people from school age to adulthood.
2. AQR is an innovative and fast growing psychometric test publisher, which works in partnership with private sector, public sector (including Government agencies in a number of countries) and educational bodies.
3. ACEVO (2012). *Youth Unemployment: The Crisis We Cannot Afford.* London: ACEVO.
4. Gregg, P. & Tominey, E. (2005). The wage scar from youth unemployment. *Labour Economics*, 12: 487–509.
5. The results of the evaluation of the Right Track project as cited here were drawn from the Interim findings of the external evaluator, Get the Data Ltd., the final evaluation report has yet to be published.

CHAPTER TWELVE

Practical applications: young people, teachers, and school leaders

Andrea Berkeley

I t's tough in today's schools. Although successive government reforms have driven up standards overall in the last ten years, there is still a national imperative to improve further. Educationally, England performs only just above OECD (Organisation for Economic Co-operation and Development) country averages in the international PISA[1] tables. The gap between the attainment of children from poor and affluent homes has remained roughly the same, in some areas it has widened, and there is a long tail of underachievement. The pressure continues, on young people, their teachers, and school leaders alike. In areas of social deprivation and educational disadvantage teachers and their leaders need even more commitment, resilience, and determination to rise to this challenge as well as to respond to the vicissitudes of education policy and social change.

> The quality of teaching and leadership in schools is the key factor in raising student achievement. For a child from a disadvantaged background, the difference between a good teacher and a poor teacher is one year's learning. That is at least one GCSE grade. Spread across five teachers, and it is the difference between a child achieving 5 Ds at GCSE and 5 Cs. (Marshall, 2013, p. 149)[2]

It has long been recognised, but not widely documented, that the emotional bond formed between teachers—especially form tutors and pastoral leaders—and young people has a significant impact on their attitudes to school, commitment to study and ultimately their ability to perform well academically. The rapport and mutual trust found in such relationships enable teachers to both challenge and support their pupils to reach their full potential. These psychological contracts between teacher and pupil are not found in standards set by the National College for Teaching and Leadership nor in the Ofsted framework for the inspection of schools but are evident to anyone who has ever attended a year eleven leaving assembly or a GCSE results day and witnessed the importance of teacher–pupil relationships.

The more teachers and tutors know about pupils, the more that they engage with the whole young person, the more likely they are to notice when something is amiss and to give specific support. A seemingly obvious feature of school relations, conducive to positive outcomes for both pupils and schools, is less easily achievable in today's state comprehensive schools, given the range of abilities and diverse backgrounds of young people, especially in the inner cities and less affluent rural and coastal areas of England. Children assessed with a wide range of special educational needs have increased exponentially. Although no longer perceived as a barrier to learning, the fact that among the student population of many schools can be found speakers of up to eighty different languages, presents a challenge for the development of literacy skills in order to access the curriculum.

Social trends that impact on teachers' and schools' capacity to meet the diverse needs of young people in the twenty-first century include a developing notion of "extended adolescence" where children spend longer in full-time education, enshrined in historical legislation in September 2013 raising the school-leaving age further, and live at home for longer, a phenomenon increasingly prevalent due to economic downturn and continuing recession. The decline of marriage and the conventional nuclear family mean that increasing numbers of children live in single parent homes or lead complex lives divided between two or more families. There is often no longer a single point of reference for home school communication. As many as a fifth to a quarter of children[3] live in poverty and the numbers of children in public care have increased.[4] These are the children most likely to be excluded[5] from school and to become involved in crime or substance abuse[6] in later life. There is a powerful association between home backgrounds and educational attainment.[7]

Teaching Leaders, a two-year leadership development programme that trains and develops high potential middle leaders (subject heads and pastoral leaders) to improve the standards of challenging secondary schools in disadvantaged areas, became interested in Dr Peter Clough's work in 2010 and seized the opportunity of piloting the MTQ48 instrument in partnership with AQR. Initially the focus was on developing mental toughness in targeted groups of young people in the responsibility of pastoral leaders in a cross section of complex urban schools.

A notable side effect of this pilot was the participants' realisation of the usefulness of the instrument for themselves personally and their own need to develop mental toughness in their leadership roles.

This in turn has led Teaching Leaders to enter into a research partnership with AQR and Peter Clough, trialling MTQ48 as part of the leadership and management development model offered by the programme and to document the results. At the time of writing 212 middle leaders have been questionnaired, the data analysed, and work begun on planning training to develop their mental toughness as leaders.

No school is an island and all serve the communities where they are located and beyond. Schools in disadvantaged areas find they are providing an oasis of calm and order for children from dislocated or chaotic homes. For many such young people school might provide the only stable and dependable part of their lives. Teachers are important figures, even when the presenting feature of such young people's behaviour manifests as hostility or aggression. Similarly headteachers and pastoral leaders become repositories for the troubles and anxieties of their parents or carers. One headteacher reported that she felt like every day she was "holding back or shoring up a tide of human misery".

Young people, especially those from disadvantaged backgrounds, need to be resilient and mentally tough if they are to succeed at school and to embark upon the lifelong learning now required for the changing nature of work and life in the twenty-first century. Furthermore, their teachers need to be equally mentally tough. The case studies and observations on practical applications of tools and techniques that follow in this chapter indicate that thinking consciously about mental toughness, how to measure it and how to strengthen it, has enormous potential for improving the life chances of young people as well as building the capacity and efficacy of leaders of teaching and learning.

Young people—mental toughness and raising aspirations

Toby Pearson, a head of year and professional mentor with both academic and pastoral responsibilities at St. George's Catholic School in West London, became particularly interested in the field of mental toughness when he changed careers from business into the teaching profession, finding that interactions within the school environment differed greatly from those he had experienced previously. Teaching Leaders gave him the opportunity of trialling MTQ48 as an assignment for an MA in educational leadership with Warwick University.

Given the pressure and time constraints of the school day, he felt the need to sharpen his communication skills in the "difficult conversations" he found he needed to have with colleagues and students, both underperforming in a complex urban school with a difficult past. Under pressure to improve, staff at the school were having to work hard at setting higher expectations and stricter behaviour boundaries and tackling the low self-esteem of most pupils. Toby wanted to build the capacity of his team of teachers in more specifically supporting pupil needs.

Tracking and monitoring pupil progress using performance data is commonplace in today's schools. Performance in each subject is measured by pupils' ability to meet targets and improve grades against a set number of National Curriculum sub-levels per term. As long as pupils hit their targets, teachers are satisfied and assumptions are made about an individual's ability to cope. However, few identify and track pupils' ability to withstand stress and overcome obstacles—and some don't even recognise it at all. Even fewer put in place interventions to counteract stress and develop mental toughness.

Toby decided to use Dr Peter Clough's attitude test with a group of sixty year nine pupils who had been identified as eligible for fast-tracking to early GCSE entry (two years prior to the usual entry age). Toby thought that this would be a suitable test group to help him and other staff gain a better understanding of how students might cope with the added pressure, providing information about their relative performance in addition to assessment grade data. Most schools collect only the latter.

His decision stemmed from an interest in psychology and learning theory and a strong belief that young people can be helped to reach their potential through developing a better understanding of their own behaviour, self-motivation and responses to all aspects of their whole experience of schooling. His focus was on how pupils handle perceived stress and what effect this had on their academic performance, an approach not commonly used in a systematic way in schools at present. Most schools will recognise the stress experienced by pupils at examination time, particularly in schools most in need of improvement and will put in place support, such as extra revision classes and one-to-one tutorials. But few have systematic strategies to help individual pupils cope with the pressure and stress associated with examinations—possibly because the teachers themselves are under stress.

The very choice of this target group is symptomatic of first the enormous pressure on schools today to fast-track students in order to boost GCSE results and improve the school's placing in the GCSE performance league tables and second, the heroic efforts of teachers like Toby, who work in the most challenging contexts, to increase the self-esteem and the life chances of young people from disadvantaged backgrounds.

Examples of possible responses in relation to the four components of mental toughness resonated with him. As an experienced teacher, he would have predicted that such a selective high-performing group of pupils would naturally score highly on commitment, "relishing the repeated opportunity to measure and prove themselves", on emotional control, "building on positive results", on life control, always completing their homework, enjoying the competition in challenge and being generally confident. He felt sure that students would be pleased that they had been selected for early entry, would rise to the challenge, having confidence in their own abilities.

However, the MTQ48 survey findings turned out to be surprising: it was clear that teachers' perceptions were very different to the pupils' own. In many cases the most academically able had the lowest mental toughness scores, clearly indicating that although they were seen to be achieving good grades they were in fact struggling with the whole experience of examinations and could improve on their performance if this were recognised and rectified. Pupils' responses fell into two main categories: those with confidence in their abilities but poor control and committed students who tend to shy away from challenge.

Toby was able to compare student mental toughness scores with achievement data and to share this with tutors, encouraging them to introduce students to mental toughness exercises after talking through with them the results of their MTQ48 diagnostics. The pupil behaviours highlighted by the tests were very familiar to tutors—and probably to most teachers. The ones with low control were the poorly organised ones, the pupils most likely to dwell on failure rather than to take responsibility for improving their performance. They are the students who arrive late, without equipment and who respond poorly to criticism, blaming others or external factors for failure.

Academically able young people who shy away from challenge are often a mystery to their teachers. They are expected to do well but teachers often underestimate the emotional impact of change—of teacher or timetable for instance—or peer pressure. These are also the ones who respond poorly to competitive environments, with some reluctant to be seen as high achievers by their peers. Any classroom teacher will recognise these "types". Simply adding more pressure—traditional teacher chivvying and nagging—does not work. Studying the MTQ48 data and associated coaching and remedial strategies, was a revelation. Toby felt that the usual strategies were failing because they were focused on the symptoms not the causes.

Toby's most powerful intervention was to interrogate and share the mental toughness test feedback alongside the usual performance data traditionally given to pupils and their parents on the school's target-setting days (days in which a school's timetable is suspended so that parents can meet tutors to discuss their children's progress and set academic targets). Enlisting the support of parents in helping their children become more organised, to think positively or to praise in order to raise self-esteem resonated with tutors and they felt more empowered to suggest practical steps and coaching techniques to both parents and tutors. In preparation for target-setting day, the two tutors of the MTQ48 test group were given the developmental reports for all test subjects and trained on how to give feedback and in coaching techniques. This enabled the tutors to set very specific personal development targets alongside the usual academic ones. These interviews with young people and their parents had a very different feel to previous ones. Pupils felt understood, cared for, and advice was well received.

Although limited in scope and reliability and without yet a control group or retest, Toby's anecdotal evidence of the efficacy of interventions following test feedback shows promise in its approaches to thinking about the whole child and personality differences in relation to examination success. In addition to sharpening up target-setting, he tried out some of the exercises designed to develop mental toughness, especially those around attentional and anxiety control and positive thinking, gently pushing students out of their comfort zones, finding them to be very receptive and thoroughly enjoying the tasks and games played.

For Toby a change in an individual's attitude was sufficient an indicator that these interventions could potentially help those who already do well to do better and to stretch them to their full potential. One or two pupils who previously seemed uninterested in tutorial sessions showed signs of real engagement and participation levels increased throughout the group. He believes that this in turn had an impact on their grades and overall achievement. Merely introducing pupils to the test made some of these pupils think about how they approach stressful and challenging situations. Indeed these interventions encouraged them to reflect on their former performance and set about improving it. As most teachers would agree, a reflective learner is a successful learner. Some of the pupils commented that they had never really thought about some of obstacles to achievement or negative aspects of their own personalities highlighted by the MTQ48. Merely naming them seemed to have an effect and they were open to reflecting on how they generally performed in certain situations and how to improve on that performance.

There is a growing interest among teachers in emotional intelligence and coaching techniques, including strategies borrowed from CBT (Cognitive Behavioural Therapy) and NLP (Neuro-linguistic programming), as well as more traditional concepts like "character building". Movements such as the Mindfulness in Schools[8] project and Curee[9] are developing apace, with teachers looking to understand the whole child rather than just "teaching to the test". These are important developments in schools dedicated to closing the achievement gap, where changing the mindsets and attitudes of both young people and their teachers is a key challenge for school leaders.

Rose Donald, director of teaching and learning at the Capital City Academy in North London, recalls an outward bound course designed for year eleven problematic students likely to underperform at GCSE—those with specific learning difficulties, persistent truants or children looked after, for instance—which had a remarkably transforming effect. They all did better than predicted and although Rose was not aware of MTQ48 at the time, with hindsight she felt that what they had acquired through the various activities was mental toughness. The experience strengthened their ability to rise to the challenge, overcome obstacles, develop resilience. It had taught them to be aspirational.

So what about teacher leaders?

The concept of mental toughness as an essential professional attribute has resonated the most with middle leaders new to their posts who often struggle with taking up authority in what is generally a very collegial profession. Many found themselves managing colleagues older or more experienced than themselves, like Katy Brown from Hampstead Comprehensive School, who was precipitously promoted to head of faculty when her line manager left suddenly or Kevin, charged with turning around A Level results in the face of dwindling resources and falling rolls. Our most needy schools are often those with the highest staff turnover, so teachers are frequently promoted to first line management with only a few years' experience and in most cases with very little training.

Schools have to fine balance increased public accountability with growing autonomy in a rapidly changing education landscape which includes burgeoning numbers of academies, free schools, federations and alliances of schools and all-through establishments with provision for early years through to post-sixteen education. Some school leaders embrace these changes and new freedoms as opportunities to improve what they offer young people and to make their own decisions closer to the action of frontline provision. Others feel crushed by continuous change and what they perceive as forced autonomy, regretting the demise or dwindling power and influence of local authorities and wearied by changes to the curriculum, examination system, and school inspection regimes.

Middle leaders in schools feel the strain most. They are the engine room of the school, producing results on the frontline. The middle leaders interviewed after taking the MTQ48 diagnostic test and receiving their feedback in a training workshop universally reported feeling anxious and under pressure in their new roles. The concept of mental toughness resounded clearly. Their battle language in response demonstrates just how much pressure there is in our schools today. They speak of climates of fear, feeling squashed and disempowered in the face of intense local competition generated by school performance league tables and funding restraints. They report "burn-out" and loss of confidence in their own abilities, and loss of control the harder they worked and the higher they achieved.

It is not surprising. Department, subject, or pastoral heads are indeed the squeezed middle. Whether it be curriculum, examination, inspection, or other policy or systemic changes, the pressure is on the "middle leader" to make it work in practice. Pressure comes from both above and below. The opportunity to make things happen, make a difference, do things "my way" joyfully seized by first-time leaders is often short-lived. Suddenly they are managing upwards as well as downwards, laterally too, in the middle arena competing with others for limited resources and conflicting ideas, and if they have been promoted internally, relationships with peers will shift and different alliances will form or break.

Although accountable, they feel less in control, no longer in charge of their own destiny. Taking up authority in role might even undermine the very achievements that led to promotion—excellent teaching abilities, for instance—which may then be experienced as a loss. They have to relearn ways of operating and motivating themselves, suppressing their personal achievement drives in the service of others. Their success stands or falls on collective achievement and the emergent leader will need to develop a different set of skills and to gain job satisfaction from enabling others to succeed and grow.

However, if standards are to rise in our schools, it is vitally important that we have mentally tough and resilient first-line teacher leaders as well as heads, who are inevitably charged with delivering improved results among their teams of teachers. There is now a solid body of research demonstrating that the quality of leadership and management is second only to the quality of teaching in ensuring effective education.

The difference between outstanding and inadequate leadership is stark. From OFSTED data, McKinsey[10] found that for every 100 schools with good leadership and management, ninety-three will have good standards of student achievement, but for every 100 schools that do not, only one will have these good standards.

The middle leaders in our sample related strongly to being given a conceptual framework with which to reflect upon their leadership demands. They know they need to be mentally tough and many spoke about the revelatory experience of having a language to talk about their own development needs in this area.

"Being able to see a breakdown of my ability to perform in stressful situations and reviewing ways to improve has helped me understand my strengths and flaws as a leader in a constructive way. To see what it is that enables me to perform at a higher level has given me the confidence to seek out more challenges in my roles as both a teacher and as a leader".

No more so is this evident than among female members of the Teaching Leaders group.

The first cut of the Teaching Leaders data shows a distinct difference between the mental toughness of male and female fellows (programme participants) particularly in relation to challenge and confidence.

Rose Donald and Sophie Grant, Curriculum Leader for English at the The Crest Girls' Academy, in a disadvantaged area of north west London found that this resonated with their own experiences climbing up the leadership career ladder. Reflecting upon male and female styles of leadership they described the emotional cost of becoming heads of department for the first time, in particular the task of holding members of their teams to account at a time of increasing accountability for schools. One described a time in her career when she shared an office with a fellow head of year, noting a difference in style. Male heads of year when dealing with a student misbehaviour or academic underperformance tended to take the no nonsense pull your socks up approach— "we'll support you but you'll bear the consequences if you don't do what I tell you"—commonly known as "tough love". In contrast female pastoral leaders tend to want to explore the underlying reasons behind behaviour giving cause for concern and are much more likely to give time consuming emotional support to pupils and their parents.

Men seem to progress up the career ladder earlier or more easily and don't agonise over failure. Their female colleagues may have more confidence in interpersonal relations but generally have less confidence in their own abilities. This view is echoed by the experiences of coaches and tutors working with trainee heads on the National Professional Qualification for Headteachers (NPQH). High calibre women often better qualified than men with similar length or depth of experience baulk at the final hurdle and feel that they just don't have the confidence to go for headship. Future Leaders, a fast track programme for potential heads of challenging schools expresses disquiet that although fifty-three per cent of Future Leaders are female, there is a lower conversion rate into headship—out of seventy heads appointed, only twenty-three are women.

Repeatedly coaches of female trainee heads—and indeed of middle leaders—report that they are tasked with addressing issues around confidence, such as having the resilience to cope with the challenges of the job but also, perhaps more worryingly, having the resilience to prepare for headship interviews, to overcome the inevitable disappointments and setbacks along the way of the interview circuit.

This imbalance is reflected in the system as a whole. While there are three times more female teachers than male in the teaching profession overall, there are almost three times as many men than women who reach secondary headship. There may be a serious issue here around recruitment not only in terms of the gender imbalance leaders but for developing the emotional intelligence, self-awareness, and emotional control that is required to lead schools in these challenging times. How do we make our female leaders more mentally tough without diminishing traditional female attributes around interpersonal relationships?

In evaluations, surveys, discussions in learning sets and coaching conversations conducted the most reported concerns of middle leaders are rarely problems with pedagogy or the curriculum but are almost universally around leading change, having difficult conversations with teachers they line manage or having to manage upwards in the face of insufficient support from senior leadership (who are of course often equally under pressure).

Given the degree and pace of change in education, it would seem important to have teacher leaders who are comfortable being stretched out of their comfort zone. Certainly the middle leaders in our sample embrace the opportunity to develop their mental toughness in the face of the challenges all around them. As in other professions, there are areas over which teacher leaders have control and influence and those that they do not. People who have a higher level of mental toughness tend to focus on areas that they can control or influence rather than those they cannot. It is more effective to spend time and energy on what you can control. The challenge is to stretch yourself to widen your circle of control. By building mental toughness training into the Teaching Leaders programme it is hoped that we can make a number of middle leaders in our most challenging schools become purposeful and positive about dealing with stressors and challenges, rather than passively accepting them along with educational failure for a significant minority of young people.

Notes

1. *Organization for Economic Cooperation* (OECD) Program for International Student Assessment (PISA) tables, 2012, OECD Publishing.
2. Marshall, P. (Ed.) (2013). *The Tail: How Britain's Schools Fail One Child in Five—and What Can be Done.* London: Profile Books.
3. *Schools, Pupils and Their Characteristics*, Department for Education, National Statistics, 2012.
4. *Children Looked After by Local Authorities in England*, including Adoption, National Statistics, 2012.
5. *Fixed-Term and Permanent Exclusions from Schools in England from academic year 2010–2011.* National Statistics, Department for Education, 2012.
6. *Outcomes for Children Looked After by Local Authorities in England: 31 March 2012*, National Statistics, Department for Education, 2012.
7. GCSE and Equivalent Attainment in England by Pupil Characteristics, January 2013, National Statistics, Department for Education, 2013.
8. Review of Studies, Journal of Children's Services 2013; mindfulnessin-schools.org.
9. Centre for the use of Research & Evidence in Education (CUREE).
10. McKinsey (2009). Capturing the Leadership Premium.

CHAPTER THIRTEEN

Parents' role in developing young people

Anna Golawski

Introduction

In my work as a parent coach, and in speaking with friends and colleagues about what they most want for their children when they grow up, the most popular answers tend to be "to be happy and healthy" or "to do their best".

This chapter will look at how mental toughness can support the development of young children and the positive intentions that parents can have for their children.

The underlying coaching approach and principle of this chapter will be to present information and ideas, yet allow the reader to choose what is most relevant to them in the development of their child and bringing out the best of their potential, talents, and abilities, whether that's in sports, drama, or academia.

I am very mindful of the fact that the definition of "happy and healthy" or "doing their best" is going to mean vastly different things to different people depending on, not least, their family set-up, dynamics, situation, and the individual needs, wants, and abilities of the child. So this chapter does not intend to be directive or prescriptive, rather it is for you to choose what is the most useful information to support your child's development and mental toughness and think about what you can do.

Development of children

The definition of development is "the sequence of physical and psychological changes experienced by human beings, which start with conception and continue throughout life" (Lindon, 2012, p. 4).

The role of parents in their child's development is to start with the foundations and building blocks in order to prepare them for later life experiences and to be better equipped to cope with the challenges and pressures that they will inevitably face at some point.

In addition to meeting the fundamental basic needs of children (i.e., home, food, clothing), parents need to support the development needs of children in the areas of:

Physical development—there are certain physical milestones that children will achieve (these will vary from child to child) and include:

- gross motor skills, which is the coordination and control of large muscles and skills such as walking, sitting, running.
- fine motor skills, which is the coordination and control of smaller muscles for activities such as holding things, writing, etc.
- vision and hearing, including the interpretation and understanding of what they see and hear around them.

Emotional development—babies are programmed to seek out the things they need by crying. As they mature, children's emotional capabilities expand to allow them to develop skills that will serve them in adulthood. Babies are born with some emotional qualities, however much of their emotional development is down to their parents who need to provide warm, attentive care, and a feeling of security. Healthy social and emotional development allows children to:

- navigate friendships and relationships, including sibling rivalry
- express and manage their own feelings
- develop persistence and attention
- self-regulate their behaviour
- develop an emotional range

- develop independence and self-confidence
- understand and empathise with other people's feelings.

Intellectual development—this involves going from "simplistic thinking" as a toddler, right through to being an adult who is capable of independent thinking and understanding of complex issues. This is a gradual and continual process which continues throughout life, and includes things such as:

- recognising different voices
- distinguishing between different objects, shapes, and textures
- understanding words
- consolidating physical development
- developing speech and language
- inquisition—asking "Why?" (a lot!)
- logical thinking and problem solving
- understanding abstract concepts.

Cognitive development and changes in children aren't so easy to spot as this is about how their brains are developing and understanding the world around them, including memory, reasoning, problem-solving, and thinking. You are likely to see changes in your child's behaviour as they learn new experiences and consequences of their actions. Cognitive development stages include:

- simple reflex actions (e.g., grasping, sucking)
- repetitive reflex actions to create interesting results (such as kicking an object)
- coordination of reactions (e.g., picking up a favourite toy)
- problem-solving
- intuition
- developing logical thought patterns.

These development stages cover things such as knowledge, curiosity, courage, confidence, independence, resourcefulness, resilience, patience, competence, and understanding (Holt, 1983) and these together support the components of mental toughness.

Parents play a vital role in the development of their children and in preparing them for managing challenges they will face later on in life as adults.

This responsibility can add pressure to parents, most often when they are juggling the demands of childcare and work, so I will also consider how important it is that parents look after their own mental toughness levels and wellbeing.

I share the view advocated by Guldberg (2009) that parents can often feel undermined by media stories and our safety-obsessed culture. I would encourage parents to trust themselves in knowing what is best for their children.

Berk (2008) has argued that transitions in family life over the past decade, such as an increase in divorce, remarried parents, and employed mothers have reshaped the family system. Each change affects the family dynamic and ultimately children's development. While family transitions have always existed, they appear more numerous and visible today than in the past.

Additional pressures of bringing up a family in the twenty-first century include less freedom and independence for children due to media stories, conflicting advice given through the media, children's access to internet information, and lower expectations about what children are capable of (Guldberg, 2009).

Over recent years there has been increased demand for parent coaching to help address these pressures, and research has given us insight into the effectiveness and results that it can achieve.

Even small changes in parent's behaviour or speech patterns can have a significant impact on children's performance, motivation, self-esteem, and confidence.

The responsibility to develop a child's mental toughness isn't just down to their time at school, and is significantly impacted by the social conditions in which a child lives and grows up.

Palmer (2006) concludes that what happens at home profoundly affects children's ability to learn and develop, and when home and school work are in harmony, children have a much better chance of success.

Needs of children

In her pioneering work, Dr Kellmer-Pringle (1986) identified the four main needs of children that need to be met in equal measure as: Love and security, new experiences, responsibility and praise and recognition.

The need for love and security is met when a child experiences a stable, continuous, dependable and loving relationship with their parents or adults (such as teachers, extended family, godparents, etc). These relationships form the basis for children's self-worth and healthy personal development (the control component of mental toughness).

New experiences are a prerequisite for intellectual and cognitive growth. A child's mastery of tasks, appropriate to each stage of their development, provides stepping stones to accomplishing more difficult tasks in later life.

It is key that new experiences are relevant to the child's development progress and that they are not continually forced to do something that they are afraid of. Holt (1983) suggests that if we push a child to do what they are afraid of, they will use their resources and energy not to explore the unknown, but to find ways to avoid pressures placed upon them. The key is finding the balance to encourage new experiences without pushing a child too far beyond the limits of their courage.

The need for responsibility is met by allowing children to achieve independence. This can first be done by allowing a young child to take care of themselves (washing, dressing, feeding, etc.) and gradually extend the responsibility to other areas as they grow and develop.

The need for praise and recognition enables a child to grow into a self-reliant adult, however it requires an extensive amount of emotional, social, and intellectual learning.

One of the key ways to improve the confidence component of a child's mental toughness is through effective praise and recognition and is a fundamental need for a child's learning, growth, and development.

In addition to the needs identified by Dr Kellmer-Pringle, I would also add that children need space and time to develop and experience an element of boredom. It is during this time that they can develop their imaginations and learn how to be self-reliant. Over recent years there has been a pendulum swing too far which has resulted in a lot of children being over-managed with various activities and clubs and ferried from one thing to another, rather than being given freedom to create their own entertainment. The trick is in finding a suitable balance and allowing them to learn to live and be comfortable with themselves without relying on others to provide feedback or entertainment.

Mueller and Dweck (1998) surveyed 400 children aged ten to twelve years. They conducted a series of intelligence tests for the children with feedback at each stage. The group of children who received praise for achievement and intelligence were less likely to enjoy the tasks and showed a reluctance to try harder. Children who were praised for effort rather than ability felt encouraged to try harder, regardless of the consequences, and were more motivated to try harder in each stage of the tests.

Hartley-Brewer (2005) also suggests that children need to be told that they are capable in order to flourish and that non-verbal praise such as hugs, smiles, and rewards have a significant part to play.

In order for praise to enhance a child's self-esteem and confidence and willingness to try new things, it has to be effective.

Matheson (2004) suggests that if praise is indiscriminate, it teaches children to lower expectations and can reduce motivation. Positive expectations can, however, help develop resilience and coping skills in preparation for life's future challenges.

Challenges facing young people

Some of the challenges facing children and young people in the twenty-first century are:

- bullying
- self-esteem
- pressure of distorted media images/unrealistic comparisons
- celebrity culture
- studying
- exam pressures
- career choices
- friendships and relationships
- peer pressure
- changing family dynamics (divorced parents, single parents, blended families, etc.).

Although some of these challenges facing children today will also have been around for previous generations, there does tend to be a general feeling that there are more pressures for young people today, which is exacerbated by the rate of technology changes and an increase in family breakups.

How can mental toughness help the development of young people?

Parents play a key role in developing mental toughness in their children which will help them cope better with the above challenges and help them to develop confidence and try new things in life.

The table below illustrates the four components of mental toughness, the issues that young people face, how parents can help develop their mental toughness to cope and the positive outcomes they can expect to achieve:

Four C's	Issues faced	How parents can help	Expected outcomes
Challenge	Exam pressures Course work Interviews First job	Attentional control Goal setting Confidence Visualising success	Exam success Developing proactive strategies to cope with stress
Commitment	Sticking to revision Drop out of college courses	Project management Time management Support/ encouragement	Complete studies Work effectively without getting burnt out Overcome setbacks
Control	Self-worth Self-esteem Emotional control Managing stress	Listening effectively Praise Empathy Helping them to relax/manage stress Understanding and managing feelings General wellbeing— diet/fitness/ stress	Choose a job/ career that they want and that they find fulfilling Feel like they are making a difference Appreciate the value of things Maturity and emotional intelligence

(*Continued*)

(Continued).

Four C's	Issues faced	How parents can help	Expected outcomes
Confidence	Bullying Peer pressure (e.g., drinking, smoking, drugs) Celebrity culture Developing friendships/ relationships Managing studies Coping in a new job	Keeping a diary/ journal of success and achievement Praise and recognition Developing assertiveness Visualising success Positive messages and being aware of the "labels" they give their children (sometimes unconsciously)	Lower reported incidents of perceived bullying Bounceback from setbacks Overcome obstacles Confidence to not be drawn into undesired behaviours by others

Parent's own mental toughness

In order for parents to support their children's development and mental toughness, it is imperative that they also look after themselves. The analogy would be on a flight, where passengers are instructed to put on their own oxygen masks before trying to help others.

Parents need to look after themselves in terms of their general fitness, wellbeing and energy levels, and this is especially important when there are the demands of work to manage as well as children.

By developing their own levels of self-awareness, parents can understand how they influence their children and be conscious of the pressures and expectations that they are putting on their children. It is about finding the balance between encouraging and supporting them to achieve their best, but without adding to the feelings of pressure and stress.

Parents need to have their support networks and ensure they take time out to relax and unwind. They are also a key role model in creating behaviours in children and need to be aware of the examples they are setting. By developing this awareness they are in a better position to break the cycles of "bad" parenting that can be passed down from generation to generation.

Conclusion

In the past we've spoken about parent's intuition, mother's wisdom, and fatherly advice, however with our busy lives in the twenty-first century and with the conflicting opinions from various parenting experts, we have lost sight of some of the fundamental needs that we need to provide for our children as part of their development stages.

Mental toughness provides us with an excellent framework to enable us to take those sound ideas and common senses and apply them to the most important aspects of family life—that of raising happy, healthy children to be the best they can and ultimately live a fulfilling life as adults who are capable of managing day to day stresses and challenges.

Having a family is probably the most important life-changing experience and children are our most treasured "possessions". However, despite our best intentions, sometimes the way we raise and interact with them, we don't always achieve our desired outcomes, and can actually sometimes be adding to the stress of our children if we have high expectations of them but without the support and guidance to get them there.

Mental toughness, and its associated interventions, provides us with a great reminder of the techniques we can bring to develop our children and enable them to reach their true potential in life. It allows parents to take a step back from living in the moment of child raising, to reflect on what they are doing well, and where they can continue to help make a positive difference.

PART III

APPLIED CASE STUDIES AND RESEARCH CASE STUDIES

CHAPTER FOURTEEN

Mental toughness in secondary schools

Helen St Clair-Thompson

In this chapter mental toughness is considered in terms of its importance within secondary schools. The results of a series of projects designed to examine relationships between mental toughness and adolescent's attainment and experiences at school are described. An overview is also given of ongoing work exploring the importance of mental toughness in education. Each project that is discussed employs the "four C's" framework of mental toughness, which is described in the earlier chapters of this book.

Introduction

Mental toughness is a popular and attractive construct within educational settings, in part due to its conceptualisation as a mindset that can be changed through psychological skills training. (You can read more about mental toughness training elsewhere in this book.) The potential malleability of mental toughness suggests that to the extent that mental toughness is important for educational outcomes, mental toughness training has the potential to improve adolescent's attainment and experiences at school. Consistent with this suggestion a number of recent projects have provided initial evidence that mental toughness training can have beneficial effects. For example, Clough and Strycharczyk (2012a) described an intervention known as "stay and succeed" which encourages learners to think about control, confidence, challenge, and commitment. This intervention encouraged participants to be better prepared for what life "throws at them", cope with difficulties and challenges, be more resilient, better organised, adopt positive thinking, and bounce back from setbacks. The results of the project were encouraging, for example they evidenced an increase in student retention rates.

The series of studies described in this chapter were therefore designed to further our understanding of mental toughness within secondary schools. In order to design successful interventions for developing mental toughness we need a clear understanding of how and why mental toughness is important within educational settings. The studies examined the relationships between challenge, commitment, control, and confidence and a range of outcomes and experiences, including scholastic attainment, attendance, classroom behaviour, and peer relationships. For a more detailed understanding the control and confidence scales of mental toughness were separated into their subscales of control of emotion, control of life, confidence in abilities, and interpersonal confidence.

The global grit project

The global grit project was an international project conducted (by Katie Lowe) at AQR, inspired by the Global Education Leaders Program. The project involved assessing the extent to which mental toughness is linked with academic success and transition in cohorts from various countries. Here the data is presented from one cohort, in the United Arab Emirates. Data was gathered on mental toughness, academic attainment, school attendance, and body-mass index. Data was available for 114 participants aged eleven to thirteen years of age.

Analysis of the data predominantly involved computing correlations between mental toughness and the other variables. As shown in Table 1 there were significant relationships between aspects of mental toughness and academic attainment. Although there were no significant relationships between mental toughness and attainment in English there were significant relationships between mental toughness and attainment in all the other subjects assessed. The analyses

Table 1. Correlations between mental toughness and attainment.

	English	Maths	Science	French	Geography	History
Challenge	0.06	0.05	0.25*	0.23*	0.08	0.11
Commitment	0.12	0.36**	0.41**	0.26*	0.24*	0.35**
Control of emotion	0.10	0.17	0.29**	0.08	0.04	0.08
Control of life	0.19	0.25*	0.34**	0.28**	0.24*	0.40**
Confidence in abilities	0.14	0.36**	0.34**	0.31**	0.24*	0.31**
Interpersonal confidence	0.18	0.19	0.18	0.24*	0.07	0.21*
Total mental toughness	0.18	0.33**	0.40**	0.34**	0.21*	0.32**

Note: ** $p < 0.01$, * $p < 0.05$.

revealed particularly close relationships for commitment, control of life, confidence in abilities, and total mental toughness.

The analyses revealed no significant relationships between mental toughness and student's attendance at school. However, they did reveal interesting associations between mental toughness and student's body mass index. These correlations are shown in Table 2. Body mass index was significantly negatively related to confidence in abilities, interpersonal confidence, and total mental toughness.

The results of this study lead to several suggestions for educational practice and also for researchers interested in mental toughness. The close relationships that were observed between mental toughness and academic attainment suggest that mental toughness training has the potential to improve adolescent's attainment at school. Schools may therefore want to consider introducing mental toughness training in to their curriculum. In particular, training focused on student's commitment, control of life, and confidence in abilities is likely to be beneficial. The relationships between mental toughness and body mass index suggest interesting avenues for future research. The results suggest that student's confidence, as well as total mental toughness is negatively related to body mass index. With correlational data is not possible to comment on the direction of causation; it could be that higher confidence and mental toughness cause lifestyle choices that result in a lower body mass index, or that a high body mass index results in reductions

Table 2. Correlations between mental toughness and body mass index.

	BMI
Challenge	−0.09
Commitment	−0.16
Control of emotion	0.01
Control of life	−0.13
Confidence in abilities	−0.19*
Interpersonal confidence	−0.29**
Overall mental toughness	−0.20*

Note: ** $p < 0.01$, * $p < 0.05$.

in confidence and mental toughness. However, future research would benefit from a more detailed examination of relationships between mental toughness, body mass index, and associated measures.

Research at the University of Hull

Relationships between mental toughness and other aspects of adolescent's experiences at school have been examined in a series of projects conducted by staff and students at the University of Hull. Projects have examined associations between mental toughness and classroom behaviour as well as adolescent's peer relationships.

In one study, conducted by Myfanwy Bugler, we were particularly interested in associations between mental toughness and adolescent's disruptive classroom behaviour. Teachers frequently report high levels of concern about disruptive behaviour, and disruptive behaviour is associated with a number of outcomes including poor academic attainment. It is therefore important to identify factors that may be related to student's behaviour, and in particular factors that can potentially be changed via intervention, such as mental toughness.

In the study 295 adolescents aged between eleven and fifteen years completed the MTQ48. Classroom teachers were then asked to complete a Conners' Teachers Rating Scale Revised Short Version (Conners, 1997) for each child in their class. This is a scale comprised of twenty-eight items assessing four dimensions of behaviour; cognitive problems/ inattention, oppositional behaviour, hyperactivity, and ADHD. Here we combined these subscales to produce an overall measure of disruptive behaviour. Again data analysis predominantly involved computing correlations between mental toughness and other variables, in this case student's behaviour.

The correlations between each subcomponent of mental toughness and student's classroom behaviour are shown in Table 3. Several aspects of mental toughness were significantly negatively related to classroom behaviour, suggesting that higher levels of mental toughness were associated with lower levels of disruptive behaviour. The analyses revealed particularly close relationships for commitment, control of life, interpersonal confidence, and total mental toughness.

Again the results of this study have important implications for educational practice. The relationships between mental toughness and disruptive behaviour suggest that mental toughness training has the potential to improve adolescent's behaviour in the school classroom. Schools may therefore want to consider introducing mental toughness training in to their curriculum, particularly if they have concerns about behaviour management. In particular, training focused on student's commitment, control of life, and interpersonal confidence is likely to be beneficial.

In another study, conducted by Jamey Spokes (also reported in St Clair-Thompson, Bugler, Robinson, Clough, McGeown, & Perry, 2014) we were interested in examining the relationships between mental toughness and adolescent's peer relationships. Peer relationships are an important aspect of child and adolescent development and are also related to outcomes including academic attainment and health

Table 3. Correlations between mental toughness and negative classroom behaviour.

	Behaviour
Challenge	−0.13*
Commitment	−0.25**
Control of emotion	−0.10
Control of life	−0.27**
Confidence in abilities	−0.06
Interpersonal confidence	−0.19**
Total mental toughness	−0.21**

Note: ** $p < 0.01$, * $p < 0.05$.

and wellbeing. It is therefore of interest to identify factors which may contribute to successful peer relationships.

In the study ninety-three students aged eleven to thirteen years of age completed the MTQ48 questionnaire, and were also asked to complete the Social Inclusion Survey (Frederickson, 1994). In this survey students are asked to answer, "How much do you like to play with—?" for each student from their tutor group, and then "How much do you like to work with—?" for each student in their group. Students responded either "I don't know them", "I like to play/work with them", "I don't mind whether I play/work with them" or "I don't like to play/work with them". The proportion of children who responded "I like to play/work with them" was calculated for each child. We examined the correlations between aspects of mental toughness and social inclusion scores.

The results of the study are displayed in Table 4. The results revealed significant relationships between confidence in abilities, interpersonal confidence, total mental toughness, and peer relationships. Thus a student's confidence is related to the extent to which other student's like to play with or work with them at school.

Together the findings of these studies suggest that mental toughness is a useful construct to consider in educational settings, and that mental toughness interventions have the potential to have beneficial effects upon several aspects of adolescents educational experiences. These include academic attainment, classroom behaviour, and peer relationships. The components of commitment and control of life were particularly related to attainment and behaviour, with the subscales of confidence also being related to attainment, body mass index, behaviour, and peer relationships.

Table 4. Correlations between mental toughness and peer relationships.

	SIS play with	SIS work with
Challenge	0.18	0.13
Commitment	0.13	0.18
Control of emotion	0.07	0.10
Control of life	0.10	0.16
Confidence in abilities	0.24*	0.26*
Interpersonal confidence	0.29**	0.24*
Total mental toughness	0.22*	0.24*

Note: ** $p < 0.01$, * $p < 0.05$.

In many ways it is not surprising that commitment was important for academic outcomes. Commitment is described as the extent to which an individual is likely to persist with a goal or with a work task. Commitment also appears to overlap with the personality construct of conscientiousness. Within the theory of hardiness previous research has revealed that commitment is closely linked to academic performance in undergraduate students (e.g., Sheard & Golby, 2007). Conscientiousness is also known to be a good predictor of academic achievement (e.g., Bauer & Liang, 2003).

Control of life was also closely related to adolescent's attainment and disruptive behaviour. Students scoring highly on control of life are described as likely to manage their workload effectively, being good at planning, time management, and prioritising. This is likely to be beneficial for attainment, and result in little disruptive behaviour. Similar suggestions are made of students who have an internal locus of control in theories of academic motivation, particularly attribution theory. If a student has an internal locus of control (arguably similar to a high level of control in mental toughness theory) they perceive achievement as a result of ability or effort, rather than task difficulty or luck. They are therefore more likely to be engaged in learning, have positive behaviours, and reach higher levels of achievement.

Both confidence in abilities and interpersonal confidence were also related to educational outcomes assessed in the current studies. Confidence is closely linked with self-esteem. Self-esteem is also important for attainment, and those who feel confident with others may be more likely to have a wider circle of friends and may contribute more eagerly in group or class activities (e.g., Cheng & Furnham, 2002). There is therefore an apparent overlap between mental toughness and constructs in motivation theory, including locus of control and self-esteem and self-efficacy. Further research would therefore benefit from developing a better understanding of how the subcomponents of mental toughness are related to constructs such as motivation.

Future research projects

Ongoing and planned research projects are examining relationships between mental toughness and other aspects of education. These projects aim to further develop our understanding of how and why mental toughness is important within educational settings. In one of these projects we are examining the relationships between mental toughness and transitions from primary school to secondary school. If mental toughness indeed acts as a resilience resource when confronted with pressure or stress then student's scoring highly on mental toughness may better cope with the transition from primary school to secondary school. As a result of proposed changes to the education system in the UK, which include curriculum subjects being assessed through large end of year examinations rather than via coursework or modular assessments we also aim to explore relationships between aspects of mental toughness and examination performance. The use of qualitative methods such as interviews or focus groups as well as quantitative analyses could also provide a more in depth understanding of the characteristics of students with high or low mental toughness. This could then inform future research into mental toughness interventions.

Future research will also examine methods for developing mental toughness within educational settings. As detailed elsewhere in this book there are several approaches to mental toughness training. These include positive thinking, visualisation, anxiety control, attentional control, and goal setting. A key part of any intervention is also self-reflection. A useful starting point for examining interventions in educational settings may therefore be to encourage students to reflect upon their own mental toughness and identify any areas of strength and weakness. This could be followed by goal setting and the implementation of strategies such as positive thinking. Given the links between mental toughness and educational outcomes that have been described in this chapter such interventions have the potential to improve adolescent's attainment and experiences at school.

Conclusion

The research described in this chapter represents a first step in understanding the role of mental toughness in education. However, from the series of studies presented it is clear that mental toughness is indeed a useful construct to consider within educational settings. If mental toughness can be developed or improved through appropriate interventions then there are many possibilities for improving the educational outcomes and experiences of children and adolescents. This may serve to allow students to realise their potential and to open doors of opportunity that were previously not considered.

CHAPTER FIFTEEN

Mental toughness in Higher Education

Helen St Clair-Thompson

In this chapter mental toughness is discussed in terms of its importance within Higher Education. The results of a series of projects designed to examine relationships between mental toughness, attainment, and attendance at university are described and data about students' life satisfaction is also presented. Finally, there is a discussion of the possible role of mental toughness in terms of success gaining employment after university. Each project that is discussed employs the four C's framework of mental toughness which is described in the earlier chapters of this book.

Introduction

As described in the previous Chapter Fourteen, mental toughness is a popular and attractive construct within educational settings. This is, in part, due to its conceptualisation as a mindset that can be changed or developed through psychological skills training. Given that mental toughness is defined as a quality which determines how people deal effectively with challenge, stressors, and pressure it seems reasonable to expect that it may be important in student's attainment and also wellbeing at university.

There is evidence that the transition to university life results in increased stress (e.g., Fisher & Hood, 1987). Demands such as coursework deadlines, examinations, the requirement to manage one's own time and learning, work/study balance, and loss of support networks (e.g., Okopi, 2011) can also cause considerable stress. Mentally tough individuals have been found to be independent and to take responsibility for their own development.

University requires a great degree of independent learning requiring students to manage their own learning to a greater extent than in secondary education. This may mean that mental toughness is even more important for success in Higher Education than in compulsory education.

Consistent with the suggestion that mental toughness is important within higher education, Peter Clough and colleagues at the University of Hull examined mental toughness in 161 university students enrolled on sports-related degree programmes. All students completed the Mental Toughness Questionnaire (MTQ48), and their end of year grades and the number of credits achieved in the first year were calculated for each student. The number of credits achieved is an important measure of progress and also of attrition.

Analysis of the data revealed that scores on all of the mental toughness subscales, as well as overall mental toughness, were significantly related to both end of year grades and credits. Further analysis revealed that life control and interpersonal confidence were the most important predictors.

The aim of the studies presented in this chapter were to examine the relationships between mental toughness and attainment in a non-sport related degree programme and to examine the relationship between mental toughness and student's life satisfaction.

Mental toughness and attainment

In one exploratory study we were interested in the relationships between mental toughness, attainment, and attendance in undergraduate psychology students.

148 students completed the Mental Toughness Questionnaire (MTQ48) at the start of their university course. At the end of the academic year their end of year grade, number of credits awarded, and number of recorded absences were calculated. We also recorded average grades

for coursework and examinations in order to explore whether aspects of mental toughness were differentially related to coursework and examination performance. The correlations between mental toughness, attainment, and attendance are shown in Table 1.

The results revealed significant relationships between commitment, attainment, and attendance, and between life control and attainment, particularly in examinations. There were no significant relationships between the number of credits and any aspect of mental toughness. However, this may have been due to a restricted range in the credit data.

Nearly all the students who participated in the study were awarded the maximum of 120 credits in their first year. It is, however, important to note that some of the correlations that were observed in the current study were relatively weak. It is likely that this was a result of the longitudinal nature of the study. Students completed MTQ48 at the start of their university course. Several aspects of university life and other experiences may have influenced mental toughness and subsequently attainment and attendance over the course of a year. You will also see in the following section that in other studies we have found much closer relationships between mental toughness and attainment.

The findings of the study nonetheless have important implications for educational practice. They suggest that there could be benefits in incorporating mental toughness training into the university curriculum,

Table 1. Correlations between mental toughness, attainment, and attendance.

	Grade	Credits	Coursework	Exams	Absences
Challenge	−0.03	−0.09	−0.13	0.01	0.04
Commitment	0.25**	0.13	0.28**	0.22**	−0.22**
Control of emotion	0.03	−0.01	0.02	0.01	−0.03
Control of life	0.19*	0.12	0.11	0.22**	−0.05
Confidence in abilities	0.07	0.03	0.05	0.06	0.02
Interpersonal confidence	−0.02	0.11	−0.06	0.06	0.13
Total mental toughness	0.09	0.01	0.05	0.12	−0.02

Note: ** $p < 0.01$, * $p < 0.05$.

perhaps as part of a "skills" module or personal development planning. In particular the findings of the current study suggest that interventions focused on commitment and life control would be most beneficial.

It is perhaps not surprising that commitment was related to attainment and attendance.

Commitment describes the extent to which an individual is likely to persist with a goal or with a work task. Previous research has demonstrated that commitment is linked to academic performance in undergraduate students (e.g., Sheard & Golby, 2007). This finding is also consistent with the results presented in Chapter Fourteen in which commitment was found to be important for attainment and behaviour in secondary school pupils.

Life control was also related to attainment, particularly in exams. Again this is consistent with the findings of Chapter Fourteen, in which life control was closely related to adolescent's attainment and disruptive behaviour.

Mental toughness and life satisfaction

In another study carried out by Amber Hardwick, a student at the University of Hull, we were also interested in the relationship between mental toughness and students' life satisfaction. Life satisfaction is an important construct within positive psychology and is considered to be an aspect of subjective wellbeing. The components of subjective wellbeing are often considered synonymous with the term "happiness". Importantly, life satisfaction and happiness precede a diverse range of positive behavioural, psychological, and social outcomes (e.g., Lyubornirsky, King & Diener, 2005). Low life satisfaction can also precede the onset of depression and psychological disorders.

In the study 129 undergraduate psychology students completed the Mental Toughness Questionnaire (MTQ48). They also supplied their university exam results to date (as students were from all years of the degree course these were from between one and five semesters of study). Finally, students completed the Satisfaction with Life Questionnaire (Diener, Emmons, Larsen & Griffin, 1985). This is comprised of five statements including "In most ways my life is ideal" and students responded to each statement on a 7-point scale ranging from 1-Strongly disagree to 7-Strongly agree. We examined the correlations between mental toughness, average grades, and life satisfaction. These are shown below in Table 2.

Each component of mental toughness, as well as total mental toughness, was closely associated with both attainment and life satisfaction. It is important to note that the relationships between mental toughness and attainment were much stronger than those observed in the previous study. This could possibly be attributed to the timing of the study. Student's completed the mental toughness and life satisfaction scales in the same testing session, and supplied their exam results to date at the same time. Considering all of this information together may have influenced the way in which students responded to questionnaire items. In addition, the closer relationships between mental toughness and attainment could also be attributed to considering grades from the entire university course. Over the three years of a degree, students are increasingly expected to engage in independent study and manage their own learning. It could be that mental toughness is particularly important for the later stages of a degree course.

Of particular interest to the present study there were also significant relationships between each aspect of mental toughness and life satisfaction. The correlations were particularly high for confidence in abilities, total mental toughness, and life control. These findings are consistent with previous suggestions that life satisfaction is related to self-esteem and self-worth (e.g. Diener & Diener, 1995) and also findings that mental toughness is related to emotional wellbeing including depression (Gerber, Brand, Feldmeth, Lang, Elliot, Holsboer-Trachsler *et al.*, 2013). The results further suggest that each component of mental

Table 2. Correlations between mental toughness, attainment, and life satisfaction.

	Grade	Life satisfaction
Challenge	0.47**	0.47**
Commitment	0.47**	0.43**
Control of emotion	0.36**	0.23*
Control of life	0.48**	0.54**
Confidence in abilities	0.39**	0.63**
Interpersonal confidence	0.27**	0.33**
Total mental toughness	0.51**	0.56**

Note: ** $p < 0.01$, * $p < 0.05$.

toughness may serve as a construct to help us understand subjective wellbeing.

These findings suggest that developing mental toughness not only has the potential to improve attainment and attendance in Higher Education, but that it also has the potential to improve students' happiness and wellbeing, which are related to a number of important developmental outcomes. Future research would benefit from exploring the effect of mental toughness interventions, some of which we have described in this book, on university students' attainment and performance but also on students' life satisfaction and components of wellbeing.

Conclusions

The studies presented in this chapter capture just some of the outcomes which are related to mental toughness; higher levels of attainment and attendance in undergraduate programmes, greater life satisfaction, and increased opportunities for employability.

Mental toughness may also be important for other aspects of Higher Education, such as the ease of the transition into university life, and the extent to which students form close friendships with their peers. Through future research we hope to develop a more detailed understanding of how and why mental toughness is important within Higher Education.

However, it is clear from the findings presented in this chapter, that if mental toughness can be developed or improved through appropriate interventions then there are many possibilities for improving the educational outcomes and employment opportunities of today's undergraduates.

Given the importance of mental toughness in several domains, including sport, occupations, wellbeing, and education, mental toughness appears to be a ubiquitous concept with implications for success.

CHAPTER SIXTEEN

Boosting career decision making and employability through mental toughness

Paula Quinton-Jones

T he global job market has never been tougher and for new and returning entrants, the ability to stay focused and motivated coupled with a strong differentiation from the rest of the talent pool is key. To offer support to international business students facing the realities of this employment challenge, Hult International Business School has embedded mental toughness into its core career services delivery. Hult has found that mental toughness is a unique and practical tool for students to use in key areas of job searching and career development:

- Identifying the most appropriate/optimal work environment to allow candidates to function at their peak performance
- Articulating skills, strengths, and behaviours in a meaningful way
- Understanding managerial style as well as how they like to be managed
- Staying motivated and maintaining focus.

It is the first two of these areas that we have found deliver most value in career coaching and we will focus on them here.

Hult is the world's largest business school by graduating class with approximately 2,000 graduates per year. This has been achieved through very rapid growth and a network of five global campuses in Boston, San Francisco, London, Dubai, and Shanghai as well as rotation campuses in Sao Paolo and New York. The student body is highly diverse with in excess of 100 nationalities represented and no one nationality makes up more than twenty per cent of the student body on any campus. Whilst many of the employment challenges faced by Hult students are the same as for any graduates entering the employment market today, there are several unique aspects of the Hult experience that intensify this challenge. The structural elements of the programmes offered, specifically the one year duration and the fact that students can choose to rotate to two additional campuses for the last four months of their programme, mean that the Hult year is out of synch with the recruitment timetable for many MBA and graduate recruiters and that for many students their time to explore career ideas and get "market-ready" is realistically only six to eight months. The result? Hult students need to be creative about finding channels to market and creating opportunities. They also need to "hit the ground running" and be prepared to make decisions and follow through with actions, sometimes in the face of limited information and often running two or three career searches simultaneously.

Whilst the diversity of the Hult student body is an advantage in many ways, it also delivers some more specific issues in terms of approach to job search and student expectations. Whilst students from Western Europe and the US are used to a degree of self-sufficiency in job search, the business school recruitment process in India centres around companies coming onto campus to source candidates with connections outside this channel not allowed. This creates an expectation of the school "delivering" jobs to students which is not Hult's approach and sets a possible tension straight away as students either feel disappointed about the school's lack of delivery against their expectations or scared by the prospect of approaching the market directly.

Even for those students not facing practical issues in terms of job search (visa regulations in the UK continue to be a barrier to market entry for non EEA (European Economic Area) students), the realities of an international career move include the need to adapt to a working culture and set of social rules (a situation that manifests early in the job search process in terms of application and interview etiquette) which can be, at best, different and at worst, at odds with native culture.

As a result of the above the role of the career services team extends beyond basic coaching on career decision-making and job search technique to supporting cultural transitions, managing expectations and helping students revise plans and maintaining motivation throughout the process; we act as cheerleaders, policemen, and confidantes.

With a starting point in identifying potential drop outs from business school, the MTQ measure has already proven its relevance in this environment; it is for this reason that the measure was initially interesting to Hult. The concept of mental toughness and its parallels with sports psychology as well as its unique perspective in a crowded market were felt to accurately reflect the Hult experience as well as the school's philosophy of innovation and alternative thinking and our practical pedagogy. We focus on an holistic experience for our students where as much learning happens outside the classroom (in teamwork exercises, mixing with colleagues, staff, and external contacts etc.) as in, and as we further investigated and developed our understanding of the measure and trialled with students, various other applications have emerged. For example, an early and simple mapping of mental toughness against GPA (grade point average) shows that it is a better indicator of academic performance than the GMAT test.[1]

When mental toughness was initially adopted by Hult as part of our career services offering, the focus was on using the measure to understand how to approach the year at Hult on an individual level (approach work, teamwork, goal orientation). As we have built mental toughness into the careers programme and wider philosophy, our use of the tool has become increasingly sophisticated and we use the concepts and associated interventions as lenses through which to view and examine various elements of the career decision-making and job search journeys.

The vast majority of the careers work undertaken at Hult centres on early career entrants and career changers. Whilst industry focused activities and speakers help students understand the mechanics and work content of various roles, students often find they are able to perform a number of different roles but don't know which will make them happy or play to their specific strengths. In situations such as this, mental toughness provides a filter to lay over the role based information; to think in more detail about the environment and work practices involved in various positions adding further granularity to career research.

Conversations around roles can vary from the basic identification of "right-fit" jobs (someone who is at the sensitive end of the scale on challenge would be best placed in a role requiring regular tasks with strong attention to detail for example actuarial work, compliance, technical drawing etc.), through to a high level of detail around the best work environment or firm for a particular student. This kind of decision information is best illustrated within the financial services industry where a student may have decided to work in corporate finance and have a challenge score of nine or ten matched with a high score on emotional intelligence. In this instance they will most likely thrive in a highly competitive (daresay ruthless) environment as they will be motivated to prove themselves as well as be able to receive criticism in a balanced way and not allow it to detract from the goal in which case they would be suited for the stereotypically high-pressure, high-reward US banks.

Case study

Finn was an MBA student with a background in the telecoms industry initially at engineer level and rose up through the ranks to a project management and implementation role, managing large-scale roll outs in remote territories including Central Africa and the Pacific Islands. Whilst he had made a firm decision to make a career change to consulting and he had the benefit of a sought-after global background in a growing industry vertical, Finn's biggest career challenge was to choose the right firm to match his career aspirations and sell himself within the cultural fit element. With an overall mental toughness score of eight and scores of eight on challenge, life control, and interpersonal confidence, Finn worked with his career coach to identify that his preference was for an environment where he could make an impact early on, express his ideas freely and have a platform to do so as well as shape his own work pattern to carve out a career path. On further investigation, they drilled down to discover that he was keen to display his credibility and build on experience to join at as high a level of possible and had full confidence in his ability to transfer the knowledge and skills he had gained as well as recognising that there was always room to learn more (verified by a confidence in abilities score of seven). Finn was keen, through his experience working in developing economies, to find an opportunity that could deliver positive social impact. On joining Hult,

Finn's plan was to join a "big name" firm such as Bain or McKinsey, but through matching these aspirations with insight gained from information and mentors provided by the school, Finn was able to identify that the lock-step career paths of the larger and more traditional strategy houses would not meet his criteria for non-hierarchical structure and the possibility to build a career within his own time frame. He also recognised that in order to start out at the highest level (thereby satisfying his need to be recognised as an expert and display his credibility) he needed to find a firm where his telecoms background would be of use. Finn narrowed his search down to mid-sized firms with strong Media and Telcos practices and on graduation received an offer from GSMA the global telecoms association, project managing the mobile money for the unbanked initiatives and working alongside colleagues with experience at McKinsey, Bain etc.

By working with his coach on mental toughness, Finn was able to objectively evaluate his career aspirations free from his views of what an MBA graduate "should" do. In the process of understanding these goals, mental toughness became increasingly valuable as an independent tool to unpack previous role dissatisfaction and assure that the next role would fulfil both technical and personal preferences.

Once students have identified the most appropriate path for them, the key to differentiation in a tough market is to be able to articulate skills and experience in a way that is distinct from other candidates and clearly demonstrates the added value that you can bring. This is a difficult task for career changers and new market entrants who do not necessarily have a direct experience. As part of Hult's research activities through Hult Labs[2] we have interviewed over 200 CEOs and Directors of Fortune 500 companies to understand what they want to see from business school graduates. Having identified MBA skill sets as "knowledge-heavy", these senior decision-makers value particular skills, and more importantly, behaviours within this talent pool. Of the ten key skills and behaviours identified by this research[3] all can be influenced and articulated through the lens of mental toughness. Some are obvious (communication, comfort with ambiguity), others are less immediate. For example, business school students are called on for sales skills in a wide variety of areas beyond the traditional sales role, whether this may be gaining buy-in from top management for a change initiative or negotiating deals and terms with suppliers. By examining their mental toughness profile a candidate may be able to identify that their success in consistently delivering against targets results from a strong mental toughness score in the areas of commitment (characterised by being excited by measures and goals as well as a clear understanding of what success looks like) and emotional control (characterised by being able to build on positive results and not be derailed by failure). With coaching from a careers adviser they can learn to weave this knowledge into their personal branding and interview preparation so that the bland statement "I have a good track record in delivering against goals" can become much more detailed, for example, "I've always found that I am able to deliver over and above my sales goals and on a sustained basis. This is because I find very definite measures of success very motivating, I know exactly what I have to do to meet them as well as being able to use my balanced view to objectively understand obstacles and not let them put me off when deadlines are tight. As a result I build a strong vision of what exactly needs to be achieved and am not distracted from that goal".

Other behaviours that have been identified as vital for business schools are self-awareness and integrity. Whilst both are difficult to measure and articulate, again, mental toughness provides a useful vocabulary for this. Integrity can be linked to a high score on life control where a candidate recognises the impact of their actions and takes full responsibility for them. It could also be articulated through a high commitment score which is characterised by the ability to see something through to its conclusion.

Another element of mental toughness is the placement of candidates on a spectrum with positive and negative outcomes at both extremes. Whilst a high score on emotional control is often valued for its evidence of calmness and "grace under pressure", overuse can result in a lack of engagement with others and being perceived as a "cold fish" which will not work well in some environments. At a basic level this is a great aid to tackling the perennial strengths and weaknesses question. In this case and example may be of a more sensitive emotional intelligence score. A candidate may acknowledge the weakness element by disclosing that they "wear their heart on their sleeve" and can be seen as passionate or too emotionally connected to their work. The key in answering this question is to demonstrate self-awareness, showing that you not only understand your flaws but also their impact on others and furthermore a willingness and ability to adapt to mitigate. In this way, the same candidate that defined sensitivity on emotional control as a weakness can use the behaviours identified at the mentally tough end of the spectrum to demonstrate the benefits of this position (authenticity and rapport building) as well as working with a coach to identify and implement interventions to demonstrate the highest level of self-awareness.

At Hult, the complexity of cultural diversity makes the need for an objective and common language to articulate skills and behaviours even more important. This is not only to balance cultural bias towards self-promotion or self-deprecation (typically those who underestimate their strengths find framing their conversation in terms of "this is what an objective assessment has shown about me" as more comfortable and less arrogant than the sense that they are simply asserting how great they are) but also to provide a useful discussion point with colleagues which allows them to calibrate their skills amongst their competition. It also opens up discussion around the workplace culture in the student's chosen location (which is typically not their home country) to better equip them for the process of changing location.

When positioned as part of the full career services offering at Hult, we have discovered mental toughness delivers a vital element of objectivity and holistic explanation and exploration of preferences and approach, providing differentiation and motivational support to young people at a period of change, high investment, and anxiety. As mental toughness becomes more widely used across Hult's global campuses and across different disciplines within career services and academics, we expect it to provide a common language and competitive advantage to our students.

Notes

1. In a mapping exercise performed by the Hult International Business School academic team it was discovered that amongst London MBA students of the class of 2012, of those with an overall mental toughness score of 8 or above, forty-nine per cent had a GPA of 3.6 or above (out of 4.0), versus twenty-five per cent for those whose overall score was 6 or 7, and twenty per cent of those with an overall score between 2 and 5.
2. Hult Labs is a new San Francisco-based research think tank for Hult International Business School. The team is composed as educators, thinkers, and writers with one goal: to innovate education as we know it.
3. The ten skills identified by the Hult Labs research are self-awareness, communication, integrity, cross-cultural skills, team skills, critical thinking, comfort with ambiguity, creativity, execution, and sales.

CHAPTER SEVENTEEN

Sex gender identity and mental toughness

Myfanwy Bugler, Helen St Clair-Thompson,
and Sarah McGeown

S ex differences or gender differences have been investigated in educational research for quite some considerable time; however the distinction between the two is often unclear. Sex refers to the differences between males and females at the biological level, whilst gender refers to the characteristics that are usually associated with being male or female. Gender identity refers to the extent to which an individual identifies with the stereotypical norms of a particular gender. The concepts of "male" and "female" are relatively easy for people to understand because these words relate to biological differences and need no explanation. But the concepts of masculine and feminine are much less closely related to biology and thus much more difficult to separate into two distinct categories. However, these dimensions seem important, and psychologists have attempted to conceptualise and measure masculinity and femininity. This has proved to be a difficult task and after many years the concept of androgyny, that is, having both masculine and feminine characteristics has appeared as an addition to the conceptual framework.

Sex differences in mental toughness

Little research has examined sex differences in adolescents' mental toughness, but when sex differences have been examined, differences are rarely found (Clough & Strycharczyk, 2012). However, in one study examining the association between mental toughness, performance, behaviour, and wellbeing (Clough, Earle & Strycharczyk, 2008) significant sex differences were reported, with males reporting higher levels of mental toughness. The authors posited that this could be the result of cultural differences in that the local area treated boys and girls differently according to social norms. Further analysis of the results was conducted analysing teacher assessments of both students' mental toughness and behaviour in addition to students' self-reported mental toughness scores. Analysis of teacher assessments of student negative behaviour revealed that teachers did indeed view boys and girls differently. Teachers associated challenging behaviour (a sign of mental toughness) as negative when exhibited by girls more so than when exhibited by boys. Therefore teachers penalised girls for challenging behaviour rather than recognising it as mental toughness. In addition, when low levels of mental toughness were found, teachers significantly identified negative behaviour in boys more so than in girls. The researcher's conclusions were that teacher perceptions of what was appropriate behaviour for boys or girls accounted for the reported sex differences in mental toughness in this study.

Interestingly, sex differences in mental toughness have also been revealed in a sports setting. For example, Nicholls, Polman, Levy and Blackhouse (2009) found that males reported significantly higher levels of mental toughness than females, with age and experience in their particular sport predicting higher levels of mental toughness. It was suggested that this reported sex difference could be due to variations in the underlying expression of the attributes related to mental toughness in males and females or alternatively it may reflect different socialisation processes (Nicholls, Polman, Levy & Blackhouse, 2009). In addition, more recent research investigating mental toughness in athletes reported sex differences with male athletes reporting significantly higher levels of mental toughness (Crust & Keegan, 2010). However, males tend to be more confident than females and as confidence is a key component of mental toughness (Clough, Earle & Sewell, 2002) this may explain these results.

Sex vs gender identity

Sex differences in mental toughness have been investigated but gender identity and its association with mental toughness is yet to be examined. It is interesting to investigate the concepts of both gender identity and sex differences in relation to mental toughness to gain a better understanding of the differences in adolescents' mental toughness. As mental toughness is reported to be a multidimensional and dynamic construct (Harmison, 2011), and influenced by an individual's environment (Bull, Shambrook, James & Brooks, 2005), it is reasonable to posit that environmentally shaped sex stereotypes as opposed to biological differences, may influence the development of this important cognitive strength construct.

In order to understand why boys report higher levels of mental toughness than girls it is important to understand which psychological factors could explain this difference in self-perceived mental toughness. An alternative approach towards understanding the differential levels of mental toughness between boys and girls may be sociological (sex-role concept). Sex-role concept refers to a set of shared beliefs that a society holds about the characteristics appropriate for individuals on the basis of their sex.

Experimental case study on sex differences, gender identity, and mental toughness

Research in sex differences in mental toughness is scant and does not address the relationship between sex, gender identity, and mental toughness. This study had two aims: to investigate the association of sex and gender identity on mental toughness in adolescents: to examine whether gender identity predicted anything over and above sex.

Procedure

In order to examine the role of sex and gender identity in self-reported mental toughness 309 adolescents (160 female, 149 male; aged between eleven and sixteen) completed questionnaires measuring their mental toughness and gender identity (i.e., the extent to which they identified with masculine and feminine traits). The students completed the MTQ48 (Clough, Earle & Sewell, 2002) to measure mental toughness and the CSRI (The Childrens' Sex Role Inventory, Boldizar, 1991) to assess gender identity.

Mental toughness: MTQ48 (Clough, Earle & Sewell, 2002)

Students were also asked to complete the Mental Toughness Questionnaire (MTQ48: Clough, Earle & Sewell, 2002). This is comprised of forty-eight items assessing six dimensions of mental toughness: challenge, commitment, control of emotions, control of life, confidence in abilities, and confidence in personal life. Challenge is defined as the extent to which individuals view problems as opportunities for self-development. Commitment reflects a deep involvement in whatever the individual is doing. Control is subdivided into two dimensions, emotional control and control of life; emotional control is the ability to keep anxieties in check and not reveal emotions to others; life control concerns a belief in being influential and not controlled by others. Confidence is also subdivided into two dimensions, confidence in abilities and interpersonal confidence. Confidence in abilities reflects the belief in individual qualities with less dependence on external support and interpersonal confidence is about being assertive and less likely to be intimidated in social events. For each item the student's agree/disagree with a series of statements on a five-point Likert-type scale (ranging from "I disagree strongly" to "I agree strongly"). A score is calculated for each of the mental toughness constructs by totalling the responses on the appropriate items.

Gender identity: the Children's Sex Role Inventory (CSRI) short form

The CSRI was used to assess gender roles (Boldizar, 1991). This instrument measures traditional masculine traits (e.g., competitiveness: "When I play games, I really like to win"), feminine traits (e.g., compassion: "I care about what happens to others") and neutral traits to act as fillers (e.g., friendly "I have many friends"). It is a self-report survey and uses a Likert scale (four, "very true of me"; three, "mostly true of me"; two, "a little true of me" and one, "not true of me at all"). Neutral items were excluded from the analysis.

Sex differences in mental toughness and gender identity

A series of ANOVAs were carried out to investigate sex differences in mental toughness.

Sex differences were found in masculine and feminine traits in accordance with stereotypical perceptions; girls identified more closely with feminine traits whilst boys identified more closely with masculine traits. However, it is important to note that the sex differences found in masculine traits was considerably narrower than the difference found in feminine traits; boys and girls differed more widely in their iden-tification with feminine traits (or traits traditionally considered to be feminine). Interestingly, when examining the mean scores for both males and females on the CSRI, it is clear that males identified more closely with the masculine traits in the questionnaire than the feminine traits whilst girls identified with both feminine and masculine traits. This may be due, in part, to cultural changes throughout the last two decades (the questionnaire was published twenty years ago). It may be the case that females, whilst identifying more with feminine traits, are also rejecting a lot of the traits that are considered to be traditionally feminine and adopting some characteristics considered to be indicative of a masculine identity.

Association between gender identity and mental toughness

Table 1. Correlations examining associations between masculine and feminine traits and mental toughness constructs (both males and females).

	Challenge	Commitment	Control of emotion	Control of life	Confidence in abilities	Interpersonal confidence	Mental toughness
M	0.39**	0.32**	0.26**	0.28**	0.22**	0.38**	0.41**
F	0.08	0.05	−0.01	0.06	0.06	0.12	0.08

Note: M = Masculine traits, F = Feminine traits. ** $p < 0.01$, * $p < 0.05$.

Masculine traits were significantly positively correlated with all the sub-components of mental toughness and overall mental toughness. However, feminine traits were not associated with any mental tough-ness constructs. Although these associations between masculine traits and mental toughness were not strong they were consistent.

Correlations were then carried out to examine differences between male and females in how masculine traits and feminine traits correlated with aspects of mental toughness.

For both boys and girls significant associations were found between masculine traits and the sub-components of mental toughness and overall mental toughness (see Table 2). In addition, for boys and girls,

Table 2. Correlations examining associations between masculine and feminine traits and motivational constructs in boys and girls.

	Challenge	Commitment	Control of emotion	Control of life	Confidence in abilities	Interpersonal confidence	Mental toughness
Males							
M	0.43**	0.41**	0.23**	0.36**	0.40**	0.43**	0.48**
F	0.12	0.08	−0.01	0.06	0.15	0.06	0.10
Females							
M	0.34**	0.18*	0.22**	0.19*	−0.03	0.35**	0.28**
F	0.15	0.12	0.21**	0.09	0.10	0.18*	0.20*

Note: M = Masculine traits, F = Feminine traits. ** $p < 0.01$, * $p < 0.05$.

identification with masculine traits were more closely associated with both the sub-components of mental toughness and overall mental toughness. These associations were stronger for boys than for girls. However, it is of interest to note that girls with high levels of mental toughness identified with masculine traits. So it would seem that mental toughness is associated with a masculine identity irrespective of sex.

Predicting sex differences using sex and gender identity

All the sub-components of mental toughness were entered into a series of regression analyses to examine whether sex or gender identity were better predictors of scores on these constructs. Interestingly gender identity (masculine identity) predicted mental toughness over and above sex for all the sub-components of mental toughness and overall mental toughness.

The results suggest that a masculine gender identity is a better predictor of mental toughness and is more closely associated with mental toughness than a feminine identity. It is important to note that whilst a masculine gender identity was correlated with, and predicted variance in mental toughness, the variance explained by this identity was relatively small. It is possible that other predictors such as cognitive skills, academic ability and other personality characteristics would also predict adolescent's mental toughness. Future research could include a range of additional enquiries to tease out the relative importance of sex/gender identity versus other traits in predicting mental toughness in adolescents.

What is interesting from the results of this study is that there appears to be a blurring of the boundaries between masculine and feminine gender identity with girls identifying with both masculine traits and feminine traits. However, for boys this was not the case as boys identified mainly with masculine traits.

Table 3. Regression analysis predicting mental toughness constructs with sex, masculinity and femininity as predictors.

	Sex	*Sex, masculine and feminine traits*
Challenge		
Sex	−0.110	−0.042
Masculinity		**0.383****
Femininity		0.025
R^2	0.012	0.153
Commitment		
Sex	−0.103	−0.043
Masculinity		**0.307****
Femininity		0.008
R^2	0.101	0.101
Control emotion		
Sex	**−0.232****	**−0.200***
Masculinity		**0.225****
Femininity		0.029
R^2	0.054	0.103
Control life		
Sex	−0.013	−0.056
Masculinity		**0.291****
Femininity		−0.019
R^2	0.000	0.081
Confidence in abilities		
Sex	**−0.123***	−0.115
Masculinity		**0.199***
Femininity		0.073
R^2	0.015	0.057

(*Continued*)

Table 3. (Continued).

	Sex	Sex, masculine and feminine traits
Confidence interpersonal		
Sex	0.018	0.103
Masculinity		**0.404****
Femininity		−0.005
R^2	0.000	0.15
Mental toughness		
Sex	**−0.129***	−0.60
Masculinity		**0.397****
Femininity		0.029
R^2	0.017	0.168

Note: $* p < 0.05$, $** p < 0.01$. Values for sex, masculinity and femininity represent final beta values.

Conclusions

This study examined gender identity as a predictor for sex differences in adolescent mental toughness and furthermore examined the relationship between masculine and feminine traits and mental toughness. The results are interesting as they suggest that both boys and girls identify with masculine traits. However, although identifying with masculine traits girls also identified with feminine traits but boys did not identify with feminine traits.

Stereotyping is a normal cognitive process that enables us to categorise the enormous amount of information we experience during childhood development. From birth to adulthood individuals are exposed to informal, potent impressions of the role it is anticipated that they will play in society. Parents and significant others cultivate masculinity and femininity by encouraging children to behave in ways and develop interests that are perceived as appropriate for the child's sex. When a child goes to school the peer group provide additional information regarding what is acceptable or unacceptable within one's own sex-role. Sex-role development consists of acquiring a gender identity, an awareness of what it is to be male or female. Much of what we consider masculine and feminine is learned via socialisation. Bandura (1977) described the role of direct reinforcement and modelling in shaping children's sex-role behaviour and attitudes. In this way socialisation and achievement experiences may play a pivotal role in the development of sex differences in mental toughness (Meece, Glienke & Burg, 2006).

Socialisation takes place at home, in the locality and at school. Eccles, Adler, Futterman, Goff, Kaczala, et al., (1983) expectancy-value model includes a parental socialisation component which highlights important pathways by which parents affect and influence children's motivation as important role models. The same may be true for mental toughness. Sex-role beliefs evolve into sex-role stereotypes when particular behaviours are applied to all males and females within a culture. Stereotypes of Western femininity comprise expectations of females to be domestic, kind, attractive, emotional, dependent, lack physical strength, and be passive. In contrast, males are perceived as being competitive and less emotional and masculinity stereotypes are perceived as being unemotional, physically strong, independent, active, and aggressive. Parental attitudes, post-school opportunities, gender roles portrayed in the media and existing inequalities by gender in the family and workplace have all been shown to influence young people's attitudes and aspirations, thereby influencing their behaviour and performance (Tinklin, Croxford, Ducklin & Frame, 2001).

Research has examined the influence of gender identity on boys' and girl's attitudes, beliefs and behaviour (Connell, 1998; Jackson, 2002–2003) and suggests that schools are crucial in the development of gender identity as they offer a complex medium through which gender identity is developed via discipline, group influence and subjects offered (Connell, 1998; Jackson, 2002–2003). Although the academic curriculum has been cited as being influential in establishing and reinforcing gender identity, the hidden curriculum is possibly more influential during adolescence. The hidden curriculum concerns everything that happens in the school that is not officially organised by the school, for example, social relations in the classroom or grounds, friendships, relationships between teachers and students, bullying and other social interactions. It is via the hidden curriculum that students convey messages, which reinforce socially accepted gendered behaviour. Thus school culture builds on established stereotypes and may reinforce gender identity during adolescence. Children spend a substantial proportion of their waking time in school and the significance of peer-group pressure in schools and the implications of this on adolescents' behaviour has been widely debated (Renold, 2002; 2004). Gender identity as a product of adolescent culture therefore offers a plausible explanation for any reported difference in mental toughness of boys and girls.

Additionally, self-perceived gender trait possession has been found to contribute significantly to observed sex differences on cognitive tasks on which boys usually perform better than girls. For example, Hamilton (1995) found that gender trait possession helped to explain performance on a three-dimensional mental rotation task. Androgyny was the important gender trait variable. In addition, gender trait measures were the only significant variables in differentiating performance on the Group Embedded Figures Test, with masculinity being the important gender trait variable (Hamilton, 1995). It is reasonable to posit that mental toughness is developed as a masculine trait in the same way.

Sex roles and gender identity are changing. In the early 1960s men and women showed a strong acceptance of gender stereotypes (Rosenkrantz, Vogel, Bee, Broverman & Broverman, 1968) but the social roles of men and women began to change during the 1960s and, according to recent research, current attitudes towards women reflect those changes (Prentice & Carranza, 2002). Prentice and Carranza (2002) also reported changes in the stereotypes for women but not for men; women were perceived as having both the traits associated with stereotypical gender roles as well as the traits necessary for achievement in non-traditional occupations. Which supports the findings of the current study. Interestingly this has also been reported elsewhere as Diekman and Eagly (2000) suggested that the traditional perception of gender differences is changing, and that changes in women's roles are occurring at a faster rate than for men. These studies indicate that attitudes towards women have become more feminist and also egalitarian over the past twenty-five years, suggesting that there has been some changes in the traditional stereotypes of women, but that attitudes towards men have not shown the same changes. It is interesting that the current study also revealed that females are taking on a masculine identity whilst still retaining a feminine identity and this more than sex differences explained the differences reported in mental toughness. The stereotype for men seems to be more stable, and men may be the victims of more stringent and resistant stereotyping than women.

CHAPTER EIGHTEEN

Sport and its role in developing young people

John L. Perry

For those who pick up news on youth sport, barely a week passes without a story discussing the ever-declining participation rates of young people in sport, competitive or otherwise. Often cited for this are two significant concerns that make this topic a real issue; one obvious reason is the future health implications associated with sedentary lifestyles, as the much-discussed obesity epidemic continues to grow. The other commonly quoted reason concerns the lack of development of psychological attributes that are associated with sport participation.

We frequently hear anecdotes of sport being good for character, teamwork, and potentially leadership. Moreover, sport inevitably leads to failure at times. Many will argue (including me) that it is experiencing failure that enables us to succeed. The key to succeeding in the face of failure is mental toughness.

Young athletes demonstrate significantly higher levels of mental toughness than non-athletes of the same age (under twenty-one years). In this chapter, I will explain why sport can play an important role in developing mental toughness in young people.

Consider again what mental toughness is; it is about dealing effectively with challenges, stressors, and pressure ... irrespective of prevailing circumstances. Now consider a logical view of sport. Firstly, it is specifically designed to be a challenge. Remember that sport requires entirely unnecessary goal-oriented actions to be successful. For example, a football team aim to score in the opponents' goal without conceding in their own. But in sport, we actually raise the challenge by imposing rules with the sole purpose of making it more difficult for the participants to achieve their aim. In this example, rules exist to prevent players using their hands, not tripping opponents, and not benefiting from an offside position. We then very clearly and objectively measure ones success (or failure) and present this as clearly and brashly to the world as possible. Participation in such a contrived situation will naturally lead to prevailing circumstances on a consistent basis. We could argue that the great benefit of sport is that it provides an ideal stage of prevailing circumstances to constantly test its participants' mental toughness. Indeed, future success often relies on how well participants adapt to such circumstances or recover from failure.

Sport, stress, and coping

By participating in sport, we are intentionally placing ourselves in a situation that will inevitably present stressors. Consequently, it is those who cope best with these stressors that will flourish. To cope well, requires mental toughness, which has been shown in a series of studies.

Coping with adversity or difficult situations is arguably the most defining factor of a mentally tough athlete. Nicholls, Polman, Levy, and Blackhouse (2009) investigated the types of strategies used by mentally tough athletes. Using a sample of 677 performers from a variety of sports, they found that mentally tough athletes use more approach coping strategies and avoidance strategies. Task-focused coping refers to strategies aimed directly at reducing stress such as mental imagery, expending more effort, controlling thoughts, and logical analysis. In Nicholls and colleagues' study, mentally tough performers would cope by using such task-focused methods. Performers with lower mental toughness tended to use more distraction or distancing based coping methods rather than tackling the problem head on. Furthermore, all aspects of mental toughness were significantly positively correlated with optimism and negatively related with pessimism.

In a follow-up study, Kaiseler, Polman and Nicholls (2009) measured mental toughness, coping strategies and coping effectiveness on 482 athletes. They found that higher levels of mental toughness lead to more problem-focused coping and less emotion-focused or avoidance. In short, when faced with a stressor, mentally tough athletes looked at ways of dealing with the problem rather than merely reducing the emotional effect. Perhaps more importantly, they tackle problems and do not bury their heads in the sand. Kaiseler and colleagues also found a strong positive relationship between mental toughness and coping effectiveness. Said differently, more mentally tough performers cope better with stress.

Sport and the four C's of mental toughness

So far, I have spoken of the relationship between sport and mental toughness in general. For the remainder of this chapter, I will explain why sport can be an effective influencer of mental toughness by considering the individual elements of the four C's model; challenge, commitment, control, and confidence.

Challenge

Earlier in this chapter, I asked you to consider a logical view of sport. In doing so, I said that sport requires goal-oriented actions; in effect, a series of challenges. So if the extent to which we approach challenge is an important element of mental toughness, surely one of the most effective ways to enhance this aspect of it is to expose young people to challenges on a consistent basis. More than simply exposure though, it is the lessons learnt from successes and failures that requires attention. Developing mental toughness doesn't happen by accident! It is through reflection and evaluation that young people can use their experiences in sport to develop mental toughness. This is achieved through feedback.

Crust and Keegan (2010) published an interesting study using sixty-nine male and thirty-six female sports competitors from a range of club to national level in a wide variety of sports, which associated mental toughness with physical risk taking. Taking educated risks in sport is seen as desirable because more risky ventures often yield greater rewards. Of the mental toughness sub scales, challenge had the strongest relationship with physical risk taking. It is worth noting though, that there was also a significant relationship between risk taking and confidence. By combining challenge and confidence, performers are able to experience the desirable psychological state of flow.

Flow is a state often described by elite athletes when referring to extremely proficient performances. It comes from positive psychology, where Csikszentmihalyi (1990) originally defined flow by nine key characteristics:

- balance between challenges and skills
- merging of action and awareness
- clear goals
- unambiguous feedback
- total concentration on the task at hand
- sense of control
- loss of self-consciousness
- transcendence of time
- autotelic experience.

Central to maximising opportunities for flow is a situation where both challenge and perceived skills, or confidence, are high. Csikszentmihalyi posited that athletes who perceive low challenge and skills will demonstrate apathy, those with high challenge but low skills will present anxiety, and those with high skills but low challenge will become bored. If we consider flow to occur when perceived challenge and skills are high, there is clearly synergy between the concepts of mental toughness and flow. This was recently examined by Crust and Swann (2013), who found that forty-five per cent of total variance in flow was predicted by mental toughness, largely coming from confidence, commitment, and challenge.

Commitment

Long Term Athlete Development (LTAD) is an approach used by many sports organisations and governing bodies to foster a talent pathway from the playground to the podium. At the very core of this approach is deliberate practice. There is a notion in sport and other recreational activities, such as music, that it takes around 10,000 hours of deliberate practice to reach an elite level. While I am quick to point out that this has not been robustly statistically examined, the sentiment correctly identifies that long, deliberate effort, not luck or sheer talent brings about success. The amount of practice required typically equates to around ten years of training. Why is this important? Because it demonstrates that much of the difference between elite and recreational performers can be explained by training and therefore, commitment.

Many people plan to train regularly, such as going to the gym, jogging, learning to play a new instrument etc., but few adhere to their own prescribed regime. At the very core of training, we are discussing commitment. Commitment explains the extent that we go to to keep promises to others or ourselves. If we say that we are going to do something, a committed person will do more to keep that promise than a less-committed person. So how does sport help commitment?

First, sport is very goal-oriented. Whether it is an upcoming match, a big competition, or a season, success in sport is highly measurable and individuals develop fairly precise expectations. With expectations comes pressure from both internal and external sources. We are now in a situation where commitment is required to succeed. Assuming that success is a preferable option to failure, we are therefore much more likely to demonstrate commitment to our goals. This is of course, also closely linked with confidence in this example, as we would need to believe that we are capable of reaching those goals as long as we remain committed to them.

The other aspect of sport to consider is teams. When participating in team sport, we are entering an unspoken agreement with teammates that we are committed to the cause, that we will work for each other and not let each other down. By fostering such an atmosphere, team sport becomes an excellent environment to develop commitment.

Some aspects of training can become highly monotonous and even boring. Imagine training for an endurance run, such as a marathon. This requires commitment to training, and managing the pain barrier. This can often include dealing with injury. Levy, Polman, Clough, Marchant, and Earle (2006) examined the mental toughness of seventy sports injury rehabilitation programme patients and found that those with higher levels of mental toughness perceived their injury to be less threatening (severe), believed they were less susceptible to further injury, and were able to cope better with pain during their rehabilitation.

Clearly, sport requires commitment to be successful; it would not be possible to put in the required hours without such commitment. This does not have to be restricted to a sporting environment though, and the commitment developed through sport could be applied in many business, health and educational settings.

Maximising performance requires adherence to development programmes. Indeed, one only need glance at a couple of person specifications to see the term "commitment to CPD" in the essential criteria. Such a valued attribute is also evident in the sports arena. As well as physical or technical training, more sports performers now undergo psychological skills training. This includes strategies such as self-talk, emotional control, and relaxation. This relationship was investigated by Crust and Azadi (2010), who found that mentally tough performers were more likely to adopt and adhere to such performance strategies. In their analysis, they found that commitment in particular was a significant predictor of seeking to enhance psychological performance.

Control

The ability to control emotion in particular within a sporting context can be a defining characteristic between success and failure. Imagine lining up a putt in golf, or taking a penalty in football, or serving for a match in tennis … these are things that those performing the task have worked at for so long. I will argue here that success in such a circumstance is more likely to be predicted by one's ability to control emotion than technical ability.

I once spoke to a tennis player who, despite serving well for the majority of a match, produced a double-fault when facing match point and lost. I asked what he did in his next training session and he responded by telling me that he practised serves for hours. He even scoffed and laughed as he said it, so certain was he that his serving ability had cost him the match. I suggested that maybe it was actually his ability to control his nervous emotion when facing match point that cost him the match and he soberly agreed. I then asked what he did in training to improve this skill … he had no answer. From then on we concentrated on how to develop pressurising training conditions and manage emotion in them.

One of the great lessons that sport can teach us is responsibility and accountability. For those performing in individual sports, this lesson comes at a very young age. We are responsible for our own fortunes. We cannot afford to simply wait for fortune. Even in team sports this lesson can be a stark one. Successful teams have individuals who are prepared to take responsibility for tasks that can maximise team success rather than waiting, or hoping, that a teammate or a coach assumes responsibility. Moreover, sport teaches us to be accountable for errors. When we accept such responsibility and accountability, we can pursue ways of ensuring that we minimise the risk of making the same errors again. By assuming such responsibility, we are learning how to gain life control.

When working with sports performers, psychologists will often discuss controllable and uncontrollable issues. For example, in a sprint race, how fast your opponents run, if the weather conditions are conducive towards quick times, or if the starting equipment becomes faulty are all uncontrollable factors. Therefore, because these factors cannot be controlled, they cannot be changed. However, being aware of how fast you are likely to need to run to win, setting goals to achieve that time, training, knowing what time you are likely to finish in, being prepared for inclement weather, and having a coping strategy for faulty equipment or unexpected delays are all controllable factors. By taking control of these, our performer will feel much more like success is in their hands.

A mentally tough performer believes that they have control over many aspects of their life, certainly inside of a sporting context and often beyond. For sport, the belief that that we produce our future is essential. If we believed that success was down to luck, what would be the point in training? The exaggerated stage that sport sets once again provides an ideal example for a transparent view that success requires hard work, which is an attitude that would serve a young person well outside of a sport domain.

Confidence

Sports commentators, pundits, supporters, and performers all recognise the importance of confidence and its effect on a sports performance. When we have a greater belief that we will succeed, we expend more effort and persist longer. More effort and persistent of course leads to improved performance. This is something generally accepted by the populous, but also shown time and again in research. I could list endless studies that have related increased confidence to improved sporting performance but this is a somewhat obvious relationship. Instead, I will consider the benefits of sport and how it may help to develop confidence in young people, considering both components of confidence in the four C's model; confidence in abilities and interpersonal confidence.

There are a host of theoretical approaches to understanding self-confidence in sport, largely related to perceived competence and one's belief that they can successfully execute a desired behaviour. Bandura's self-efficacy theory (1977; 1986; 1997) suggests that the biggest predictor of efficacy expectations (self-confidence) is performance accomplishments. This means that if we have performed the desired action successfully before, we are more likely to believe that we can do it again. This seems perfectly appropriate and one of the benefits mentioned earlier is that sport provides an exaggerated level of challenge. With more challenge, one would expect more success and therefore, more confidence in reproducing that level in the future. However, this is true only of a very specific situation, such as performing gymnastic movement correctly, making a putt in golf, or making a free throw in basketball.

Vealey (1986; 2001) explained that while state-specific self-confidence exists (i.e., being able to perform a given task at a given time), there is also a trait element (i.e., a more stable personality characteristic). This type of self-confidence is more transferable across domains. More recent research of confidence in sport considers the sources of this confidence. In particular, it appears that confidence is often derived from feedback. In sport, we obtain constant feedback from ourselves, teammates, coaches, supporters, and the statistical representation of our performance (e.g., goals scored, tackles made, greens in regulation, runs per over etc.). Therefore, by performing in sport, a young person is exposed to more feedback than they would be normally. It is from this feedback that confidence can be drawn. There is of course an important caveat here regarding the quality and nature of feedback provided! In senior positions within a team or in a coaching context, it may be the young person that offers feedback to others. This can build a more interpersonal type of confidence.

Interpersonal confidence is the extent to which we are prepared to assert ourselves and our preparedness to deal with challenge or ridicule. This can be developed through sport in a number of ways including taking on leadership roles and accepting responsibility. Consider a team environment, which could be for a specific team sport or a group of performers from an individual sport such as a development squad/academy. This group will have complex dynamics and individual members assume certain roles. By assuming some of the more leading roles in the group, we learn to assert ourselves more. In time, this may become a team captain role or even a coach. This requires a significant amount of communication skill, team building capability, and strong decision-making. All of these are desirable attributes outside of sport but are routinely developed inside sport by taking on leadership roles. Considering the second part of the definition of interpersonal confidence, being prepared to deal with challenge and potentially ridicule is inherent in all competitive sport. By exposing oneself to such challenges and the potential for things to go wrong, over time we clock up more successes. With more successes, comes greater confidence.

Summary

By its very nature, sport provides challenge, which leads to prevailing circumstances. Sport requires great commitment in training to reach ones potential. It presents high-pressure situations, which require great control, and it pushes people to their limit, which requires great confidence. It is for these reasons that sport is a prime way of developing mental toughness in young people.

CHAPTER NINETEEN

Performance, behaviour, and career aspirations of students in secondary education—mental toughness case study

David Ayre and Damian Allen

odern society and the demands of twenty-first century life constantly challenge us to deal with difficult and often stressful events that change our lives. Many people react with a flood of strong emotions and a sense of uncertainty. Yet, people, particularly young people, generally adapt well over time to life-changing situations and traumatic conditions. Why are we sometimes able to do this well and in others cases, with little or no success?

The point that children anywhere can achieve, irrespective of their background, is an important one, but it is essential to see resilience within the broadest possible set of determinants. This is an emerging area of debate that is far from clear, but it is well understood that it is important to gain a more complete understanding of the cognitive function of children and young people so we can better help them develop. With developments in neuroscience and psychology this is increasingly possible.

To a large degree, this course of action requires mental and emotional resilience and toughness—an ongoing process that requires time and effort, and engages people in taking a number of steps, or very often, predetermined and well planned interventions.

Developing mental toughness and resilience is a personal journey—individuals and in particular young people, do not all react the same way to pressure, demands, and stressful life events. An approach to building mental toughness and resilience that works for one person might not work for another.

The ever increasing understanding of, and appetite for, resilience and mental toughness building interventions means that there is the potential to impact not only on children and young people, but on the institutions that support them, as it aids their strategic commissioning and allows them to target their resources to an intervention that clearly has a positive impact.

The impact of various different pieces of Government legislation and policy positioning, it was felt, did not do justice to the necessity of considering the impact on the resilience of children and young people. From the removal of the EMA (Education Maintenance Allowance) grant for students, to the implications of the Tickell and Wolf reviews, there is a great body of evidence that leads to the conclusion of specified support for children and young people being a prerequisite for their success, without being explicit.

The work of eminent academics such as Sarah Jane Blakemore[1] at University College London has seen the subject of neuroscience come to the fore in the last three years, and a paper on adolescent brain development by the DofE research department was the first indication of the Government beginning to take the subject area as a serious concern.

Underpinned by the work of John Abbott,[2] and various international studies, we were keen to explore the potential benefits for ourselves, and continued to build on this for over six years.

Initial pilots in Knowsley

In Knowsley we measured the resilience of our students, using the mental toughness MTQ48 questionnaire. This work showed that there is a close correlation between an individual's mental toughness and their performance in tests, their aspirations and their wellbeing. However, it also revealed a negative skew in the results of cohorts of pupils, indicating the effect of a broader cultural deficit at play in the borough.

The evidence would suggest that the ability of a young person to achieve cannot simply be explained by a genetic or innate predisposition; the effects of poor conditions in localities such as

Knowsley impacts on the mental toughness and resilience of the children and young people that live there. In effect, this prevents them from developing the levels of resilience necessary to fulfil their full potential.

Mental toughness was first established in Knowsley as part of the "Targeted Youth Support Pathfinder"[3] which began in 2006. This project was to test the hypothesis that mental toughness is related to performance, behaviour, and wellbeing.

The whole mental toughness concept was originally used with year ten and year eleven pupils in helping them to achieve maximum attainment and to help them fulfil their potential.

In 2007, All Saints Centre for Learning participated in the Deep Support Programme, which aimed to increase students' level of self-worth and resilience.

In 2009 the Firm Foundations Programme[4] (a cross-borough programme across secondary schools focused on improving English and maths GCSE performance) used the MTQ48 with those pupils at risk of underperforming. Staff were trained in giving feedback and providing interventions.

These pilots built on a commitment from senior management to mental toughness, and were underpinned by the Mental Toughness Strategy. Following work on SEAL (Social and Emotional Aspects of Learning) and TaMHS (Targeted Mental Health in Schools) it was decided that the work, whilst promising, failed to yield the defensible evidence that was craved.

The schools in Knowsley were broadly supportive of the work, and once presented with the evidence of the efficacy of the interventions, were keen to see the work continue.

What we sought to implement, why, and how we went about this

There is evidence, both nationally and internationally, of the efficacy of mental toughness and the psychometric test used to monitor change, MTQ48. In education, mental toughness can be applied to all ages from pre-school through to higher education and evidence has shown significant relevance to outputs such as performance, behaviour, employability, wellbeing, social behaviour, and completion of studies. It is also a major factor in transition at every key stage and a range of studies have shown development in various aspects of the adolescent brain, linked to mental toughness.

Knowsley had long been keen to explore ways of improving the personal and social development of its children and young people, and as such trialled interventions such as SEAL and TaMHS.

These interventions garnered little, if any, quantifiable evidence that a demonstrable difference had been made to the development of the skills of young people.

However, mental toughness proved to do just that, and on the basis that it is definitively improving levels of resilience in young people, we sought to further embed the practice across youth work and education.

In Knowsley, we saw individual improvement due to the implementation of interventions such as: coaching for success, mentoring, one-to-one tuition and examination preparation, and practice techniques.

This has the potential to impact not only on children and young people, but on the institutions that support them, as it aids their strategic commissioning and allows them to target their resources to an intervention that clearly has a positive impact.

As such, we set up working groups with the schools, each of which had a nominated mental toughness lead, and held a series of workshops to identify and design the interventions which we believed had the greatest potential impact. We stressed that mental toughness was not something that you could teach, and shouldn't be factored into the timetable, but rather that it was an approach that should permeate every aspect of the school day, and constantly be of benefit to pupils, teachers, and parents alike.

The pupils were then tested at the beginning and end of the academic year, with the interventions being run in the intervening period. What this saw was a great deal of collaborative working between schools, who shared similar characteristics but were able to understand the need to adapt their practice to best reflect their own individual circumstances.

All the data that was analysed at the end of the year showed that there was a direct correlation between increased mental toughness and increased levels of school attendance, uptake of free school meals, and academic performance, with further work ongoing to identify potential links with childhood obesity.

These insights allowed schools to better target their resources so that they could meet the needs of the children who were affected by low levels of resilience and provide them with tailored support, along with support for their parents and the platform for them to achieve to their full potential.

How we are seeking to embed mental toughness at The Children's Society

At The Children's Society, we are committed to working with children and young people to increase their levels of resilience and mental toughness. We are set to work with local authorities across the country so that we can coordinate our work more effectively, and help to ensure that children and young people are able to make the most of the opportunities that life presents.

Many, if not the majority, of The Children's Society's programmes, services, and children centres work with children, young people, and families who are struggling with issues of mental health and/or emotional wellbeing and many refer on to and work in close partnership with mental health services.

The Children's Society's practice base has not used this approach before. We are currently exploring avenues for how work can be done with children and young people either through schools or through other community or group settings. The approach requires both service design and monitoring; service design would require the implementation of evidence-based interventions and coaching reports, monitoring would require the use of the specifically designed test, the MTQ48.

This would be a new approach for The Children's Society's direct practice work, and involves a different way of conceptualising the issues faced by children and the method of improving the situation that children are facing. With a move towards integrated working, trialling this method, and particularly in the event of a wider roll-out, would have implications for the stance and messaging of the organisation.

We have a long-standing interest in the wellbeing of children, and are keen to build from this internationally renowned evidence base to further incorporate the measurement, evaluation and intervention necessary to establish mental toughness as a complimentary service.

There are currently pockets of work that are emerging across the organisation, with work in Greenwich with a cluster of schools being established, and through a project with the drug and alcohol service in Essex which seeks to increase the resilience of young people.

As we seek to expand the range of locations and interventions, we will seek to be locally responsive, understanding that with mental toughness, context is an imperative consideration.

The London Borough of Newham and the Young Foundation have done some fascinating work[5] on wellbeing and resilience, which has explored links between inequality and resilience, and the euphemism of how resilience is seen as masking state withdrawal, when really it is more about seeing social capital as a community asset.

The work that we are doing around wellbeing and resilience will define what strengthens it, what acts as a barrier to it and identify how and where we can work to have the greatest possible impact.

Our work will see The Children's Society move away from the model of the negative perception of a resilience deficit towards an adaptive resilience model, whereby we can highlight and learn from how children and young people have increased their resilience through a mixture of direct support and collaborative resourcefulness.

The reason for seeking to embed the approach at The Children's Society boils down to two fundamental points: first, we have a commitment to working with the most disadvantaged children and young people, and second, resilience is always brought to the fore in terms of austerity, but so far there has been inadequate definition and focused work to drill down into what it means and how it can be best harnessed.

The disruptiveness of the welfare cuts will have a serious, negative impact on the resilience of both individuals and communities, and are a counterbalance to the embryonic stages of promising work across the country.

There are clear links to empowerment, and the concept of "resilient movers"[6], coined by Angie Hart, Professor of child, family and community health at the University of Brighton, is an emerging area of debate that we believe is well worth further exploring.

Further emergence of resilience as a concept and how it's profile is growing.

Some insights from neuroscience are relevant from the development and use of adaptive digital technologies. These technologies have the potential to create more learning opportunities inside and outside the classroom, and throughout life. This is exciting given the knock-on effect this could have on wellbeing, health, employment, and the economy.

There is great public interest in neuroscience, yet accessible high quality information is scarce. Caution is urged in the rush to apply so-called brain based methods, many of which do not yet have a sound basis in science. There are inspiring developments in basic science, although practical applications are some way off.

The emerging field of education neuroscience represents opportunities as well as challenges for education; it provides means to develop a common language and bridge the gap between educators, psychologists, and neuroscientists.

The research has shown that puberty and pre-puberty heralds the beginning of a rapid and considerable reorganisation of the brain. Immediately prior to puberty a "second wave" of grey matter development and synaptic over-production is thought to take place (the first "wave" having taken place in early childhood).[7] This is followed in adolescence by a time of "massive" synaptic pruning, with substantial loss of grey matter,[8] while at the same time myelination and axon growth is occurring, increasing the speed with which information is communicated in the brain.

Breakthroughs in understanding provided by such research, and supplemented by more readily accessible texts such as the Young Foundation report for Camden Council,[9] or the work of the charity Mothers Against Gangs,[10] which has based a great deal of its work on the concept of resilience in youth, the community, and the police force, means that there is a wider appreciation of the changes that children and young people go through, and the need to adapt practice and policy to better reflect this.

A more in depth piece of work was undertaken by Oldham Council,[11] who looked to work in partnership with both its secondary schools and colleagues from National Strategies to implement a programme, entitled Accelerate, which sought to close the attainment and progress Free Schools Meals (FSM) gaps as measured in GCSE results and KS2-4 progress data.

Five of Oldham's ten secondary schools participated in the programme, with a focus on FSM students in year ten. In terms of attainment and progress, the Accelerate cohort did not present a normal distribution pattern, but was skewed to the middle and lower groupings. There were individual exceptions, but the overall picture was of a cohort of students who would gain lower grades at GCSE and would be less likely than average to make three levels of progress between KS2 and 4.

The undertaking of such work is a critical step in the development of a wider understanding of cognitive development and how resilience affects academic behaviour in adolescents.

We have found that using the four C's mental toughness model, and its related measure, have provided a structure and evaluation mechanisms that been used effectively in a wide range of settings working with young people.

Notes

1. www.ted.com/talks/sarah_jayne_blakemore_the_mysterious_workings_of_the_adolescent_brain.html last accessed 29 October 2013.
2. http://www.ccl-cca.ca/pdfs/21stCentury/library/When_will_we_ever_learn.pdf last accessed 4 December 2013.
3. www.education.gov.uk/publications/eOrderingDownload/DCSF-RR016.pdf last accessed 29 October 2013.
4. www.aqr.co.uk/sites/default/files/Knowsley%20Update%20case%20study.pdf last accessed 4 December 2013.
5. www.youngfoundation.org/wp-content/uploads/2012/10/The-State-of-Happiness.pdf last accessed 29 October 2013.
6. www.rihsc.mmu.ac.uk/events/docs/2011-RIHSC-Conference-programme.pdf last accessed 29 October 2013.
7. Giedd, J. N., Blumenthal, J., Jeffries, N. O., Castellanos, F. X., Liu, H. *et al.* (1999). Brain development during childhood and adolescence: a longitudinal MRI study. *Nature Neuroscience, 2, 10*: 861–863.
8. Spear, L. P. (2000). The adolescent brain and age-related behavioral manifestations. *Neuroscience and Biobehavioral Reviews, 24*: 417–463.
9. www.youngfoundation.org/wp-content/uploads/2012/10/uts_on_some_of_the_most_vulnerable_in_Camden_2.pdf last accessed 29 October 2013.
10. www.mothersagainstgangs.co.uk/ last accessed 29 October 2013.
11. www.thersa.org/__data/assets/pdf_file/0011/785279/2020PSH_Oldham_report.pdf last accessed 29 October 2013.

PART IV

DEVELOPING MENTAL TOUGHNESS

CHAPTER TWENTY

Can mental toughness be developed in young people?

Doug Strycharczyk

Given that the succeeding chapters are about approaches to develop mental toughness in young people, the answer to the chapters opening question has to be "yes" and "perhaps". There are three important issues to be addressed in this chapter.

First, do we really change someone's mental toughness if we do something with them or do they simply learn to adopt the behaviours and actions of more mentally tough people and find it works for them too? Second, which tools and techniques work ... and why do they work? Finally, how can we make sustained change?

But before that there is one more consideration to examine. We are often accused of subliminally suggesting that everyone should be mentally tough. That is far from the case. The mentally sensitive can be very effective, they can lead fulfilling lives and they can be capable of achieving great things too. Learning more about this will be a focus for research and development in the future. More casually, in our work we have found that where mentally sensitive types are successful they are also very self-aware. They know they are mentally sensitive and they work around that.

One person with whom Doug has worked with has been assessed as scoring sten 3 on the interpersonal confidence scale. The person is also a senior manager for a very successful large organisation. She agrees that the score, which places her in the lowest sixteen per cent of the population, is an accurate reflection of her mindset. She doesn't enjoy presentations and meetings. Both figure prominently in her life. She has learned to master doing presentations with coaching support and by progressively building this confidence starting with short presentations to same audiences to the point where she now addresses hundreds for one and a half hours. So gently pushing herself (and allowing herself to be gently pushed by people she trusts) seemed to have worked.

Her approach on managing meetings is also interesting. In her role she has to call many meetings—it's a valuable way of managing many issues. She will call the meeting, set the agenda, ensure that the correct people are invited but she won't chair it—she delegates that role to another. She uses her self-awareness to remain effective. In Covey's word she uses the "strengths of others".

Despite this, the evidence shows that statistically the mentally tough seem to get a better deal in life in many important respects. They get jobs and they get better jobs, they are better paid, they enjoy better health and wellbeing and so on. Statistically this means that most of the mentally tough enjoy the above mentioned benefits but not all the mentally tough do. Similarly much fewer of the mentally sensitive enjoy these benefits but some do.

So there is an argument for developing mental toughness in many if not most people.

It is also important to remember that mental toughness is a (narrow) personality trait and that it is only one of the characteristics that make up our persona—there are other personality traits and abilities and skills which come into play to make a person. These interact with mental toughness and its components and will either exaggerate strengths and weakness or mitigate any downsides that might arise.

However individual mental toughness is often significant. So it matters.

Back now to the first issue. When working with mental toughness development do we actually change the mindset of the individual or are we equipping them with the tools and techniques that mimic the effective behaviour of the mentally tough? And does it matter?

The answer is that we probably achieve both. If we equip someone to deal better with the challenges of life, does it matter which we actually achieve? We are making a difference whichever way we go.

Nevertheless there is small and growing body of circumstantial evidence to show that we can indeed change the mindset of people (young people). There is also research to suggest that mental toughness does change through experiential learning.

We know for instance that studies looking at mental toughness levels at differing ages show that mental toughness steadily develops as one grows older. As one experiences more of life it does seems that people learn from those experiences. A specific small scale study shows that when exposed to situations which create anxiety for mentally tough adolescents not only do they deal with these stressors better than their mentally sensitive colleagues but they also develop their mental toughness further which the mentally sensitive do not do. This provides a degree of evidence that experiential learning is important for developing resilience and mental toughness.

It doesn't appear that young people can be taught to be mentally tough. They appear to need to be taught "how to learn" to be mentally tough.

Nevertheless there is also some evidence to show that you can show young people how to cope with stressors and pressures without necessarily changing their essential nature. They can be taught to adopt tools, techniques, and strategies which enable them to manage challenges, change, and adversity.

For many, learning about these tools and techniques might turn out to be a stage in the process of becoming fundamentally more mentally tough. It's one of the ways we develop our personality—we adopt a behaviour or a set of actions and find these work. So they become habitual and, hey presto!, they are now part of our make-up.

So ... what do we know about what works.

The vast majority of interventions that seem to work are experiential in nature. People, and young people in particular, will learn to be more resilient, confident, and risk taking if they try things, find they work and are encourage to repeat them until they find they work repeatedly. This means that there have to be some consistent key ingredients in most mental toughness development activity. These are:

- Experiential learning works best. Encourage young people to try activities which need mental toughness or some component of mental toughness if the activity is to produce a satisfactory outcome for them. The mentally tough—the top twenty-five per cent of the population—do this anyway. They are naturally inclined to experiment and to try things.

- Reflection. Experiential learning only works if you reflect on the outcome every time you do something. It the activity works, reflection helps to understand why it works and encourages you to do more. If the activity hasn't worked, reflection helps to understand why it might not have worked and what might be needed to try again. If that doesn't happen it's too easy to slip into "I've tried that before and it didn't work".

  Many young people will be good at reflection. Many won't be. This is one of the reasons why support activity such as coaching, counselling, and mentoring can be extremely valuable in developing mental toughness. For many this type of guided reflection is essential.

  Parents, guardians and teaching staff can also be an important source of this support too. The only problem is that few parents are taught how to do this and not too many teachers are equipped with these skills either.

- Measurement or evidencing progress. One of the challenges in persuading young people into trying a new intervention is that they need to believe that it will work or that it does work. A competent, trusted, and enthusiastic coach, teacher, or counsellor may be able to engage a young person sufficiently for that young person to agree to try something new. That's a good start.

  However behaviour change happens incrementally and the increments can be tiny. For the individual these can be imperceptible. If the young person doesn't see, think, feel, know that something is changing and for the better then they will not believe in the intervention and will stop applying them.

  Creating awareness in young people that these interventions work for them is an important part of the reflection process. It is important therefore to introduce some form of measurement or assessment of progress into the application of a new tool or technique and to build it into the reflective process.

  This will be easier for some types of interventions. The number grid exercise described in the attentional control chapter does that perfectly. It is straightforward to show a young person that their scores are improving and that this reflects their increased ability to concentrate.

It will be harder for positive thinking exercises where there is no clear output which can be used as a score. But it is possible to introduce simple mood measures which over time will show an individual that they are developing in a useful way.

- Purposeful Practice. Change in behaviour or mindset only happens when the new behaviour becomes a habit. This requires repeated application. In the world of sport this is known as purposeful practice. Championed by Matthew Syed in his book *Bounce: the Myth of Talent and the Power of Practice*, he ascribes much of his own development as a world champion table tennis player to purposeful practice. His coaches could introduce new techniques, stances etc. to him but they only worked if he applied many hundreds of hours of purposeful practice to embed them into his overall technique.

  That's true for almost everything. We don't all need to be world champions although we should all want to be the best that we can be. Some commitment to practise a new technique until it becomes a habit is required. Some hours, maybe not hundreds of hours.

  The world of sport is littered with good examples and, usefully, young persons are often moved by those examples. It's now part of football folklore how Eric Cantona moved to Manchester United and helped to transform the club. He astonished all his colleagues by staying behind after training every day to practice more—and he was already the most skilful player.

  The issue of purposeful practice does pose a challenge for those involved in developing young people. It can often require frequent attention from a parent, teacher, or coach which is not easy to do in many cases. We are experimenting with the use of technology. Most young people appear to possess mobile phones. These are now much more than phones—they are mini computers. This can play an increasing role in supporting purposeful practice.

- Selecting interventions that work. This is not as straightforward as it seems. Interventions come in all shapes and sizes and from many sources. Many of the best have been developed by sports coaches and sports psychologists. Others come from areas such as Cognitive Behavioural Therapy (CBT), Psychology, Neuro-Liguistic Programming (NLP) etc. Although we find that these disciplines often claim techniques as their own when they are fairly generic across all disciplines.

There are many hundreds of tools and techniques. It's an interesting truth that most seem to work. But they don't all work for all people. One important requirement for the selection of interventions is to know, with a good degree of accuracy, what the young person needs. This is where the mental toughness measure is helpful. Working with people who work with young people we often find that the need is misdiagnosed. The tendency is to label young people as under confident and to treat that. One study we carried out in a school in Knowsley, UK, showed that almost half of the young people assessed as under confident in fact had reasonable levels of confidence. Their issues were about commitment and challenge. The coaches working with the young people were seeking to boost their confidence—to little effect. The real issues were receiving little or no attention whatsoever.

Another concern here is that a lot of interventions are faith based. The user believes they work but, other than some personal anecdotes, they often have little or no real evidence for the interventions they use. This will change in the future. This is now becoming the main thrust of our research—but it takes time. This requires long-term studies to show that an intervention makes a difference and that the difference is sustainable.

Yet another issue is why an intervention might work. Is it the intervention? Or is it is the person passionately delivering the intervention? Is it the nature of the recipient? Is it the support they have from parents, friends etc.? It's probably down to a combination of all of these factors.

Having painted a cautious and thoughtful picture, are there interventions that work? There are. You can continue reading. These will be described in more detail in the following chapters but the interventions appear to fall into five broad groupings plus the need for self-awareness. Those groupings are:

1. **Positive thinking**—affirmations, self talk, turning negatives into positives, etc.
2. **Visualisation**—guided imaging, using your head to practice, etc.
3. **Anxiety control**—relaxation techniques, controlled breathing, etc.
4. **Attentional control**—focus, dealing with interruptions, mindfulness, etc.
5. **Goal setting**—SMART, balancing goals, how to deal with big goals, etc.

These all help to develop the capability to deal with stress, pressure, and challenge, and where appropriate, to cope with these. Most of these are known to most competent coaches, teachers etc. The one area which is regularly overlooked is attentional control. There is growing awareness of its importance. The most common response for practitioners to the understanding of the mental toughness model is "I now know how to make better use of the knowledge and skills I possess". The key lies in understanding the concept of mental toughness and its components and to link it to what people already do to develop others.

Helping young people to be self-aware about their mental toughness and to show them how it explains a lot of their behaviour, performance, and wellbeing is becoming considered a sixth area of intervention. One of our projects in Knowsley produced an interesting observation. Young people who were assessed as average and above average mentally tough would often require only a little further support. They responded well to new ideas and were more likely to go away and do something about them. Almost as if their innate mental toughness was "kicking in". The mentally sensitive didn't do this to nearly the same extent.

Again, in a world where we have scarce resources, this indicates a strategy for keeping all young people according to need.

Finally, when working with young people, developing mental toughness appears to be suited to individual and to group intervention. We are beginning to see examples of group coaching and group development which is producing good results. It does appear that working with groups who have a shared need (e.g., they all have low commitment scores) is more effective than mixing mentally tough and mentally sensitive people. Individual are more empathetic towards each other. Moreover when an intervention works for one it quickly spreads to the others in the group.

Similarly Peter Clough working with large numbers of students at Hull University found that matching the coach or tutor to the young person was also beneficial—it produced better results. Again the opportunity for empathy seems to help.

Let's now look at interventions in more detail …

CHAPTER TWENTY-ONE

Positive thinking

Doug Strycharczyk

T he power of positive thinking has been well understood down the years. We can think ourselves into action and we can think ourselves out of action. The underlying principle here is "we are what we think".

Positive thinking takes the notion of we are what we think and transforms it into an approach that encourages ideas, words, and images into the mind that are conducive to performance, wellbeing, growth, and success. Everything we know, feel, and believe is based on our internal thoughts.

Positive thinking relies on two interrelated themes:

- Avoid negative or demeaning statements in your language or in your mind
- Adopt a positive approach in everything you do, say, or think.

You reinforce self-limiting beliefs every time they slip into your conversation or mind.

Unfortunately we are more often aware of the negative aspects of mindset than we are of the positive aspects. If we list everything we typically do in a busy day we might find that we have done say a hundred different things. We might have even done some of them to an exceptional standard and received some form of recognition. We will also have come across a few problems and setbacks. That is the nature of life—it's full of ups and downs. At the end of the day, just before going to bed, if asked to recall the most significant moments in your day which are you more likely to remember? The hundred or so things that you handled perfectly well or the half dozen or so that didn't work out so well? For the vast majority it will be the latter.

Positive thinking (or its polar opposite—negative thinking) impacts upon:

• Control—both emotional control and life control (self-efficacy)
• Commitment
• Challenge
• Interpersonal confidence.

It requires experience and maturity to learn how to be more positive and deal with all the challenges that arise in life. Young people don't have that experience and rarely possess the maturity to see things positively as a default response to an adverse situation.

Positive thinking is also an approach that appears in almost all models of resilience, mindset and optimism. Dweck's "growth mindset" is essentially about building belief in one's ability to achieve anything. Seligman's "learned optimism" is very much about developing the ability to see the sunny side of things. In his 2012 book *Flourish*, he introduces an acronym PERMA which he claims represents the five building blocks of wellbeing and happiness:

• Positive emotions—feeling good about onself
• Engagement—being completely absorbed in activities
• Relationships—being authentically connected to others
• Meaning and purpose—purposeful existence
• Achievement—a sense of accomplishment and success.

Positive emotions or positive thinking is, according to Seligman, the cornerstone of this approach.

So how can you change negative thought patterns and get young people to take a more positive view of their world? More formally, how can we prepare young people to:

- See problems and difficulties as challenges rather than problems
- Confront mindsets which automatically default to "I can't do that"?
- Ultimately taker a positive view about life and all that it entails— even the difficult stuff.

We cannot remove hurdles, challenges, and create a world free from setbacks. At the same time we cannot just tell young people to be more positive, they need to be shown how to be positive.

There are now hundreds of tools and techniques which support the development of positive thinking. They appear within CBT, NLP, sports coaching, and positive psychology. We will describe a few for which there is some evidence here. They tend to fall into two broad groupings:

- Those that develop a positive mindset
- Those that turn negative thoughts into positive ones.

Developing a positive mindset

Self talk

Probably the best evidenced of all the positive thinking techniques, self talk is widely used in sports coaching where it is closely associated with developing a winning mindset. We are becoming better aware that the language we use in our speech and in our heads and the way we process language has a significant effect on how we approach tasks, work, challenges etc.

Words often conjure up images and meaning beyond the simple dictionary definition of the word. It is this "additional" meaning that can influence us. A good example is the word "exam". The dictionary meaning might describe it simply as a test of ability.

In September 2008 I was present at the start of a new academic year when the year tutor addressed a group of year ten students. During that address, the year tutor spoke about the fact that the students were starting a lengthy run in towards their CGSE exams. It was immediately observable that some students responded positively to talk about "exams". They sat upright. They smiled and they looked alert. Others visibly shrank. They looked uncomfortable and looked as if they wanted to ignore this bit of the presentation.

So use the word "exam" in conversation with students and you will get a range of responses. These will determine performance, wellbeing, and success.

Some students will hear the word "exam" and will associate it with an eagerly anticipated opportunity to show the examiner what they can do. They associate the word with opportunity. The link is provides a positive experience. They may even feel a surge of excitement (coupled with some nerves).

Others hear the word "exam" and respond quite differently. They associate it with something to be avoided. In their mind the exam is more than a test, it is a situation which will reveal how little they know about the topic being assessed. Anxiety swamps any attempt at positivity.

Both groups of students may have equal abilities and they may have attended exactly the same classes and programmes but they are thinking differently and the results will almost certainly be different.

We see this behaviour replicated in many walks of life. Whether it is on the sports field playing with your team in an important match, in a leisure activity such as performing in a drama group or doing some activity at home. The way they approach the "match", the "performance" or the "job" may affect significantly how these are handled.

One exercise could be to challenge students in teams to reduce or even eliminate the use of negative words. They keep a score of how often others use negative words. They earn bonus points if they offer a positive substitute. Agree that for the duration of the exercise they omit negative words, such as "don't", "can't", "not", "won't", and "no." Unless of course they are entirely appropriate.

When subject to anxiety or pressure, try persuading the young person to talking themselves through it. Examples include:

- "These feelings will fade away—they won't last forever"
- "I know how to control these feelings. I must concentrate on relaxing myself"
- "I will begin to feel better soon"
- "No-one is looking at me. I am not going to make a fool of myself"
- "This is perfectly natural and normal. I know what is happening to me".

Exercise: self talk—think of three positive statements which would work for you.

1.

2.

3.

There is a scientific/biological explanation for how self talk works. The MRI brain scan study described earlier in the book confirmed that the challenge scale in the mental toughness model is closely associated with the part of the brain called the fusiform gyrus. This is the part of the brain which is responsible for the visual word form (written not spoken) and semantic processing and language comprehension. These are all likely to play a part in "self talk".

Think three positives

This is the authors' favourite exercise. It works time after time. It requires little equipment other than a diary and a pen. Most young people get through most days getting most things right. They can, if they reflected diligently, see that they have completed most of them perfectly well. Mostly they don't.

Mostly however, when they get to the end of the day and ask themselves "how did things go?" they default to thinking about what went wrong. That's not necessarily a bad thing to do—we have to confront our mistakes and problems. However if they spend every day thinking about what went wrong they can easily develop the feeling that they aren't doing terrible well.

A useful and highly effective activity is to get the young person to write down at the end of each day (or some suitable time) a reminder of, say, three things that have gone well for them. This reminds them that they do get some things right and doing this repeatedly restores a sense of balance—"I make mistakes but I mostly get it right".

It is also a perfect exercise with which parents can engage with their children. The propensity for negative thought can often be attributed to lack of positive, or overly critical, comment from parents when their children are in their formative years.

Affirmations

These are short statements or phrases that mean something to you. When subjected to stress, pressure, or challenge their use can enable you to adopt a more positive approach. Affirmations are essentially a way of saying to yourself "I can do it!".

One useful way of assessing impact is to ask the young person to assess their mood after using these affirmations. Do they feel more positive after using these sentences or phrases? If asked to do something they would consider challenging, do they know feel more positive about attempting it.

Examples of affirmations include:

Affirmations
• I am a calm, methodical, and efficient student • I can make a difference • I can do things that stretch me • I work well under pressure • I enjoy doing my coursework • I love that feeling when I deliver an assignment • I enjoy being calm when others around me are not.

To make affirmations effective they should:

1. Be made in the present tense. Affirmations need to be stated in the "now". There is a temptation to make affirmations in the future sense—describing what you will do. "I am ..." works much better

than "I will ..." because the subconscious recognises "I am" as something being done now, not in the future.

2. Have an emotional reward. Affirmations that are not personal to you won't work very well for you. So they should be expressed in the first person. Again this helps the subconscious mind recognise that this is something it is supposed to go to work on. Affirmations should begin with "I" or "my" instead of "you".

3. Be positively phrased. Affirmations rarely work when expressed as a negative. The mind isn't good at recognising the concept of "not". Its use can inadvertently reinforce the behaviour you are seeking to change.

Affirmations work because it is broadly equivalent to someone else telling you that "you can do it". If you work with a coach or mentor who consistently reinforces your ability to do something, you will probably come to believe that it is so. You are helping a young person create that person "in their head" who is doing exactly the same thing.

What will I do tomorrow?

At the end of each day, encourage the young person to identify one, two, or three things that they are very confident they can accomplish the next day. The fewer the better—they need a virtual guarantee of success. The tasks must be achievable.

This operates by reinforcing/applying the old adage "success breeds success". Most people like the sense of winning and it banishes the sense of failure like nothing else.

Once a more positive mindset is achieved they will be moved to take on more challenging tasks.

The positiveness hunt

This positive thinking exercise involves purposely seeking out and recording the positive aspects of a young person's day.

1. They'll need a small pocket-sized notebook and in it write: "The good things that happened to me today."

2. Each day, they go out and seek out the positive things that happen around them. If someone offers them something unexpectedly, they

make a note of it. They do the opposite so easily? This encourages them to recognise and seek the positive instead?

You can make it competitive. They can form teams and see which team finds the most positives and which finds the most unusual or striking positive.

3. They can also challenge themselves each day to beat the previous day's amount of positive events. This can be developed to illustrate goal setting too.

Looking at heroes/heroines

This encourages young people to look at people they admire and identify positive qualities about each which they can seek to mimic. They may need help to get behind some of the positive qualities. Young people will often identify with people from the sport and music worlds. What they may not always realise is how hard some of these have to work to get to the position where they are admired.

Ask the person to identify someone they admire and one positive quality that this person demonstrates. Then they are challenged to develop the same or similar behaviour.

Turning negatives into positives

The "glad" game

The character Pollyanna from the Disney movie plays a positive thinking game she calls "the glad game". The game helps increase positive thinking habits. It works very well as a group exercise.

One person brings up a negative event, such as losing a job, doing badly in a test, getting a poor mark for an essay, being dropped from the school team etc. They start off saying something like, "I've just lost my job and I'm trying not to panic."

Others provoke the first person and others to think positively by responding with positive phrases, such as, "But now I've been dropped, I'll have time to—blank." The first person or one of the others fills in the blank with a positive word or phrase, like "watch the team and work out how I might do better," or "have the time to do that job I need to do."

Searching for the silver lining in setbacks is the optimistic basis for the "glad game."

Reframing

Inevitably there are times when we all get it wrong.

If something didn't go well enough or something went wrong, ask the young person to identify what might be the positive in the situation. It is very rare that anyone gets everything so wrong that there are no positive aspects in failure.

Listen to sports coaches talking about their team after a defeat. Most will acknowledge the defeat but they will also identify what went well and will often identify the mistakes as opportunities for improvement. The important thing here is to understand that things do go wrong and we do make mistakes but very rarely is it fatal in any way.

Instead get the young person to acknowledge and give themselves credit for what they have done, remind them that they are not perfect and that they can do better next time.

A good discipline is to take time out to consider;

- What kind of thing always makes me think negatively?
- What kind of thing always makes me think positively?
- What advice would you give to a friend who consistently showed these negative thoughts?
- How could they identify the positives in these situations? (this is very effective if they work in groups).

Thought stopping—physical and mental cues

Again widely used in sports coaching, this is a powerful and often quick to apply technique which is closely related to affirmations and self talk. A cue is a device that you activate when experiencing negative thoughts. It is useful in dealing with worry, panic, and anxiety.

The essence of thought stopping is that you consciously issue a "Stop!" command when you experience negative thoughts. The negative thought is then replaced with something more positive and realistic.

The way thought stopping works is straightforward. Essentially, it is a form of controlled distraction which abruptly and firmly turns one's thoughts from the negative to something that is more controllable. Without some form of positive intervention, negative thoughts can "accumulate" and become the normal response. This will influence the way you behave and feel.

If coupled with positive and reassuring statements, it is possible to break negative thought patterns.

Thought stopping can arise through the use of mental or physical cues or a combination of both. The process is typically as follows;

- Identify a situation where you frequently find yourself thinking negatively
- Identify the negative statement you make when in this situation
- Prepare yourself with some form of relaxation
- Find a phrase or cue you can use to stop your negative thoughts.

A physical cue can be as simple as pinching yourself. Sports people will use elastic bands on the wrist and "thwack" themselves when a negative thought arises.

Mental cues will include:

- Positive statements which are activated when the negative thought arises
- Mentally or even orally shouting "STOP!"
- Replacing a poor image with a positive image
- Associating the negative image with it's consequence.

The positive thinking (attitude) ladder

Fiona Mackay Young developed a useful scale which she called an attitude ladder. It consists of a range of statements that change incrementally from "I won't try" to "I will do it". This is shown below.

I did it!
1. I will do it
2. I can do it
3. I probably can do it
4. I will try to do it
5. I'll think about trying to do it
6. I do want to do it …
7. I wish I could—I'm not sure I can
8. I don't know how to do it
9. I can't do it
10. I won't try because I know I can't …

The ladder works as a device to get someone to benchmark current mindset.

- What is their typical response when asked to do something? Does that affect performance and/or wellbeing?
- What do they think is a better response? How will that impact on performance or wellbeing?
- How do they think that could be achieved?

It is important to provide recognition as their default response creeps up the ladder.

Finally, the last word goes to Groucho Marx:

> Each morning when I open my eyes I say to myself: I, not events, have the power to make me happy or unhappy today. I can choose which it shall be. Yesterday is dead, tomorrow hasn't arrived yet. I have just one day, today, and I'm going to be happy in it. (Marx)[1]

Note

1. http://people.virginia.edu/~jfo/quotes/quotes6.html last accessed December 2013.

CHAPTER TWENTY-TWO

Anxiety and anxiety control

Sharon Bryan

Anxiety is something that can affect anyone no matter what age, background, sex, status, or social grouping. Mentally tough individuals are better able to deal with this.

This chapter describes some work carried out with young people in relation to stress management. It is a personal account and is deliberately written from a practitioner's perspective. I hope you find some of the tools and techniques helpful.

At some point in their life, many young people experience anxiety. This can vary from the classic "exam nerves" through to something as extreme as OCD (Obsessive Compulsive Disorder).

From our experience of working with both young people and adults, we know that many such conditions can go undiagnosed and unaddressed for years.

We all form our own unique "maps of the world" during adolescence. In this development period, our ability to deal with stress begins to be defined, sometimes for better, sometimes for worse. It can be argued that if we can learn how to be anxious, which is certainly part of the growing up process, we can learn how not to be!

When working with young people we have noticed that anxiety for some is a debilitating factor and a major issue. This is clearly

221

linked to all four of the mental toughness aspects: control, commitment, challenge, and confidence. We have also observed that individuals often experience difficulty in expressing or discussing how problems relate to stress and anxiety.

Arguably, one of the key differences when working with young people, as opposed to adults, is a relative lack of developed awareness. Whereas most adults have learned what anxiety is, and how it affects them, some young people are cast adrift in a sea of confusion. This lack of understanding and self-insight can be hard to deal with and may eventually be an added cause of anxiety. A classic vicious circle!

Anxiety is perfectly normal. At some point, every one of us will experience it.

The presence of anxiety can be beneficial to us, for example, when a situation poses a threat of harm or danger.

The problem is, when anxiety is debilitating and has no potential beneficial effect.

We experienced this when working with one young girl who could not function if she came into contact with buttons—"button girl". She suffered from a condition that was seriously hampering her ability to enjoy life.

The girl was fourteen at the time, and was finding school problematic. She was unable to take part in certain activities; simple things like going shopping with her friends were impossible. She had already received CBT therapy from her doctor but to her the situation was becoming untenable. She was feeling unhappy, frustrated, and upset. She had experienced the following issues and challenges:

- worry and upset
- nausea and vomiting
- becoming dizzy and starting to shake
- passing out
- thinking "really bad things" that she may do
- calling herself "mad", "crazy" and "lunatic".

All of the above frequently culminated in the onset of extreme panic attacks. Whilst this case was extreme, it shows the devastating effects of anxiety on some people.

What we have found to be universally beneficial in helping reduce anxiety is to help the person understand what was happening to them.

Breaking this down takes care and considerable time. However, it is sometimes possible to take a more straightforward approach.

For example, our "button girl" didn't need to know why she had this particular challenge—she just wanted to stop the feelings of anxiety and the impact this had on her mentally and physically.

By understanding anxiety we can understand why we feel the way we do and this helps to change the cycle.

Anxiety is like anything else. The more we do it the better we get at it.

Think about that statement for a moment.

How would you feel if you thought about your anxiety for five minutes, then extend this to an hour ... a day ... a week?

The more we burden ourselves, the stronger the anxiety becomes unless we break the cycle.

It's the "fear of fear". It can hold us back!

The more we avoid the issue the more our feelings grow and the more we think negatively. Next time we have to face our anxiety!

Understanding and familiarity are the greatest allies to dealing with anxiety and help us to learn how to control our feelings and reactions.

As an example I will briefly describe our work with two rock school students. One had anxiety issues that impacted on their performance; the other had issues which impacted on their ability to sing.

When working with these students we used the ABC strategy to start the process of controlling and understanding anxiety. This simple approach gives an insight into the individuals and allows them to begin to explore safely how to deal with the anxiety.

ABC simply means:

A—Awareness   What causes the anxiety and how do you react?
B—Balance   There is a fine line between positive and negative anxiety. How much can you cope with before it becomes negative?
C—Control   What can you do to help yourself combat the negative effects of anxiety and stress?

For example, our two rock school students were very different.

Our performer had what a layman would call "stage-fright". He was fine and had no issues whatsoever in rehearsals. However, at the point of the dress rehearsal, knowing that the performance was imminent, the anxiety cycle started for him. The resulting anxieties transposed into him being "fixed to the spot".

Dealing with his anxiety was about stripping things down and taking the ABC approach. For him, recognising when his feelings of anxiousness starting was critical (we actually did much more work to ascertain what was causing the issues which is something for another book!).

Once he knew when his anxiety started, he was able to work with us to set himself a "trigger" that he could fire whenever he needed to. Similar to anchoring in NLP, this involved setting up an alternative stimulus and response for him.

Whenever he felt the physiological triggers, described as a "black cloud starting in his stomach", he knew when to fire his trigger. Using positive affirmation and visualisations he could disperse the cloud and thus reduce the physical symptoms. This then allowed him to keep anxiety to a level that was right for him.

For our other student, his anxiety was hampering his ability to actually sing. He would be affected by his anxiousness and quite simply he would lose his voice and ability to sing. This was a very different case and therefore we adopted different methodologies.

We used simple relaxation techniques linked to breathing and the use of biorhythms so that he could understand how his physical anxiety came about and impacted on him. By understanding this, he was able to use techniques to slow down his breathing to reduce, and actually stop the anxiety response.

There are a number of other techniques to aid anxiety control. These try to deal with three main aspects of anxiety:

- Physical arousal—the feelings that give the terror or panic
- Tension feelings—the tension that links and correlates to anxiety and stress
- Mental stress—we simply cannot stop thinking about what it is that causes the anxiety and all of those distressing thoughts and terrible things that go with it.

We can't list every technique but we have included some of the things that we have found beneficial when working with young people.

LISTENING—self talk can be a fantastic tool.

The issue is—do we have the right channel tuned in?

With young people we find that negative self talk can overwhelm the positive to such a degree that the positive words simply get lost!

Understanding and challenging self talk helps to combat the anxiety that is caused by negativity.

To stop listening to the negative is, to some extent, a choice.

We have worked with one young girl who was suffering panic attacks leading up to her veterinarian nursing practical examination. After talking to her it was apparent that it was not her exam that was causing her stress, rather it was the thought of letting her grandfather down. We simply asked "How many times have you failed?" and, "How many times have you let your grandfather down?" She could give no examples of either of these.

After discussion she adopted a method of telling herself that her anxiety was simply her way of making sure she remembered everything and she could turn it up and down as she needed to.

SHOWING—quite often, and certainly with young people, we find that anxiety can get transposed very quickly into anger and a defensive stance.

One young man that we worked with found any challenge to his work unacceptable and would in effect "throw a tantrum". He was working on an apprentice scheme and this was obviously not the best approach for him and was hampering the potential possibility of succession.

We used two techniques to help.

First, we used perceptual positions. This means the individual can explore a real situation and ascertain possible alternative situations which give different results. Second, to deal with the anxiety anger, we used a simple stopping technique. Each time he felt angry he, with agreement of lecturers and employer, would write down what he was angry about.

Transposing anger to written word changes the way an individual feels and the anxiety is reduced.

CREATING FUN—laughter is a fantastic way to make you feel better and to discharge tension.

For young people having something that makes them laugh or just feel good can discharge anxiety very quickly. This was one of the tactics we used with "button girl"—making things funny helped her to cope with the contact.

TURNING OFF—we often fail to do this.

It's a bit like keeping a computer running all of the time with lots and lots of applications open. Stopping or just slowing down a bit, gives us chance to cool off. Relaxing, as well as holidays, having down time, hobbies and the like, are really valuable. We have found that using metaphor and simile with young people helps them to switch off for a time. Writing a story, or a song, gives a valuable recharge as well as developing focus.

Other techniques that are helpful include:

* planning techniques
* self-coaching
* understanding strengths—making worry work
* anchoring
* managing time
* relaxation

  o Progressive—relax your body and your mind will follow
  o Applied—one muscle group after another
  o Meditation—mind focused.

* Cognitive Behaviour Therapy—target unhelpful thinking
* Transactional analysis—personality and systemic growth (Parent–Adult–Child)
* EMDR—Eye movement desensitisation and reprocessing—stored memories
* EFT—Emotional freedom—negative emotion relief.

Anxiety is something that we will all experience in our life.

Understanding where this comes from for each of us, and learning which tools and techniques best suit us, is what aids in the development of mentally tough individuals.

Remember we learn to be anxious so we must be able to learn not to be!

CHAPTER TWENTY-THREE

Goal setting

Doug Strycharczyk

Goal setting has long been recognised as one of the most valuable ways that an individual can motivate themselves to achieve something important and significant in their lives.

That's fine as long as the individual's mindset is such that it responds positively towards seeing the goal and the process of setting goals. Then goal setting is a marvellously uplifting activity. It's just as often that case that individuals don't understand what a goal looks like and how to set off towards its attainment. For these goals can be confusing and in many circumstance threatening and debilitating—anything but motivating.

Does this matter for young people? Young people are set goals and targets and are expected to learn how to set their own goals and targets almost every day of their young lives. It's one of the most important life skills that they can learn. That's true for most adults too!

Brian Tracy (2010) in his review of education in the USA makes the same claim. Goal setting is the most important life skill for an adolescent. Yet only three per cent of students in the USA ever receive training in goal setting skills. When they do—they emerge as top performers.

In this chapter we are primarily working with young individuals developing the ability to set goals for themselves and learning how to manage goals that are set for them.

Goal setting impacts upon the following components of mental toughness and resilience:

- Life control (self-efficacy)
- Commitment—clearly this is where goal setting is the heart of the matter. Commitment is all about the preparedness to set goals and the desire to achieve and to surpass them
- Challenge
- Confidence in abilities (self belief). Achieving goals builds this like no other activity.

Much of the pioneering work on goal setting has been carried out by Dr Edwin Locke. He found amongst other things that well-constructed goal setting has the ability to act as a mechanism that motivates the individual towards the goal.

With his colleague Latham (2006), he found that goals appear to motivate by:-

- Improving attention on activities directly relevant to the goal
- Serving as an energiser; interestingly Locke found that the more challenging the goals and the more specific it is, the harder the individual will work towards its attainment
- Affecting commitment
- Activating cognitive abilities and strategies that allow people to cope with their situation.

Locke and Latham originally confirmed the need to set specific and difficult goals and identified three other factors which appear important in goal setting to motivate individuals, goals must have:

1. Clarity: Setting SMART goals. Clarity focuses the individual on the goal.
2. Challenge: Identifying challenging goals which are perceived as difficult but achievable.
3. Commitment:

   - How important is the ultimate goal?
   - A belief in the ability to achieve the goals.
   - The extent which promises are made to self and to others.

4. Feedback: This enables the sense of progress and provides the opportunity to flex or adapt.

5. Task complexity: The more complex the task the more difficult it will be to achieve. Individuals can take on too much without giving themselves a realistic chance of achieving the task.

Our experience in the full spectrum of applications suggests that there are four aspects of goal setting which are important:-

• Understanding what a goal is and accepting their relevance
• Setting clear, realistic achievable goals—the SMART process is a good way of achieving this
• Dealing with big goals.—How do you eat an elephant? Setting milestones
• Balancing Goals.

Understanding what a goal is and why it's important

Almost all young people have dreams about what they want to be and what they want to achieve. They stay dreams unless they have some direction. Like most techniques in building resilience, this too has to be learned.

A useful exercise is to get a young person to make a list of about twenty-five dreams, then take a day or two to think about them. If they cannot then explain why they want to achieve a particular dream on the list, that one should be removed. The list may include academics, sports, relationships, health, personal fulfillment, extracurricular activities, family goals and finances. If it is important enough that the young person can develop the dream and explains why he wants or needs it, then it is an acceptable goal.

Another good exercise is to ask the "miracle question". If a young person has a problem or a task to handle, ask them this "What would it feel like to go to sleep tonight and wake up tomorrow and find the task is done or the problem is solved?—a miracle has happened". This enables the person to projects themselves in to a point where the goal has been achieved and to feel the sense of buzz that goes with it.

Setting achievable goals—SMART(ER) goals

For goals to be effective they should be SMARTER: This is a seven-letter acronym which describes the key steps in effective goal setting. It is often found in the abbreviated original format SMART which describes the first five steps. Either is effective.

Specific	You must be able to define them clearly and concisely.
	The clearer the goal the more effective it is. "I want to do well at school" is better replaced with "I want to get four grade A passes in my A level exams".
Measurable	You must know when you have achieved success and what success will look like. Measures are usually unambiguous and tangible—they remain in sight and progress can often be monitored.
Achievable	Sufficiently challenging but not impossible. Generally the evidence shows that most young people make progress by "gently" stretching themselves.
Relevant	It should be relevant to their needs and have a real impact.
Time bound	There must be a deadline to work towards. To say "I'll write that essay soon" is very different to "I will write that essay by the last day of the month".
Exciting	They should inspire enthusiasm and commitment. The benefits and impact should be assessed as worthwhile or valuable.
Reviewable	There must always be provision for reviewing and re-establishing targets to take account of changing circumstances.

Eating the elephant—Dealing with big goals and setting milestones

Many goals are big goals and some may appear to be big but they may not be. If we are not careful the goal can appear overwhelming to a young person. The trick is to take these significant goals and turn them into something which is realistic and achievable.

QUESTION: How do you eat an elephant?
ANSWER: A slice at a time.

The key to achieving big goals is to break the task down into smaller relevant tasks which when completed are clear steps towards the achievement of the big goal. These intermediate tasks should each have SMART goals attached whereupon they are called "milestones".

A useful technique which works well is the 2-4-8 rule.

This simply takes a big goal that has to be achieved at some time in the future (say two weeks) and work out what you would need to have achieved by the mid-point (one week) if you are to be on track for the big goal. These milestones should begin to appear to be more achievable.

Then you repeat the exercise. What has to be done by the new mid-point (four days away) of this shorter period to be on track for the mid-point and end goal? These will often now appear to be eminently achievable. An example might be:

- I have to write a 1,500 word essay in two weeks
- By the end of one week—I should have a plan to write that essay in two evenings in the final week
- By the end of four days—I should have researched the subject and done some reading to get ideas. I can then create a mind map in the second half of the week to enable a plan to form.

These actions will typically be "smaller" actions which are more easily handled. They don't look so daunting and the whole project now feels doable.

If it's a bigger project, review progress regularly at each milestone point. Its useful to do that with someone else to ensure some form of discipline.

At any point the individual should ask themselves:-

- Does the next milestone appear achievable? Are you more confident that you can achieve this target? Do you fell more in control?
- What might stop you achieving each target—have you planned to deal with it? Are there lead times you need to take into account? Are you procrastinating?
- How confident do you feel that you will now hit the big target?

A psychological perspective on goal setting

Most of the research into goal setting has been focused on how to max-imise the technique. Much less attention has been paid to the underpin-ning psychology.

What we can say is:

- Goal setting works better for some people. Certain personalities are drawn to it; others find it limiting and stifling. Everyone can benefit—not everyone wants to.
- It reduces anxiety. By allowing an individual to deal more effectively with demands.
- Nearly everybody puts things off. Goals help to alleviate this. The reasons for procrastination are many—including self-handicapping (giving yourself an excuse), fear of failure, low self-esteem and attribution distortions.

CHAPTER TWENTY-FOUR

Attentional control

Pauline Bowe

When facilitating mental toughness development programmes this statement usually elicits nods of agreement from delegates. It is one of the most important qualities we can possess and yet, for generations of adults it has never been on the curriculum. The importance of this quality becomes even more apparent when those same delegates are asked to complete practical exercises and they suddenly realise they may not be very good at maintaining attentional control. Differences in this ability are highlighted when comments such as "I can't concentrate when other people walk into the room as I am more interested in what they have to say, even though I have a deadline to meet" and in contrast, "I can get so engrossed in my work people startle me because I didn't hear them come in".

Further questioning reveals that the person who is able to focus is able to achieve more and feels more in control over their lives. Those that struggle report feelings of not being able to finish tasks, have difficulty in managing their time effectively and procrastination. One can only guess how much more successful they may have been, had they learned to concentrate as children. The advantages of being able to focus on a task whilst ignoring other distractions enables a young person to confidently learn new skills or knowledge, pass examinations, and furthermore, to achieve exceptional results in further or higher education and the world of work.

So what is attentional control?

Attentional control can be seen as a self regulatory process that underpins both mental and emotional functioning and in recent years has been identified by researchers in child development as a feature of effortful control (EC) "the efficiency of executive attention, including the ability to inhibit a dominant response and/or to activate a subdominant response, to plan, and to detect errors" (Rothbart & Bates, in press).

Our modern world has provided us with amazing new discoveries in science and technology that have enabled us to have greater access to a whole variety of information and resources. The breadth, depth and even speed of information that we process on a day-to-day level would be alien to our grandparents. However, since the late twentieth century toddlers have been socialised into manipulating machinery to a point that observers would perceive it as innate. Consider the toddler who can operate the DVD player better than the adult! However, for some young people, this new way of life can present problems in their ability to forgo the immediate gratification of a computer game or TV programme in favour of completing their homework, revision, or learning to play the piano or even embarking on a new sport.

The marshmallow test is a prime example of this. A marshmallow was presented to children and those who had higher levels of self control and didn't eat it were rewarded with two marshmallows at the end of the test. Follow-up research found that those children who delayed gratification were more successful in life. For some children there are far too many distractions and their attention is being diffused across a range of unimportant stimuli which ultimately means educationally they can underperform.

Why can some maintain attentional control and others struggle?

In recent years researchers have highlighted correlations between attachment styles, positive parenting and self regulation. These studies have identified a link between a child's positive bond with a main caregiver, offering a general view that positive parenting can impact on a child's emotional regulation, motivation states, and how they respond to events. Researchers also suggest that such children also exhibit lower levels of anxiety, which positively impacts on their ability to self regulate their thoughts and behaviours. Much of this research focuses on the genetic *vs* environmental determinants of psychopathology and the onset of Attention Deficit Hyperactivity Disorder (ADHD) which is more specifically related to attentional control. Whilst the formation of attentional and effortful control have been deemed to be part of a person's temperament and, thus partially genetic, it is also clear from such attachment studies, that they are also learned as a result of early experiences socialising or shaping how children react to others and the environment.

The proliferation of the use of FMRI scans has enabled us to learn more about why this is so, and the concept of neural or synaptic plasticity have enabled us to dispense of the old saying "give me a boy at seven and I will give you the man". Our brains are flexible and can adapt by developing new neural networks in response to learning new things or being in new environments. Even the Flynn effect that highlights how IQ in developing countries has improved since the second world war sheds new light on what was once thought of as a genetic trait that couldn't change. This is good news for those in education or development roles who have concerns that any interventions employed are unlikely to work because of genetics.

Research conducted by Peter Clough aimed at developing mental toughness in young people in schools in Knowsley is a point in case. His work employed the use of an interesting piece of technology called Mindball. This machine was designed to develop attentional control and concentration by harnessing the ability to relax and focus on moving a ball across a table whilst your opponent simultaneously does the same. Participants wear electrodes on their head that monitors brain waves. These signals are then used to enable the ball to move across the table. This game acted as a biofeedback device which enabled young people to monitor their own progress and adjust their behaviour or thoughts to elicit a response. The winner was the player who was able to concentrate the most. However, there are simpler methods of developing attentional control and, as you will see most of these have been employed by sports psychologists to assist in the coaching of elite athletes.

Attentional control and mental toughness

The ability to maintain attentional control pervades all aspects of mental toughness. Mentally tough individuals are more likely to identify and adhere to important goals (commitment), be able to focus and see the opportunity of doing so when under pressure (challenge), manage or eliminate distractions and regulate their own behaviour (life and emotional control). They will have the self belief that they can focus on what needs to be done even when the task may be difficult or in the face of strong opponents (confidence in abilities and interpersonal relationships).

For many years, sports psychologists have emphasised the importance of developing mental toughness in players and, specific to attentional control are the functions of information processing and selective attention. The basic idea here is that in order to attend to a stimulus we need to be able to hold a memory of it and to retrieve that memory to make decisions about how we will respond (Keele, 1973). In order to do this we also need the ability to "gate out" unimportant information to attend to the target. Think back to the last football or basketball game you watched and the many distractions that players have to ignore in order to score. These include the spectators cheering or booing, opponents trying to prevent them from scoring, team members offering encouragement and, their own internal dialogue.

In order to develop mental toughness and to stay at the top of their game, professional sports men and women routinely practice the art of attentional control. Imagine a scenario where they weren't able to do this and they were telling the crowd to be quiet or asking opponents if they could kindly move out of their way!

Practice is the key

The tools and techniques used in sport can be just as easily applied in the classroom or the workplace and do not require equipment as expensive and elaborate as Mindball. It is also important to remember the key to success with any of the tools and techniques in this book is practice. Carol Dweck's work on mindset dispels the myth that innate abilities create geniuses and highlights the importance of practice in developing expertise in a particular skill. In other words, when Mozart was a lad he practiced for hours a day, it didn't just come naturally. This point cannot be stressed enough. Sometimes mental toughness development programmes are delivered to people who know a lot of the tools and techniques but they never actually practice them or, timetable space in their lives to do so. As a result their ability to manage stress and achieve peak performance appears to be no better than those that have never heard of the concepts.

A caveat to this is provided by psychologist David Marchant, who argues that practicing to concentrate doesn't necessarily mean that we improve at it. However, the more proficient we become at a task, for example, learning and manipulating mathematical formulae, the easier it becomes. We then spend less effort attending to it and distractions are less likely to bother us. He suggests that practicing tasks that are similar to the ones you wish to develop will help.

Tools for developing attentional control

So far you will have noticed that tools for developing mental toughness are presented in this book as separate categories. However, it is worth noting that practicing these will also contribute to the development of attentional control in the following ways;

Goal setting—provides a clear pathway to the desired result. The process helps a person to identify the focus of attention out of many possible options.

Positive thinking—helps to reduce negative internal dialogue that can act as a distraction to achieving the goal.

Anxiety control—enhances emotional control required to attend to the goal.

Main attentional control techniques

First things first, minimise unwanted distractions. Whilst recent research by Clough and colleagues has found that working environments do not affect mentally tough people, for those who are still learning a new skill, reducing distractions can initially help them to learn to focus. Once proficient these distractions are less likely to be noticed. Educationalists will be familiar with the need to encourage students to create a quiet space at home to enable them to study but, this is not always possible in a busy school, college, or university where other people are likely to be the main distraction. In this instance a growing trend is for people to wear headphones (with no music blaring from them). This sends a visible cue to others not to disturb you whilst you work.

Enabling young people to become self-aware whilst practicing attentional control techniques is important because we don't always know what it feels like to concentrate. Some commentators describe this as a flow state or the awareness of being fully engaged in the task, almost as if the task and the person are merged together. Typically when learning a new skill we are aware of everything around us, (and within us) and that we are not very good at what we are doing. We may feel uncomfortable, even anxious at the thought of failing. The more we practice and move around the learning cycle, the more we get into a flow state and become proficient at the task.

You will notice that the exercises presented are both cognitive and physical tasks. Number or word grids can highlight awareness in the ability to focus on cognitive tasks whilst the stork stand or waste paper basketball exercises aid in gaining greater awareness of hand-eye coordination or balance required to focus on a task.

The number grid

The number grid is a ten by ten grid containing numbers from zero to ninety-nine. The task is to mark off the numbers consecutively from zero to ninety-nine in ninety seconds. When given to groups of people it is clear that the person who reaches the highest number in that time is the one who is able to concentrate.

Stroop test

The basic idea with a stroop test is to identify words that describe a colour, written in their own colour amongst words describing colours that are written in different colours. There are different versions of these available including a version on the Nintendo DS Brain Training game. Once again this is a timed exercise and those that are able to concentrate are able to focus on the task.

Both of these exercises require people to focus on the target word or number against a backdrop of distractions, these being other numbers or words and the pressure of lack of time. When given the opportunity to practice with different number and stroop grids people become more proficient at these tasks and typically describe the "numbers or words jumping out at me". They are able to identify this sensation as their flow state with these particular tasks and are asked to consider other situations when they have experienced this and also when this skill may be advantageous to them.

Games

Many games such as card games and chess are excellent tools to develop focus. Although the idea of the lunchtime chess club may not be appealing to some students, the sessions provide an ideal backdrop against which to "gate out" distractions and focus on beating your opponent. In addition to the complexity of the game itself, your opponents threatening glare, the shuffle of chairs, mobile phones ringing, coughing etc are distractions to be overcome and when brought into the conscious awareness of young people can help to improve their game and enhance their ability to focus in other situations.

One of the most successful (and enjoyable) training tools for both young people and adults is the use of bop it. The player is required to follow oral instructions to "pull it, twist it, flick it, spin it or bop it" using the corresponding attachments on the machine. There is also a musical beat playing in the background and the player only has a limited time to complete the task before the next instructions is quickly issued. Those that score higher in this game are those that are able to concentrate well. When using these toys within a training session there are usually eight bop it toys in play at any give moment which creates a greater level of complexity to the game. This time the player has to hear their own bop it whilst all the others are also in play. This is analogous to any classroom or work situation where one has to ignore the distractions and focus on their own task.

The use of this toy in training is also a lesson in practice. Trainers are typically adept at using the game because they have had to practice it to demonstrate it and can walk through the group playing the game with very little difficulty in hearing their own toy above the others. This is pointed out to the group as evidence that practice can make it easier to concentrate on a task.

Other complex games such as computer games usually provide ample opportunity to focus on a task at the expense of attending to other more complex stimuli. Again the key here is to encourage young people to develop self-awareness about their own ability to focus.

The stork stand

This is a yoga exercise that requires the participant to stand clear of any objects such as chairs, desks, or other people and to begin standing on one leg whilst the arms are raised perpendicular to the body. The easy version (which is recommended for those who are unfamiliar with the task) is to focus on an object straight ahead and if this exercise is being undertaken in a group, create an element of competition by asking who is going to stay in this position for the longest. The harder version is to ask participants to close their eyes whilst undertaking the task. Those who are more competitive will persevere with this task even if they are tired because they are determined to win. This makes it an appealing exercise as the motivation to win is likely to encourage a greater commitment to the task.

Waste paper (zen) basketball

Most classrooms and offices have bins and paper and an easy way to practice attentional control is to roll up pieces of paper into compact balls and practice throwing them into a bin. Again as a group exercise an element of competition and also performance anxiety (and thus an opportunity to control anxiety) is inherent in the exercise as participants watch each other attempting hit their target. This is a simple yet affective exercise and one that can also develop a greater level of hand-eye coordination.

Conclusion

The lives of our young people are dominated by instant access to information that many an eminent scientist would have taken months or even years to access a hundred years earlier. The requirement to focus on a target or task at the expense of other distractions is probably more important now than at any other point in history. Positive early experiences may enable a young person to become more adept at this self regulatory behaviour but, neuroscience and epigenetics have also taught us that we can develop this quality by practicing simple and practical techniques. In doing so we are improving our mental toughness and our ability to achieve excellence in any area of our lives we choose to develop.

CHAPTER TWENTY-FIVE

Mindfulness for young people

Liz Hall

Mindfulness is no longer widely viewed as the preserve of hippies and monks. In recent years, it has gone mainstream, extending into secular settings including employment, mental health, parenting, and education.

Mindfulness has roots in Buddhism although there is a tradition of contemplation within most religions, including Christianity. Its secularisation and growth in popularity is due in part to the work of people including Jon Kabat-Zinn, founder of the Center for Mindfulness in Medicine, Health Care, and Society at the University of Massachusetts Medical School. His Mindfulness-Based Stress Reduction (MBSR) programme has been implemented worldwide, along with many variations in all sorts of settings.

We are living in times of unprecedented complexity, choice and change and our young people, of course, are not immune to what goes on around them. We are seeing rises in depression and anxiety, including among young people, and the growing evidence base for mindfulness indicates it has much to offer here. Mindfulness-based therapy is now recommended by the UK government body the National Institute of Health and Clinical Excellence, as the go-to therapy for recurrent depression.

Benefits

There is a burgeoning mass of research on mindfulness, including from neuroscience. There have been many evaluations carried out on MBSR and variations including Mindfulness-Based Cognitive Therapy (MBCT), as well as MBSR-informed programmes offered within education such as the Mindfulness in Schools Programme (MiSP).

The research points to an impressive array of benefits. Here are some: greater compassion to self and others; heightened emotional intelligence; boosted creativity; being more able to see the bigger picture, make better decisions and focus more; greater ability to manage stress and anxiety, and enhanced physical wellbeing (see Table 1).

Table 1. Impact of mindfulness-based interventions.

How mindfulness impacts the mind and body

Regular meditation:

- Increases grey-matter in brain regions, including those involved in the learning and memory processes, emotion regulation, and perspective-taking (Hölzel, Carmody, Vangel, Congleton, Yerramsett, Gard & Lazar, 2011).
- Improves psychological functions of attention, compassion and empathy (Carter, Presti, Callistemon, Ungerer, Liu, *et al.*, 2005; Tang, Ma, Wang, Fan, Feng, *et al.*, 2007; Lazar, Kerr, Wasserman, Gray, Greve, *et al.*, 2005; Lutz, Brefczynski-Lewis, Johnstone & Davidson, 2008).
- Activates the parasympathetic nervous system, calming the autonomic nervous system and decreasing cortisol (Tang, Ma, Wang, Fan, Feng, *et al.*, 2007).
- Boosts the immune system (Davidson, Kabat-Zinn, Schumacher, Rosenkranz, Muller, *et al.*, 2003).
- Improves medical conditions including type II diabetes; cardiovascular disease; asthma; premenstrual syndrome and chronic pain (Walsh & Shapiro, 2006).
- Improves psychological conditions e.g anxiety, insomnia, phobias, eating disorders (Walsh & Shapiro, 2006).

What is mindfulness?

Kabat-Zinn (1994) defines mindfulness as paying attention in the present moment, but in a non-judgmental way. Mindfulness offers a set of techniques to train the mind, but also includes paying attention to the body and the world around us, with compassion and curiosity.

In mindfulness, we practice bringing our attention to what arises in our field of experience again and again (the mind naturally wanders), with compassion and non-judgment. So we are enhancing our ability to:

- Control our attention, choosing our subject of focus and bringing our attention back again and again
- Attend to the present moment, to whatever arises
- Stay with difficult emotions/thoughts/feelings
- Be compassionate to ourselves and others
- Drop evaluation and judgment
- Reframe positively.

How does it work?

Practising even just a little mindfulness rewires the brain, according to brain scan studies using functional Magnetic Resonance Imaging (fMRI). Although the most striking changes are observed in long-term meditators, brain changes can also be seen in people who have only been meditating for eight weeks for an average of under half an hour a day. Such studies have not yet been carried out on children but it seems reasonable to assume we would see similar changes.

These brain changes include greater blood flow and a thickening of the cerebral cortex in areas associated with attention and emotional integration, for example increased grey-matter density in the hippocampus, associated with learning and memory, and greater density in structures associated with self-awareness, compassion, and introspection (Davidson & Lutz, 2008). Practising mindfulness also appears to decrease grey-matter density in the amygdala, known to play an important role in anxiety and stress (Hölzel, Carmody, Vangel, Congleton, Yerramsetti, Gard *et al.*, 2011).

Resilience/mental toughness

Much of the research underlines how practising mindfulness increases resilience and the ability to deal with stress and anxiety, countering negative affective processes implicated in depression, anxiety, and schizophrenia (Frederickson, 1998).

It helps us:

- Regulate our emotions, generate positive emotions and manage difficult ones (e.g., Boyatzis & Jack, 2012; Frederickson, 1998)
- Reframe/reappraise positively, which is associated with positive health outcomes (e.g., Carver, Pozo & Harris, 1993)
- Improve attentional control, which is associated with heightened resilience (Marchant, 2012 in Clough and Strycharczyk (2012))
- Be more present and attuned to others (Siegel, 2010)—we know that interpersonal confidence is important to resilience.

Mental wellbeing

Around one in five children and adolescents experience problems severe enough to warrant the intervention of mental health services. Mindfulness offers young people strategies to "nip things in the bud".

Over time, humans have evolved two different neurological processes: the behavioural inhibition system (the avoidance system) and the behavioural activation system (the approach system) (Gray, 1981). The approach system is reward seeking and is associated with feelings such as hope and joy, whereas the avoidance system is sensitive to danger or punishment, holds us back from moving to goals, and is associated with emotions such as fear, anxiety, and disgust. This system helps to keep us safe but it can become chronically overactive, leading to anxiety, and depression and stamping out creativity and the ability to see the bigger picture.

Meditation helps to strengthen the approach pathways while switching off the over-activated avoidance pathways for example, Urry, Nitschke, Dolski, Jackson, Dalton *et al.* (2004).

We can explain to young people that human beings have developed a number of "superpowers", which have helped our species. We have developed a sense of the past and of the future, allowing us to see patterns in what has happened before to help us avoid repeating potentially fatal mistakes and allowing us to plan for better futures. However, even "superpowers" have drawbacks, and so we often find ourselves "stuck" in the past and future. Or our switch becomes jammed in hyper-alert "oh-no-there's-a-sabre-toothed-cat" mode. It may be appropriate for a young person to feel terror because a bully is targeting them at school, or because they feel their social standing is in jeopardy because they have been "fraped" on Facebook. However, it´s not a matter of life and death if they are unable to make it to a party because they have an assignment to complete, for example. Explaining to young people that they have a choice over how they frame situations, that it´s common to get stuck in panic mode and that there are techniques they can learn such as mindfulness can be enormously helpful.

Much of the current theoretical and empirical literature supports the view that young people with positive social and emotional skills demonstrate resilience when confronted with stressful situations (Greenberg, Domitrovich & Bumbarger, 2001). There appears to be a positive correlation between measures of children's social and emotional skills such as emotional regulation and measures of later psychological health (Greenberg, Domitrovich & Bumbarger, 2001) according to much of the research. This suggests that the earlier the better when it comes to interventions such as mindfulness training, which can develop social and emotional skills early before mental health difficulties emerge.

Education

Secondary school students taking part in a mindfulness programme report reduced indications of depression, anxiety, and stress up to six months later. They are also less likely to develop pronounced depression-like symptoms, suggests a study of 400 students aged between thirteen and twenty by Professor Filip Raes (Faculty of psychology and educational sciences, KU Leuven), The study is thought to be the first to examine mindfulness in a large sample of adolescents in a school-based setting, using a randomised controlled design.

In addition to the .b programme run through the MiSP, there are many mindfulness initiatives being rolled out for young people within education, including in a number of states in the US under the Association for Mindfulness in Education (AME) initiative.

Benefits include improved wellbeing, calmness, relaxation, improved sleep, less reactivity, increased self care, self-awareness, and a sense of connection with nature, according to a study of an MBSR and Tai Chi programme for eleven to thirteen year olds in the US included (Wall, 2005).

Mindfulness can be easily incorporated within social and emotional learning (SEL) programmes. Katherine Weare, Emeritus professor at the Universities of Exeter and Southampton, suggests the two share goals and to some extent techniques. SEL programmes generally attempt to develop students' social and emotional skills, attitudes and capacities, including self-awareness, the ability to manage the emotions, optimism, persistence and resilience, empathy, and the ability to make relationships, all of which are also goals for mindfulness, through providing a spiral curriculum of explicit learning opportunities (Weare, 2012).

The mental toughness framework and mindfulness

Mindfulness supports the development of the four mental toughness (MT) components, particularly control, challenge, and commitment.

Control

Marchant says, "If there is one factor that underpins people's ability to perform at their best, it's their ability to focus and control their focus of attention effectively" (Marchant, 2012, p. 247). He also highlights estimates that in the UK the average attention span of young people dropped to seven to eight minutes at the start of the twenty-first century, compared to ten to twelve two decades earlier.

Practising mindfulness helps young people improve their attentional control. One study (Semple, Lee, Dinelia & Miller, 2010) found nine to thirteen year old children who were struggling academically who took part in a twelve-week MBCT-based programme enjoyed significant improvements on measures of attention, as well as reductions in anxiety and behaviour problems compared to non-participants.

Another study (Schonert-Reichl & Hymel, 2007) reviewed the MindUP programme developed by the Hawn Foundation, which fosters the development of wellbeing traits using social, emotional, attentional, and self-regulation strategies, including mindfulness exercises. Teachers noticed improvements in nine to thirteen year olds behaviour, attention, and focus.

Adolescents with attention and/or behaviour control deficits also reap benefits from mindfulness, including significant increases in personal goals, sustained attention, happiness, and mindful awareness (Bögels, Hoogstad, van Dun, de Schutter & Restifo, 2008) and improvements on tasks measuring attention and cognitive inhibition, and in externally observed and self reported anxiety and depressive symptoms (Zylowska, 2008).

Challenge

A study by Kabat-Zinn and colleagues found people who had completed an eight-week MBSR programme scored highly on a number of resilient traits identified by Kobasa, 1979 and Antonovsky 1993. They were also more likely to see challenges as opportunities rather than threats (Weissbecker, Salmon, Studts, Floyd, Dedert & Sephton, 2002; Dobkin, 2008).

Young people face numerous challenges, including many new beginnings and endings and shifts in relationships with peers and others. The way they perceive these challenges is an important factor in how mentally tough they are.

Key elements here are non-judgment and compassion, which we encourage in mindfulness. Encouraging young people to turn towards whatever is there, including difficult emotions such as sadness or anger can feel counter-intuitive. However, it's not about being self-indulgent, but about "sitting with" feelings without adding another layer of judgment, or harsh self-criticism. By turning towards difficult emotions, these very often dissipate.

For young people, each day can bring a new emotional rollercoaster and although young people often move rapidly from one emotion to another, this does not detract from the intensity. For many, realising that they are not their thoughts and that thoughts and feelings are transient rather than the truth, is a huge eye-opener.

Meanwhile, the meta-cognitive aspect of mindfulness has been well-researched—practicing mindfulness helps us see the bigger picture and pay attention to more data, not only within ourselves, but in others and the world around us. Garland, Gaylord and Park (2009) propose, for example, that it's this aspect that allows us to shift from "avoidance" to "approach" mode. With young people, I often talk of mindfulness helping us to develop "goat vision"—goats' rectangular pupils allow them periphery vision.

Confidence

Mindfulness helps develop confidence in both of the sub scales identified by Clough—abilities and interpersonal confidence. By becoming more compassionate to ourselves (and others), we feel more able to try new things. It also enhances focus and delivers a range of cognitive improvements, which can enhance confidence in abilities. Furthermore it enhances emotional intelligence, which boosts interpersonal confidence.

Emotional intelligence

Practising mindfulness helps us make meaningful relationships, accept experiences as they truly are, manage difficult feelings, and to be calm, resilient, compassionate, and empathic (Baer, 2003; Salmon, Sephton, Weissbecke, Hoover, Ulmer & Studts, 2004).

A US study of an MBSR-derived mindfulness programme, "Learning to BREATHE", for seventeen to nineteen-year-old students in an American independent girls' school showed decreases in negative affect, and increases in calm, relaxation, self-acceptance, emotional regulation, awareness, and clarity (Broderick & Metz, 2009).

Commitment

Being able to stick to a commitment—to others and to oneself—is another core component in mental toughness, and certainly it's one many young people struggle with. Mindfulness can help those practicing mindfulness get in touch with what really matters to them and to feel more connected to others, and as we have seen, it helps them to see the bigger picture, which may strengthen their commitment.

Introduction to mindfulness for young people: the .b programme

Duration: eight weeks, with daily home practice encouraged in-between sessions.

Content: weekly two-three hour group sessions, with opportunity for discussion, and a focus on the following elements:

- Directing one's attention
- Turning towards calm
- Dealing with worry
- Being "here now"

- Mindful movement, such as "mindful walking"
- "Stepping back" (understanding thoughts are not facts, for example)
- Befriending the difficult (including understanding stress and how we personally deal with stress).

Activities

Practices include an introductory practice such as the raisin meditation where participants are encouraged to approach a raisin (or chocolate!) as if for the first time, really taking the time to explore what it looks like, smells like, and feels like before slowly and mindfully eating it. Another is beditation (a variation on the body scan practice) in which the idea is to mindfully scan the body from head to toe, exploring sensations with curiosity and without judgment.

Other activities include ones such as FOFBOC (feet on floor, bottom on chair), which encourage young people to bring their attention away from their brain to their body, allowing them to "come to their senses" both physically and metaphorically.

The .b programme has been developed by the mindfulness in schools project

What young people say

Marcus (aged thirteen) "(the) lessons are fun and relaxed as well as providing great techniques to take into everyday life. Mindfulness has helped me reduce headaches, concentrate before exams and perform in football. "

Molly (aged thirteen) "Beditation (a mindfulness practice taught on the .b programme) really helps me sleep and makes me calm in everyday life."

James (aged fourteen) "It helps relieve any anxiety for exams, auditions etc."

Zoe (aged fourteen) "Mindfulness helps to control emotions when they get out of hand and to live in the moment."

Our son, Dylan (then aged eleven), who is taught mindfulness at his new school, says: "Mindfulness helps me to relax when I'm stressed. It also can calm me down when I'm angry."

Source: Participants on the .b-derived programmes including Mindfulness4teens, run by Raymond Freeman (a trained .b teacher) and Liz Hall (mindful coach and author of Mindful Coaching*).*

Conclusion

To conclude, mindfulness has much to offer in the development of mental toughness in young people, as well as supporting them in many other ways, such as to be ethical, compassionate, creative, and joyful members of society.

There appear to be no disadvantages to sharing mindfulness techniques with young people and many benefits. Within the mental health and educational arenas, in particular, mindfulness has much to contribute.

REFERENCES

Adams, M. (2012). Problem-focused coaching in a mainstream primary school: Reflections on practice. *The Coaching Psychologist, 8, (1)*: 27–37.

Antonovsky, A. (1993). The structure and properties of the sense of coherence scale. *Social Science & Medicine, 36*: 725–733.

Avey, J. B., Wernsing, T. S., & Luthans, F. (2008). Can positive employees help positive organization change? Impact of psychological capital and emotions on relevant attitudes and behaviors. *Journal of Applied Behavioral Science, 44*: 48–70.

Baer, R. A. (2003). Mindfulness training as a clinical intervention, a conceptual and empirical review. *Clinical Psychology: Science and Practice, 10*: 125–143.

Bandura, A. (1977). *Social Learning Theory*. New York: General Learning Press.

Bandura, A. (1977). Self-efficacy: Toward a unifying theory of behavioural change. *Psychological Review, 84*: 191–215.

Bandura, A. (1986). *Social Foundations of Thought and Actions: A Social Cognitive Theory*. Englewood Cliffs, NJ: Prentice Hall.

Bandura, A. (1997). *Self-efficacy: The Exercise of Control*. New York: Freeman.

Bauer, K. W., & Liang, Q. (2003). The effect of personality and precollege characteristics on first year activities and academic performance. *Journal of College Student Development, 44*: 277–290.

Berg, I., & Szabo, P. (2005). *Brief Coaching for Lasting Solutions*. London: Norton Professional.

Berk, L. (2008). *Child Development*. (8th Edition). Needham Heights, MA: Allen & Bacon.

Biswas-Diener, R. (2010). *Practicing Positive Psychology Coaching: Assessment, Diagnosis, and Intervention*. New York: John Wiley.

Biswas-Diener, R., & Dean, B. (2007). *Positive Psychology Coaching: Putting the Science of Happiness to Work for Your Clients*. Hoboken, NJ: John Wiley.

Bogels, S., Hoogstad, B., van Dun, L., de Schutter, S. & Restifo, K. (2008). Mindfulness training for adolescents with externalizing disorders and their parents. *Behavioural and Cognitive Psychotherapy, 2*: 193–209.

Boldizar, J. (1991). Assessing sex typing and androgyny in children: the sex role inventory. *Developmental Psychology, 27*: 505–515.

Boyatzis, R., & Jack, A. (2012). Coaching with compassion: An fMRI study of coaching to the positive or negative emotional attractor. Presented at the Academy of Management Annual conference, Montreal.

Brand, S., Lemola, S., Kalak, N., Gerber, M., Clough, P. & Holsboer-Trachsler, E. (2012). Sleep well, our tough heroes!—Mental toughness, sleep and psychological functioning in adolescents. Poster presented at the twenty-first congress of European Sleep Society.

Bresser, F., & Wilson, C. (2010). What is coaching? In: J. Passmore (Ed.), *Excellence in Coaching: The Industry Guide* (pp. 9–26) (second edition). London: Kogan Page.

Briggs, M., & van Nieuwerburgh, C. (2010). The development of peer coaching skills in primary school children in years 5 and 6. *Procedia—Social and Behavioral Sciences, 9*: 1415–1422.

Briggs, M., & van Nieuwerburgh, C. (2011). Ways of working. *Coaching: An International Journal of Theory, Research and Practice, 4*: 163–167.

Broderick, P. C., & Metz, S. (2009). Learning to BREATHE: A pilot trial of a mindfulness curriculum for adolescents. *Advances in School Mental Health Promotion, 2, (1)*: 35–45.

Bull, S. J., Shambrook, C. J., James, W. & Brooks, J. E. (2005). Towards an understanding of mental toughness in elite English cricketers. *Journal of Applied Sport Psychology, 17*: 209–227.

Burns, R. (1785). To a Mouse. In: *Kilmarnock volume*. Kilmarnock: John Wilson.

Campbell, M. A., & Gardner, S. (2005). A pilot study to assess the effects of life coaching with Year 12 students. In: M. Cavanagh, A. M. Grant & T. Kemp (Eds.), *Evidence Based Coaching: Volume One. Theory, Research and Practice From the Behavioural sciences* (pp. 159–169). Bowen Hills, Queensland: Australian Academic Press.

Carter, Presti, Callistemon, Ungerer, Liu, *et al.*, (2005). *Meditation alters perceptual rivalry in Tibetan Buddhist monks, Curr Biol, Jun 7, 15(11)*: R412–3.

Carver, C. S., Pozo, C., Harris, S. D., *et al.*, (1993). How coping meditates the effect of optimism on distress: a study of women with early stage breast cancer. *Journal of Personality and Social Psychology, 65, (2)*: 375–390.

Cheng, H., & Furnham, A. (2002). Personality, peer relations and self-confidence as predictors of happiness and loneliness. *Journal of Adolescence, 25*: 327–339.

Clough, P., & Strycharczyk, D. (Eds.), (2012a). *Developing Mental Toughness: Improving Performance, Wellbeing and Positive Behaviour in Others*. London: Kogan Page.

Clough, P., & Strycharczyk, D. (2012b). Mental toughness and its role in the development of young people. In: C. van Nieuwerburgh (Ed.), *Coaching in Education: Getting Better Results for Students, Educators and Parents* (pp. 75–91). London: Karnac.

Clough, P., Earle, K., & Sewell, D. (2002). Mental toughness: the concept and its measurement. In: I. Cockerill (Ed.), *Solutions in Sport Psychology* (pp. 32–43). London: Thompson Publishing.

Clough, P., Earle, K., & Strycharczyk, D. (2008). Developing resilience through coaching. In: J. Passmore (Ed.), *Psychometrics in Coaching*. London: Kogan Page.

Collins, J. (2001). Good to Great. www.jimcollins.com/article_topics/articles/good-to-great.html Last accessed 30 October 2013.

Connell, R. W. (1998). Teaching boys: new research on masculinity and gender strategies for.

Conners, C. K. (1997). Conners' rating scales-revised. Multi Health Systems Inc. US. schools. *Teacher's College Record, 98*: 206–235.

Creasy, J., & Paterson, F. (2005). *Leading Coaching in Schools*. London: National College for School Leadership.

Crust, L. (2009). The relationship between mental toughness and affect intensity. *Personality and Individual Differences, 47*: 959–963.

Crust, L., & Azadi, K. (2010). Mental toughness and athletes' use of psychological strategies. *Journal of Sport Science, 10*: 43–51.

Crust, L., & Clough, P. J. (2005). Relationship between mental toughness and physical endurance. *Perceptual and Motor Skills, 100*: 192–192.

Crust, L., & Keegan, R. (2010). Mental toughness and attitudes to risk-taking. *Personality and Individual Differences, 49*: 164–168.

Crust, L., & Swann, C. (2013). The relationship between mental toughness and dispositional flow. *European Journal of Sport Science, 13*: 215–220.

Csikszentmihalyi, M. (1990). *Flow: The Psychology of Optimal Experience*. New York: Harper & Row.

Cullen, K. (2011). *Child Psychology, A Practical Guide*. London: Icon Books.

Davidson, Kabat-Zinn, Schumacher, Rosenkranz, Muller, *et al.*, (2003) *Alterations in brain and immune function produced by mindfulness meditation, Psychosom Med.; 65, (4)*: 564–570.

Davidson, R., & Lutz, A. (2008). Buddha's brain: neuroplasticity and meditation. *IEEE Signal Processing Magazine, 25, (1)*: 176–174.

Dewhurst, S. A., Anderson, R. J., Cotter, G., Crust, L., & Clough, P. J. (2012). Identifying the cognitive basis of mental toughness: Evidence from the directed forgetting paradigm. *Personality and Individual Differences, 53*: 587–590.

Diekman, A. B., & Eagly, A. H. (2000). Stereotypes as dynamic constructs: Women and men of the past, present, and future. *Personality and Social Psychology Bulletin, 26*: 1171–1188.

Diener, E., & Diener, M. (1995). Cross-cultural correlates of life satisfaction and self-esteem. *Journal of Personality and Social Psychology, 68*: 653–663.

Diener, E., Emmons, R. A., Larsen, R. J. & Griffin, S. (1985). The satisfaction with life scale. *Journal of Personality Assessment, 49*: 71–75.

Dobkin, P. (2008). Mindfulness-based stress reduction: What processes are at work? *Complementary Therapies in Clinical Practice, 14, (1)*: 8–16.

Dobson, J. (2009). Why Do the People Hate Me So?: The Strange Interlude.

Douglas, C. A., & McCauley, C. D. (1999). Formal development relationships: A survey of organizational practices. *Human Resource Development Quarterly, 10*: 203–220.

Dweck, C. S. (2012). Mindset: How You Can Fulfil Your Potential. Constable & Robinson.

Eccles, J., Adler, T., Futterman, R., Goff, S., Kaczala, C., Meece, J. & Midgley, C. (1983). Expectancies, values, and academic behaviours. In: J. Spence (Ed.), *Achievement and Achievement Motives* (pp. 78–147). San Francisco: Freeman.

Evans, G. (2011). Second order observations on a coaching programme: The changes in organisational culture. *International Journal of Evidence Based Coaching and Mentoring, (special issue 5)*: 70–87.

Fishbein, M., & Ajzen, I. (1977). Attitude behaviour relations: a theoretical analysis and review of empirical research. *Psychological Bulletin, 84*: 888–918.

Fisher, S., & Hood, B. (1987). The stress of the transition to university: A longitudinal study of psychological disturbance, absent-mindedness, and vulnerability to homesickness. *British Journal of Psychology, 78*: 425–441.

Flynn, J. R. (1984). The mean IQ of Americans: massive gains 1932 to 1978. *Psychological Bulletin, 95*: 29–51.

Frankl, V. E. (1959). *Man's Search For Meaning*. Boston: Beacon Press.

Fredrickson, B. L. (1998). What good are positive emotions? *Review of General Psychology, 2*: 300–319.

Frederickson, N. H. (1994). *Social Inclusion Survey*. Windsor, Berkshire: NFER-Nelson.

Gable, S. L., & Haidt, J. (2005). What (and why) is positive psychology? *Review of General Psychology, 9*: 103–110.

Garland, E. L., Gaylord, S., & Park, J. (2009). The role of mindfulness in positive reappraisal. *The Journal of Science and Healing, 5, (1)*: 37–44.

Gerber, M., Brand, S., Feldmeth, A. K., Lang, C., Elliot, C., Holsboer-Trachsler, E. *et al.*, (2013). Adolescents with high mental toughness adapt better to perceived stress: A longitudinal study with Swiss vocational students. *Personality and Individual Differences, 54*: 808–814.

Gerber, M., Kalak, N., Lemola, K., Clough, P. J., Pühse, U., Holsboer-Trachsler, *et al.*, (2012). Adolescents' exercise and physical activity are associated with mental toughness. *Mental Health and Physical Activity, 5*: 35–42.

Gerber, M., Kalak, N., Lemola, K., Clough, P. J., Perry, J. L., Pühse, U. *et al.*, (2013). Are adolescents with high mental toughness levels more resilient against stress? *Stress Health*. In Press.

Giedd, J. N., Blumenthal, J., Jeffries, N. O., Castellanos, F. X., Liu, H. *et al.*, (1999). Brain development during childhood and adolescence: a longitudinal MRI study. *Nature Neuroscience, 2*: 861–863.

Gordon, K. (2012). Applying mental toughness to career guidance and career planning. In: P. Clough & D. Strycharczyk (Eds.), *Developing Mental Toughness: Improving Performance, Wellbeing and Positive Behaviours in Others*. London: Kogan Page.

Grant, A. M. (2003). The impact of life coaching on goal attainment, meta-cognition, and mental health. *Social Behavior and Personality, 31*: 253–264.

Grant, A. M., Green, L. S., & Rynsaardt (2010). Developmental coaching for high school teachers: Executive coaching goes to school. *Consulting Psychology Journal: Practice & Research, 62*: 151–168.

Gray, J. A. (1981). A critique of Eysenck's theory of personality. In: H. J. Eysenck (Ed.), *A Model for Personality* (pp. 246–276). Berlin: Springer-Verlag.

Green, L. S., Oades, L. G., & Grant, A. M. (2006). Cognitive-behavioural, solution-focused life coaching: Enhancing goal striving, well-being, and hope. *Journal of Positive Psychology, 1*: 142–149.

Green, S., & Spence, G. B. (manuscript in preparation). Evidence-based coaching as a positive psychology intervention. To appear in: A. C. Parks & S. M. Schueller (Eds.), *The Wiley-Blackwell Handbook of Positive Psychological Interventions*. Oxford: Wiley Blackwell.

Green, S., Grant, A. M., & Rynsaardt, J. (2007). Evidence-based life coaching for senior high school students: Building hardiness and hope. *International Coaching Psychology Review, 2, (1)*: 24–32.

Green, S., Oades, L. G., & Robinson, P. (2012). The role of positive psychology in creating the psychologically literate citizen. In: J. Cranney & D. S. Dunn (Eds.), *Educating the Psychologically Literate Citizen: Global Perspectives* (pp. 119–130). Oxford: Oxford University Press.

Greenberg, M. T., Domitrovich, C., & Bumbarger, B. (2001). The prevention of mental disorders in school-aged children: current state of the field. *Prevention and Treatment, 4:* 1–59.

Gregg, P., & Tominey, E. (2005). The wage scar from youth unemployment. *Labour Economics, 12:* 487–509.

Goldman, R., & Papson, S. (1999). *Nike Culture: The Sign of the Swoosh.* California: Sage.

Guldberg, H. (2009). *Reclaiming Childhood. Freedom and Plan in an Age of Fear.* London: Routledge.

Hamilton, C. J. (1995). Beyond sex differences in visuo-spatial processing: the impact of gender trait possession. *British Journal of Psychology, 86, (1):* 1–20.

Harmison, R. J. (2011). A social cognitive framework for understanding and developing mental toughness in sport. In: D. F. Gucciardi & S. Gordon (Eds.), *Mental Toughness in Sport: Development in Theory and Research* (pp. 47–68). Oxford, UK: Routledge.

Hart, T. (2004). Opening the contemplative mind in the classroom. *Journal of Transformative Education, 2, (1):* 28–46.

Hartley-Brewer, E. (2005). *Raising and Praising Boys.* London: Vermillion.

Holt, J. (1983). *How Children Learn.* London: Penguin Books.

Hölzel, B. K., Carmody, J., Vangel, M., Congleton, C., Yerramsetti, S. M., Gard, T. *et al.,* (2011). Mindfulness practice leads to increases in regional brain gray matter density. *Psychiatry Research: Neuroimaging, 11, (1):* 36–43.

Horsburgh, V., Schermer, J., Veselka, L., & Vernon, P. (2009). A behavioural genetic study of mental toughness and personality. *Personality and Individual Differences, 46:* 100–105.

Jackson, C. (2002). 'Laddishness' as a self-worth protection strategy, *Gender and Education, 14:* 37–51.

Jackson, C. (2003). Motives for 'Laddishness' at school: fear of failure and fear of the 'feminine'. *British Educational Research Journal, 29:* 583–598.

Kabat-Zinn, J. (1994). *Wherever You Go, There You Are: Mindfulness Meditation for Everyday Life.* London: Piatkus.

Kaiseler, M., Polman, R. C. J., & Nicholls, A. R. (2009). Mental toughness, stress, stress appraisal, coping and coping effectiveness in sport. *Personality and Individual Differences, 47:* 728–733.

Karasek, R. A. (1979). Job demands, job decision latitude and mental strain: Implications for job redesign. *Administrative Science Quarterly, 24:* 285–308.

Kauffman, C., & Scoular, P. A. (2004). Towards a positive psychology of executive coaching. In: P. A. Linley & S. Joseph (Eds.), *Positive Psychology in Practice* (pp. 287–302). New York: John Wiley.

Keele, S. (1973). *Attention and Human Performance*. California: Goodyear.

Kellmer-Pringle, M. (1986). *The Needs of Children*. (Third edition). London: Routledge.

Kemp, T., & Green, L. S. (2010). Executive coaching for the normal "non-clinical" population: fact or fiction? Paper presented to the Fourth Australian Conference on Evidence-based Coaching, University of Sydney.

Kline, N. (1998). *Time to Think: Listening to Ignite the Human Mind*. London: Cassell.

Kobasa, S. C. (1979). Stressful life events, personality, and health: An inquiry into hardiness. *Journal of Personality and Social Psychology, 37, (1)*: 1–11.

Kyriacou, C. (1987). Teacher stress and burnout: An international review. *Educational Research, 29*: 146–152.

Kyriacou, C. (2001). Teacher stress: Directions for future research. *Educational Review, 53, (1)*: 27–35.

Lazar, S. W., Kerr, C. E., Wasserman, R. H., Gray, J. R., Greve, D. N., *et al.*, (2005). Meditation experience is associated with increased cortical thickness, *Neuroreport, 16*: 1893–1897.

Leavis, F. R. (1968). *A Selection from Scrutiny: Volume 2*. Cambridge: Cambridge University Press.

Levy, A. R., Polman, R. C. J., Clough, P. J., Marchant, D. & Earle, K. (2006). Mental toughness as a determinant of beliefs, pain, and adherence in sport injury rehabilitation. *Journal of Sports Rehabilitation, 15*: 246–254.

Lindon, J. (2012). *Understanding Child Development, 0–8 Years*. (Third edition). London: Hodder Education.

Linley, P. A., & Joseph, S. (Eds.), (2004). *Positive Psychology in Practice*. Hoboken, NJ: Wiley.

Lewin, K. (1951). *Field Theory in Social Science*. Harper and Row, New York.

Locke, E. A., & Latham, G. P. (2006). *New directions in goal-setting theory*. R. H. Smith School of Business, University of Maryland, and 2Rotman School of Management, University of Toronto.

Loehr, J. E. (1983). *Athletic excellence: Mental toughness training for sports*. Denver: Forum Publishing Company.

Luthans, F., Youssef, C. M., & Avolio, B. J. (2007). *Psychological Capital: Developing the Human Competitive Edge*. Oxford: Oxford University Press.

Lutz, A., Brefczynski-Lewis, J., Johnstone, T., & Davidson, R. J. (2008). Regulation of the Neural Circuitry of Emotion by Compassion Meditation: Effects of Meditative Expertise. *PLoS ONE 3, (3)*: e1897. doi:10.1371/journal.pone. pdf

Lyubornirsky, S., King, L., & Diener, E. (2005). The benefits of frequent positive effect: Does happiness lead to success? *Psychological Bulletin, 131*: 803–855.

Mackenzie, S. V., & Marnik, G. F. (2008). Rethinking leadership development: How school leaders learn in action. *Schools: Studies in Education, 5*: 183–204.

Madden, W., Green, S., & Grant, A. M. (2011). A pilot study evaluating strengths-based coaching for primary school students: Enhancing engagement and hope. *International Coaching Psychology Review, 6, (1)*: 71–83.

Maddi, S. R., Kahn, S., & Maddi, L. K. (1998). The effectiveness of hardiness training. *Consulting Psychology Journal, 50*: 78–86.

Marchant, D. C. (2012). In: P. Clough & D. Strycharczyk, D. (Eds.), *Developing Mental Toughness: Improving Performance, Wellbeing and Positive Behaviour in Others* (pp. 247–256). London: Kogan Page.

Marchant, D. C., Clough, P. J., & Crawshaw, M. (2007). The effects of attentional focusing strategies on novice dart throwing performance and their task experiences. *International Journal of Sport and Exercise Psychology, 5*: 291–303.

Marchant, D. C., Greig, M., & Scott, C. (2008). Attentional focusing strategies influence bicep EMG during isokinetic bicep curls. *Athletic Insight, 10, (2)*: 11.

Marchant, D. C., Polman, R. C. J., Clough, P. J., Jackson, J. G., Levy, A. R. & Nicholls, A. R. (2009). Mental toughness: Managerial and age differences. *Journal of Managerial Psychology, 24*: 428–437.

Marshall, P. (2013). *The Tail: How Britain's Schools Fail One Child in Five—and What Can be Done*. Profile Books.

Marshall, P. (Ed.) (2013). *The Tail: How Britain's Schools Fail One Child in Five—and What Can be Done*. London: Profile Books.

Maslow, A. H. (1943). A theory of human motivation. *Psychological Review, 50*: 370–396.

Masten, A. S., & Motti-Stefanidi, F. (2009). Understanding and promoting resilience in children: promotive and protective processes in schools. In: T. B. Gutkin & C. R. Reynolds (Eds.), *The Handbook of School Psychology* (Fourth edition, pp. 721–738). New York: Wiley.

Matheson, D. (2004). *An Introduction to the Study of Education*. (Second edition). London: David Fulton.

Meece, J. L., Glienke, B. B., & Burg, S. (2006). Gender and motivation. *Journal of School Psychology, 44*: 351–373.

Mental Health Foundation. (2010). Be mindful. http://www.mentalhealth.org.uk/publications/be-mindful-report/

Mento, A. J., Steel, R. P., & Karren, R. J. (1987). A meta-analytic study of the effects of goal setting on task performance: 1966–1984. *Organizational Behavior and Human Decision Processes, 39, (1)*: 52–83.

Mischel, W., Ebbesen, E., & Zeiss, A. (1972). Cognitive and attentional mechanisms in delay of gratification. *Journal of Personality and Social Psychology, 21*: 204–218

Mueller, C. M., & Dweck, C. S. (1998). Praise for intelligence can undermine children's motivation and performance. *Journal of Personality and Social Psychology, 75*: 33–52.

Mukherjee, S. (2012). Does coaching transform coaches? A case study of internal coaching. *International Journal of Evidence Based Coaching and Mentoring, 10*: 76–87.

Murray, H. A. (1938). *Explorations in Personality: A Clinical and Experimental Study of Fifty Men of College Age*. Oxford University Press: Oxford.

Nicholls, A. R., Polman, R. C., Levy, A. R. & Blackhouse, S. (2008). Mental toughness, optimism, and coping among athletes. *Personality and Individual Differences, 44*: 1182–1192.

Nicholls, A. R., Polman, R. C., Levy, A. R. & Blackhouse, S. (2009). Mental toughness in sport: achievement level, gender, age, experience and sport type differences. *Personality and Individual Differences, 47*: 73–75.

Nisbett, R. E., Flynn, J. *et al.* (2012). New findings and theoretical developments. *American Psychologist, 67*: 130–159.

Noble, T., & McGrath, H. (2008). The positive educational practices framework: A tool for facilitating the work of educational psychologists in promoting pupil wellbeing. *Educational and Child Psychology, 25*: 119–134.

Okopi, F. (2011). Risk behaviours and early warning signals for ODL dropout students in Nigeria: Implications for counselling. *International Journal of Psychology and Counselling, 3*: 40–47.

Palmer, S. (2006). *Toxic Childhood. How the Modern World is Damaging our Children and What We Can Do About It*. London: Orion.

Passmore, J., & Brown, A. (2009). Coaching non-adult students for enhanced examination performance: A longitudinal study. *Coaching: An International Journal of Theory, Research and Practice, 2, (1)*: 54–64.

Peterson, C. (2006). *A Primer In Positive Psychology*. Oxford: Oxford University Press.

Peterson, C., & Barrett, L. C. (1987). Explanatory style and academic performance among university freshmen. *Journal of Personality and Social Psychology, 53*: 603–607.

Pink, D. (2011). *Drive: The Surprising Truth About What Motivates Us*. Scotland: Canongate Books Ltd.

Prentice, D. A., & Carranza, E. (2002). What women and men should be, shouldn't be, are allowed to be, and don't have to be: the contents of prescriptive gender stereotypes. *Psychology of Women Quarterly, 26*: 269–281.

Quartz, K. H. (2003). Too angry to leave: Supporting new teachers' commitment to transform urban schools. *Journal of Teacher Education, 54*: 99–111.

Renold, E. (2002). Presumed innocence: (hetero) sexual, homophobic and heterosexist harassment amongst children in the primary school. *Childhood, 9*: 415–433.

Renold, E. (2004). Other boys: negotiating non-hegemonic masculinities in the primary school. *Gender and Education, 16*: 248–266.

Rogers, C. (1957). The necessary and sufficient conditions of therapeutic personality change. *Journal of Consulting Psychology, 21*: 95–103.

Rosenkrantz, P., Vogel, S., Bee, H., Broverman, I. & Broverman, D. M. (1968). Sex-role stereotypes and self-concepts in college students. *Journal of Consulting and Clinical Psychology, 32*: 287–295.

Ross, J. A. (1992). Teacher efficacy and the effect of coaching on student achievement. *Canadian Journal of Education, 17, (1)*: 51–65.

Salmon, P., Sephton, S., Weissbecke, I., Hoover, K., Ulmer, C. & Studts, J. I. (2004). Mindfulness meditation in clinical practice. *Cognitive and Behavioural Practice, 11*: 434–46.

Schonert-Reichl, K. A., & Hymel, S. (2007). Educating the heart as well as the mind: why social and emotional learning is critical for students' school and life success. *Education Canada, 47*: 20–25.

Seligman, M. E. P. (2006). *Learned Optimism: How to Change Your Mind and Your Life.* USA: Vintage Books.

Seligman, M. E. P. & Csikszentmihalyi, M. (2011). Positive psychology: An introduction. *American Psychologist, 55*: 201–207.

Semple, R., Lee, J., Dinelia, R. & Miller, L. (2010). A randomized trial of mindfulness-based cognitive therapy for children: promoting mindful attention to enhance social-emotional resiliency in children. *Journal of Child and Family Studies, 19*: 218–229.

Sheard, M., & Golby, J. (2007). Hardiness and undergraduate academic study: The moderating role of commitment. *Personality and Individual Differences, 43*: 579–588.

Shidler, L. (2009). The impact of time spent coaching for teacher efficacy on student achievement. *Early Childhood Education Journal, 36*: 453–460.

Siegel, D. (2010). *The Mindful therapist: A Clinician's Guide to Mindsight and Neural Integration* New York: WW Norton.

Spear, L. P. (2000). The adolescent brain and age-related behavioral manifestations. *Neuroscience and Biobehavioral Reviews, 24*: 417–463.

Spence, G. B., & Grant, A. M. (2007). Professional and peer life coaching and the enhancement of goal striving and well-being: An exploratory study. *The Journal of Positive Psychology, 2*: 185–194.

St Clair-Thompson, H., Bugler, M., Robinson, J., Clough, P., McGeown, S. P., Perry, J. (2014). Mental toughness in education: Exploring relationships with attainment, attendance, behaviour and peer relationships. *Educational Psychology 2014*. Published online 11 March 2014.

Syed, M. (2011). *Bounce: The Myth of Talent and the Power of Practice*. London: Harper Collins.

Tang, Y. Ma, Y., Wang, J., Fan, Y., Feng, S. *et al.*, (2007). Short-term meditation training improves attention and self-regulation. *PNAS, 104*: 17152–17156.

Tinklin,T., Croxford, L., Ducklin, A., & Frame, B. (2001). Gender and pupil performance in Scotland's schools. Report to the Scottish Executive Education Department, Edinburgh: Centre for Educational Sociology, University of Edinburgh.

Tracy, B. (2010). *Goals!: How to Get Everything You Want—Faster Than You Ever Thought Possible*. California: Berrett-Koehler.

Urry, H. L., Nitschke, J. B., Dolski, I., Jackson, D. C., Dalton, K. M., *et al.* (2004). *Making a life worth living: neural correlates of well-being, Psychol Sci.; 15, (6)*: 367–372.

van Dick, R., & Wagner, U. (2001). Stress and strain in teaching: A structural equation approach. *British Journal of Educational Psychology, 71*: 243–259.

van Nieuwerburgh, C. (2012). Coaching for mental toughness. In: P. Clough & D. Strycharczyk (Eds.), *Developing Mental Toughness: Improving Performance, Wellbeing and Positive Behaviour in Others*. London: Kogan Page.

van Nieuwerburgh, C. (Ed.) (2012). *Coaching in Education: Getting Better Results for Students, Educators, and Parents*. London: Karnac.

van Nieuwerburgh, C. (2014). *An Introduction to Coaching Skills: A Practical Guide*. London: Sage.

van Nieuwerburgh, C., & Passmore, J. (2012). Coaching in secondary or high schools. In: C. van Nieuwerburgh (Ed.), *Coaching in Education: Getting Better Results for Students, Educators, and Parents* (pp. 63–74). London: Karnac.

van Nieuwerburgh, C., & Tong, C. (2013). Exploring the benefits of being a student coach in educational settings: A mixed-method study. *Coaching: An International Journal of Theory, Practice and Research, 6, (1)*: 5–24.

van Nieuwerburgh, C., Zacharia, C., Luckham, E., Prebble, G. & Browne, L. (2012). Coaching students in a secondary school: a case study. In: C. van

Nieuwerburgh (Ed.), *Coaching in Education: Getting Better Results for Students, Educators, and Parents* (pp. 191–198). London: Karnac.

Vealey, R. (1986). Conceptualization of sport confidence and competitive orientation: Preliminary investigation and instrument development. *Journal of Sport Psychology, 8*: 221–246.

Vealey, R. (2001). Understanding and enhancing self-confidence in athletes. In: R. Singer, H. Hausenblas, & C. Janelle (Eds.), *Handbook of sport psychology* (Second edition, pp. 550–565). New York: Wiley.

Veselka, L., Aitken, J. Schermer, R., & Vernon, P. (2010). Laughter and resiliency: a behavioral genetic study of humor styles and mental toughness. *Twin Research and Human Genetics, 13*: 442–449.

Wall, R. B. (2005). Tai Chi and mindfulness-based stress reduction in a Boston public middle school. *Journal of Paediatric Health Care, 19*: 230–237.

Walsh, R., & Shapiro, S. L. (2006). The meeting of meditative disciplines and western psychology: A mutually enriching dialogue. *American Psychologist, 61*: 227–239.

Weare, K. (2012). Evidence for the impact of mindfulness on children and young people. *The Mindfulness in Schools Project in association with Mood Disorders Centre.* Available at http://mindfulnessinschools.org/ Last accessed 13 June 2013.

Weiner, B., & Sierad, J. (1975). Misattribution for failure and enhancement of achievement strivings. *Journal of Personality and social Psychology, 31*: 415–421.

Weissbecker, I., Salmon, P., Studts, J. L., Floyd, A. R., Dedert, E. A. & Sephton, S. E. (2002). Mindfulness-based stress reduction and sense of coherence among women with firbomyalgia. *Journal of Clinical Psychology in Medical Settings, 9*: 297–307.

Whitmore, J. (2009). *Coaching for Performance: GROWing Human Potential and Purpose: The Principles and Practice of Coaching and Leadership.* (Third edition). London: Nicholas Brealey.

Wiley, C. (2000). A synthesis of research on the causes, effects and reduction strategies of teacher stress. *Journal of Instructional Psychology, 27*: 80–87.

Willetts, D. (2011). *The Pinch: How the Baby Boomers Took Their Children's Future—And Why They Should Give it Back.* London: Atlantic Books.

Zylowska, L. (2008). Mindfulness meditation training in adults and adolescents with ADHD: A feasibility study. *Journal of Attention Disorders, 11*: 737–746.

INDEX

Principal coverage is entered in **bold**.